Assessment Centers in Human Resource Management

Assessment Centers in Human Resource Management

George C. Thornton III

Colorado State University

▲
▼▼ ADDISON-WESLEY PUBLISHING COMPANY

Reading, Massachusetts • Menlo Park, California • New York
Don Mills, Ontario • Wokingham, England • Amsterdam • Bonn
Sydney • Singapore • Tokyo • Madrid • San Juan • Milan • Paris

Dedicated to my parents:

Wanda, who gave me a love for learning,
and
George, who inspired me to pursue an education.

Library of Congress Cataloging-in-Publication Data

Thornton, George C. , 1940–

   Assessment centers in human resource management /George C. Thornton III.

            p.   cm.

      ISBN 0-201-55403-8

      1.   Employees—Rating of.   2.   Personnel management.
I.   Title.
HF5549.5.R3T48   1992
658.3'125—dc20

                                                         91-28799
                                                              CIP

ISBN 0-201-55403-8
1 2 3 4 5 6 7 8 9 10-BA-9594939291

The Addison-Wesley Series on Managing Human Resources

Series Editor: John Parcher Wanous, The Ohio State University

Merit Pay: Linking Pay Increases to Performance Ratings
Robert L. Heneman, The Ohio State University

Assessment Centers in Human Resource Management
George C. Thornton III, Colorado State University

Fairness in Selecting Employees, Second Edition
Richard D. Arvey, University of Minnesota and
Robert H. Faley, Kent State University

Organizational Entry: Recruitment, Selection, Orientation, and Socialization of Newcomers, Second Edition
John P. Wanous, The Ohio State University

Increasing Productivity through Performance Appraisal
Gary P. Latham, University of Toronto and
Kenneth N. Wexley, Michigan State University

Managing Conflict at Organizational Interfaces
L. David Brown, Boston University

Managing Careers
Manuel London, AT&T and Stephen A. Stumpf, New York University

Managing Employee Absenteeism
Susan R. Rhodes, Syracuse University and
Richard M. Steers, University of Oregon

Foreword

This is an exciting time for the Managing Human Resources Series. Originally conceived in 1977, the first six books were published between 1979 and 1982. These books were uniformly well received by academic and business professionals alike. They have been extensively cited by researchers in human resources as state-of-the-art monographs. Moreover, students—both undergraduate and graduate—have found the series books to be both readable and informative.

The series is now in its second phase. *Fairness in Selecting Employees* (1979) by Rich Arvey was revised by Arvey and Robert Faley and published in 1988. This was followed by *Managing Employee Absenteeism* by Susan Rhodes and Rick Steers. My own book on *Organizational Entry* (1980) has been revised and reissued in 1992. Two new titles also appear in 1992. The first is *Merit Pay* by Rob Heneman, and the second is *Assessment Centers in Human Resource Management* by George Thornton. The commitment from Addison-Wesley to continue and expand the series has been crucial.

As always, this series is dedicated to the articulation of new solutions to human resources problems. My charge to authors has been to produce books that will summarize and extend cutting-edge knowledge. These authors must be intellectual leaders. In addition, they must make their books readily accessible to college students and human resource professionals alike. Readability need not and must not be sacrificed at the altar of academic scholarship. Both are achievable, as evidenced by the first books in this series. The present ones continue this tradition.

John Parcher Wanous
Series Editor

Preface

Assessment centers work! For some time now, the evidence has been convincing to all but the most die-hard skeptics that assessment centers help human resource managers and operations managers accurately predict future performance of job applicants and candidates for promotion. That evidence has been published in many sources, and it will be summarized again here.

Why, then, do we need another book on the assessment center method? For many reasons. First, not all the research is positive—some studies show that assessment centers do not work the way they are supposed to. Thus, there is a need to explain the discrepant findings. Second, even though most would agree that assessment centers work, some have suggested that we do not know *why* they work; therefore, we need to explore further the reasons why assessment centers work. Third, assessment centers are being used in new and uncharted ways; we must question whether their use in the realm of diagnosis of training needs and development of managerial skills is supportable. Fourth, we are seeing many innovations in the assessment center method, including the use of computers for presenting testing material, recording responses, and integrating judgments. These innovations are due, in part, to the need to reduce the time required for managers to carry out assessment duties. Do these changes undermine or enhance the accuracy of the assessment center method? A full discussion of these and many other issues is sorely needed.

The purpose of this book is to provide an up-to-date review of the "state of the art" of assessment center research and practice in both public and private organizations. Three objectives guided my efforts: description, analysis, and prescription. In each chapter, there is a description of current practices, along with the results of studies evaluating those practices. In-depth analysis of several controversial issues is provided for each element of the assessment center method, e.g., the attributes to be assessed, the types of exercises used, and the ways in which results are observed and integrated. Each chapter begins with a presentation of two or more key concepts, followed by a discussion of how different organizations are handling the issue and, where available, evidence of the effectiveness of alternative approaches. Various psychological theories are provided to help the reader see the issue in broader perspective. So that readers can decide where they stand on each issue, sufficient information is provided for the readers to make informed judgments. My own position is stated at the end.

The intended audience for the book includes students in psychology and human resource management at the upper-division undergraduate level and the beginning graduate level, as well as practicing human resource managers in public and private organizations. The book provides a basic description of the assessment center method, but quickly moves to the analytical process of deciding how assessment centers should be designed differently for different purposes.

While the book is not a "how-to" manual for assessment center operations, presentation of research and theory regarding the key issues of assessment operations will help the practitioner make the numerous decisions needed for the design and implementation of an actual assessment center. Further, the book is not intended for the academician looking for a set of specific research studies. On the other hand, since the analyses show unresolved questions, the book is a rich source of ideas about what topics need further study.

Against the advice of some of my colleagues, I've included considerable research and theory, some of which is quite complex. I have attempted to present this material in a way that is understandable to a college-educated audience. Readers' efforts to comprehend this material will be well rewarded as they decide where they stand on many of the issues concerning assessment center effectiveness.

The assessment center method has matured considerably in the last ten years and moved in directions unforeseen in the early 1980s. Some of these innovations include

- assessment of applicants for entry-level positions in high-technology manufacturing
- assessment of a wider range of attributes needed for success in highly competitive environments (e.g., "vi sion" among managers, the quality of "kaizan" among manufacturing employees)
- computer-administered exercises
- mechanical aids for the integration of behavioral observations and judgments.

The time is ripe for an appraisal of these innovations. They raise fundamental issues about the assessment center method. What is "essential" to the definition and integrity of the assessment center method? How many changes can be made in the method before it becomes something other than an "assessment center"? More importantly, what difference does it make if there are changes, as long as the technique works? Each of these innovations, the issues they present, and directions for the future are discussed in this book.

I wish to thank the many people who contributed in large and small ways to the completion of this book. Major portions of the manuscript were written while I was on sabbatical leave in 1990 at Bar Ilan University, Tel Aviv, Israel, where Shaul Fox provided moral, financial, and professional support. Bill Byham, Barbara Gaugler, John Wanous, and an anonymous reviewer deserve special mention for reviewing the entire manuscript. Colleagues at Colorado State University, including Kevin Murphy, Jan Cleveland, Russell Cropanzano, and Jack Hautaluoma provided an environment that is both challenging and supportive. Each of these folks critiqued portions of the manuscript and provided valuable direction. Advanced graduate students in industrial/organizational psychology at Colorado State in a seminar on assessment centers provided a valuable test bed for my ideas and gave valuable feedback on the manuscript; they may not recognize many sections of the book that were modified as a result of their spirited input. Becca Anhalt was especially helpful with editorial matters during the closing phases of production. Comments from undergraduate students in a seminar with Barb Gaugler at Rice University gave me a fresh perspective on how that segment of my audience might respond to the book. Finally, I wish to thank Mary Balderrama for her secretarial support as we learned the tricks of submitting a manuscript on word processing disks. Any faults that remain, of course, are my responsibility.

Ft. Collins, Colorado   G. C. T. III

Contents

1

Assessment Centers and Human Resource Management Decisions

The assessment center method is a procedure used by human resource management (HRM) for evaluating personnel in terms of human attributes or abilities relevant to organizational effectiveness. Even though all assessment centers share common features, the process can be adapted in many ways to achieve different objectives. The theme of this book is that each assessment center must be tailor-made to fit the purpose of the particular human resource decision to be made. Three human resource activities will be studied in detail: deciding who to promote into management, diagnosing strengths and weaknesses in work-related skills as a prelude to development, and training managerial and teamwork skills. The human resource manager must design the assessment center with a specific purpose in mind and then make choices in order to build an assessment center that adequately serves that purpose. Throughout this book alternative ways of setting up each element of the assessment center are discussed, and a rationale for deciding what procedures to follow is provided. Recommendations for assessment center practice are based on theory and research relevant to each element of an assessment center, as well as the experience of many assessment center practitioners.

This chapter describes the assessment center method and compares it with other assessment procedures, lists several types of human resource decisions, and shows how assessment centers have been used to facilitate these decisions. Chapter 2 presents three cases that show how assessment centers are used to solve three very different types of human resource management problems.

The Assessment Center Method

An essential feature of the assessment center method is the use of situational tests to observe specific behaviors of the participants. Situational tests include exercises requiring participants to prepare a written report after analyzing a marketing problem, make an oral presentation, answer mail and memos in an in-basket, or talk with a customer about a service complaint. Often several participants are observed discussing an organizational problem or making business decisions, although group exercises are not essential unless group interactions are a part of the target job. Trained assessors observe the behaviors and make independent evaluations of what they have seen. These multiple sources of information are pooled by the assessors in an integration discussion. The result of this discussion is usually an evaluation of each participant's strengths and weaknesses on the attributes being studied and, in some applications, a final overall assessment rating. When assessment centers are used for training and development purposes, individuals can learn new management skills, and groups can learn to improve organizational effectiveness.

A Typical Assessment Center

Here's how one assessment center works. (I hasten to emphasize that there's really no typical or universal way that assessment centers are set up or conducted.) On Monday morning, twelve participants, or "assessees" (e.g., supervisors being considered for promotion to higher-level management), six assessors (e.g., third-level line managers and HRM staff members), and an administrator report to a site away from the organization, such as a hotel. Prior to this time, the assessors have been trained to conduct the assessments, and the assessees have been briefed about the program. At the assessment center, the administrator provides orientation, makes introductions, and reviews the schedule. Over the next two days, the participants take part in a series of situational exercises and are observed by the assessors. While six participants are engaged in a group problem-solving discussion, the other six are individually analyzing a case study of an organizational problem and preparing a written report on it. Each participant then conducts a performance review session with a problem employee, makes a presentation of ideas for improving operations, and responds to paperwork that has accumulated in a manager's in-basket.

Assessors watch the exercises and take notes. After each exercise they write a report summarizing the types of decision making, as well as interpersonal and communication behaviors demonstrated by each individual they were assigned to observe. These assignments are rotated so that each participant is observed by at least three assessors.

After two days of these exercises, the assessees go back to work, and the assessors spend the next two days discussing their observations and making evaluations of management potential. Each assessee is discussed at length. Assessors take turns reporting the behaviors they observed relevant to the performance dimensions. After all the reports are given, the assessors individually rate the assessee on each performance dimension, using a five-point scale. These independent ratings are posted on a chart, and any differences are discussed until assessors reach agreement. Next, individual ratings of the probability of success as a higher-level manager are made and discussed until consensus is reached. In many programs, the assessors then discuss the development needs of the assessee and make suggestions for what might be done to improve job effectiveness.

At a later time, each assessee receives an oral and written report on how well he or she did. Reports are also given to higher-level managers who will be making promotion decisions. When the assessment center is used to diagnose training needs, there may be a feedback meeting with the assessee and his or her immediate supervisor to plan follow-up actions.

It is important to note that this is just one example of assessment center operations. (Chapter 2 describes how three other organizations designed their assessment centers.) There are many variations on the basic theme. In particular, very different procedures are useful in integrating behavioral observations. In the example above, assessors discuss their ratings until consensus is reached. Another procedure gaining wider acceptance is the statistical integration of ratings. For example, some organizations compute an average of the individual assessors' ratings to derive the final dimension ratings; others use a formula to combine final dimension ratings into an overall prediction of success. The advantages and disadvantages of various data integration methods are discussed in Chapters 6 and 7.

Comparison with Other Assessment Procedures

The assessment center method is similar to some assessment procedures and quite different from others. Alternative personnel assessment methods include paper-and-pencil tests measuring mental abilities, interests, and personality characteristics (Guion, 1965); background interviews and application blanks reviewing educational and work experiences (Gatewood & Feild, 1987); single performance tests or work-sample tests measuring specific competencies (Anastasi, 1988); performance appraisals evaluating effectiveness on the current job (Bernardin & Beatty, 1984); peer evaluations (Kane & Lawler, 1978); and clinical assessments by individual psychologists using various combinations of tests and interview methods (Ryan & Sackett, 1987, 1989). Each of these methods has strengths, and many have been found effective in predicting managerial success.

What is special about the assessment center method is the way various individual assessment procedures are used in combination with each other. An assessment center involves several different types of assessment techniques (e.g., tests, situational exercises, interviews), more than one situational exercise representing important elements of the target job, observation of complex behaviors relevant to managerial competencies, multiple assessors (usually including higher-level managers), and a systematic process of pooling observations and integrating the evaluations. The result of an assessment center is an evaluation of several managerial competencies and, in many cases, an overall evaluation of potential to succeed in the target jobs.

Situational exercises are one of the distinguishing features of the assessment center method. They provide the opportunity to observe complex behaviors of candidates as they interact with other people, solve problems, and act upon their analyses.

These exercises need not be actual work samples. A work sample is a detailed replica of one segment of the actual work situation. For example, a typing test is a replica of one critical element of a secretarial job. An assessment center exercise for managers *may* be a work sample (e.g., an actual problem confronting the organization), but it does not have to be a complete replica of a job element. Instead, exercises may be only partial simulations of the job. The question of how similar assessment center exercises must be to actual work situations is explored in depth in Chapter 5. At this point, it is sufficient to say that the assessment center exercises only need to represent the essential features of the target job and organization.

Human Resource Management Decisions

Assessment centers can contribute valuable information to a large number of functions that are carried out by any human resource management (HRM) system in an organization. These functions are designed to ensure that the organization recruits, selects, trains, compensates, and evaluates its personnel in ways that support the organization's objectives.

The following paragraphs summarize many of the HRM functions carried out in most organizations (Cherrington, 1983; French, 1982). In each one, a brief example is given to show how assessment centers have been used in actual organizational settings.

Recruitment

Any organization must attract a steady stream of talented and motivated people ready to move into all positions in the organization (Wanous, 1992). The source of new personnel may be located outside the organization, in the form of applicants, or inside the organization, in the form of promotions and transfers. Diamond Star Motors, a joint venture between Chrysler and Mitsubishi, used the assessment center method to show applicants what they would experience in the Japanese management system (Henry, 1988). This orientation attracted many and led others to withdraw from the application process. The assessment center results were also used for making selection decisions. At Lawrence Livermore Laboratories, an assessment center was used to show engineers and scientists what management entails and to give them an opportunity to discover some of their own managerial strengths.

This experience was helpful in attracting some of the participants to management positions.

Selection

Organizations must decide whom to select and whom to reject among the many applicants for a job opening. Selection procedures, therefore, should be nondiscriminatory and help identify individuals who are likely to succeed on the job. The Police Department of Fort Collins, Colorado, developed a set of situational tests that presented applicants with difficult interpersonal problems encountered on the job and observed their ability to remain calm and avoid reacting aggressively when confronted by angry citizens (Gavin & Hamilton, 1975). Other organizations have used assessment centers to select employees for entry-level positions, such as assembly jobs (Henry, 1988); for team workers and team leaders in manufacturing (Team Columbus, 1990); and for high-level executive positions, such as plant manager, general manager, and senior government official (Byham, 1986).

Placement

There are often several possible jobs that can be assigned to a new employee. Ideally, the assignment results in a good match of job requirements to the individual's strengths. In a program for recruiting management trainees, Sears (Bentz, 1980) used an assessment center not only to select among applicants, but also to place new recruits in positions where there was an optimal fit. For example, recruits skilled in oral communication were placed in jobs requiring frequent presentations, whereas recruits who tested weak in planning were placed under managers with strong planning skills.

Training and Development

Training is the process of imparting the appropriate knowledge, skills, abilities, and other characteristics needed by an individual for effective organizational functioning. Assessment centers have been used to diagnose employee deficiencies and to provide skill training in selected areas (Byham, 1971; Thornton & Byham, 1982). For example, Cochran, Hinckle, and Dusenberry (1987) designed a developmental assessment center for a government agency in which feedback was given on nine managerial skills. Participants then listed target areas for improvements. In another application, the United States Army War College (Beitz, 1985) designed a set of assessment center activities that relied heavily on self-assessments. Using these self-assessments, senior officers gained insight into their own developmental needs and then designed the best educational activities for their academic year at the college. Chapter 2 includes a detailed case study of a diagnostic assessment center.

Performance Appraisal

Organizations need procedures for evaluating the job proficiency of employees. In most cases, the immediate supervisor provides a performance appraisal on an annual basis. In other cases, assessment centers have been used to certify the competence of individuals to perform required technical skills. In these situations, the exercises are often work samples. The American Board of Professional Psychology (1988) uses an assessment center to evaluate the skill of clinical psychologists in diagnosing a client's personal problems.

Organizational Development

Organizational development refers to a set of procedures that improve the effectiveness of a department or of an entire organization. Organization development is different from management development, where the objective is to improve an individual's skills. Many organizations use large-scale, complex organization simulations as a means of promoting organization development (Stumpf, 1988). For example, Martin Marietta uses a complex organization game much like an assessment center to help high-level managers work cooperatively in a team and communicate more effectively (Teresa Philbin, personal communication, March 14, 1988).

Human Resource Planning

Effective organizations forecast future demand for particular skills and determine the supply of those skills in their current work force. Kodak's Colorado Division found that one by-product of its assessment center was the identification of a general deficiency among its first- and second-level managers in the skill of management control, i.e., the application of techniques to determine whether a work process or project was being completed in an accurate and timely manner. Kodak used this information to design a new training program to improve its employees' management control skills (Thornton, 1976).

Promotion and Transfer

Giving an employee a new and higher level of responsibility is a major decision for that individual and for others whom he or she will supervise. AT&T and many of the Bell Companies have used assessment centers for over thirty years to identify individuals' potential for success in managerial positions (Bray & Grant, 1966; Bray, Campbell, & Grant, 1974). Of course, the candidate's performance on the current job is also considered very carefully. This type of program is described more fully in Chapter 2.

Layoffs

When an organization must reduce its work force for economic reasons or because of changes in its structure, it is faced with difficult decisions about whom to release and whom to retain. The security division of the Hoffman Company used an assessment center to simulate the job requirements of the restructured department. Each employee was given a chance to demonstrate his or her capabilities for the new assignment. Participants reported that they believed the assessment center provided a fair chance to demonstrate relevant skills. They preferred this process over one in which the decision was based solely on seniority or on their supervisors' performance evaluations of their current jobs.

Summary

These brief examples show the wide variety of applications of the assessment center method. All this should not be interpreted to mean that all assessment centers are alike or that there is only one way to conduct an assessment center. Quite the opposite is true. The design of an assessment center depends on the purpose it will serve, and on the type of climate the organization wishes to create. The organization's human resource management system and its organizational climate are closely intertwined.

The Relationship of Human Resource Management Systems and Organizational Climate

Organizations differ dramatically in the type of human resource management systems they use. Some are rigid and mechanistic, others are quite flexible and humanistic (Schein, 1970). Assessment processes are one manifestation of these different orientations to employees in the organization; they will differ from organization to organization, depending on the character of the organization, the demands of the context, and the image the organization wishes to project. HRM specialists have just begun to explore the relationship of an organization's characteristics to its personnel practices. Jackson, Schuler, and Rivero (1989) have shown that organization characteristics—such as industry sector, emphasis on innovation, the manufacturing technology, and the organization structure—are related to several personnel practices in areas such as performance appraisal, compensation, employment security, and training.

At a more theoretical level, Lawrence (1984) has argued that even though all organizations carry out each of the human resource functions listed above, the particular manner in which these functions are carried out varies considerably from one organization to another. The HRM style of an organization should be compatible with the more general philosophy of management that the organization wishes to perpetuate. Every organization should be aware that its HRM practices—specifically, its evaluation procedures—have a strong effect on the attitudes and behavior of applicants and employees. Applicants and employees form an implicit contract (Schein, 1970) with an organization as a result of the way they are evaluated in selection, training, and performance appraisal procedures. If they are treated in a routine and mechanical way, employees may put forth only limited efforts, but if they are treated in a caring and individualized way, they are more likely to put forth extra effort on behalf of the organization.

Applicants to an organization begin to form impressions of the organization on the basis of their first experiences with recruiting and selection practices (Rynes, Heneman, & Schwab, 1980). Organizational brochures give information about policies and practices; interviewers treat applicants with respect or condescension; tests may appear relevant and fair or irrelevant and invasions of privacy; and contacts in the employment office may be supportive or demeaning.

All of these interactions with representatives of the organization form the basis of initial impressions. What is even more important is that these perceptions of the organization's personnel functions tend to generalize quite widely to other features of the organization (Thornton, in press). The applicant begins to form an impression about other organization policies, other members of the organization, and the general organizational climate. Even more importantly, these initial impressions form the basis of subsequent attitudes toward the organization and of the employee's commitment to that organization (Wanous, 1992). Ultimately, the employee's effort, job performance, and decision to stay or leave the organization are affected by attitudes that may have been formed during these early contacts.

Types of Human Resource Management Systems

The way in which HRM functions are carried out reflects an organization's philosophy toward its human resources. Lawrence 1984) has observed that human resource management systems have gone through several phases in the history of labor in the United States. Up to the mid 1800s, a craft arrangement predominated in which apprentices worked their way up to journeyman and master craftsman. Subsequently, a market system emerged in which unskilled employees worked for a supervisor and were paid by a piece-rate system. Lawrence characterized human resource management between World War I and World War II as a technical system, with fine division of labor and hourly pay based on the value of jobs, determined by job evaluation. Recently, a career-oriented system of HRM has begun to predominate in which the individual works for a long period of time for one organization in a series of jobs and gets paid a salary based on merit and seniority. According to Lawrence, the United States is now moving toward a commitment-based system in which individuals work in semiautonomous work groups for a base salary plus bonus.

Even though one of these patterns may have predominated in the past, all of them are still present in organizations today. Lawrence goes beyond a description of these systems to assert that the commitment-based system is preferable and leads to better organizational effectiveness. It can also be argued that each of the patterns of personnel management has its place in organizations. While a commitment-based system has clear advantages in the world economy and fits with trends in values among many American workers, each of the other patterns of relationship between employer and employee is viable.

What is important, then, is that an organization match its HRM practices to the management philosophy it wishes to perpetuate. The assessment center is flexible enough that it can be adapted for use as part of a craft, market, career, or commitment-based human resource management philosophy. The assessment center can simulate the type of relationship the organization wishes to develop with its employees. For example, in line with the craft arrangement, Anheuser-Busch uses work sample procedures for assessing skilled craft positions, such as journey-level mechanics and plumbers. AT&T and a number of operating companies in the telephone industry follow a merit-based selection model by using an assessment center for making promotions to first-level supervisor. Kodak's Colorado Division followed a career growth model in implementing a series of assessment centers to foster career growth among technical personnel, first-level supervisors, and department heads. In seeking employees to work in its assembly plant, managed with a commitment-based philosophy, Diamond Star Motors used an assessment center to simulate a factory setting requiring close teamwork and constant improvement in methods.

There is much evidence to suggest that the assessment center method is viewed quite favorably by participants. Studies of participants' reactions to assessment centers used for a variety of purposes have been conducted (Dodd, 1977; Thornton & Byham, 1981). Applicants for management trainee positions see the procedure as a fair selection process. Candidates for promotion believe the method gives them a fair chance to show their management potential. Both successful and unsuccessful assessment center participants have positive reactions. Minority applicants believe the method is unbiased. When used for developmental planning, high-rated as well as low-rated individuals use the information and engage in follow-up improvement activities.

Criticisms and Limitations of the Assessment Center Method

Numerous criticisms have been made of the assessment center method. Some criticisms are practical in nature: the process is complex and requires time for key managers to serve as assessors. People have questioned whether the benefits outweigh the costs, especially in comparison with less costly assessment procedures. Other criticisms have arisen as a result of research that has not supported some of the typical assessment center procedures. For example, there is a mixture of support for the use of different types of procedures for observing, reporting, and combining behavioral observations. Still other criticisms are theoretical in nature; they challenge some of the basic assessment center assumptions about the perception of other people's behavior and the accuracy of social judgment. Throughout this book, these and many other controversial issues are raised. Arguments and research data on both sides of each issue are presented so the reader can form his or her own opinion. I will give my position on each of these issues also.

Summary

The assessment center is a flexible procedure for assessing a wide variety of personnel for various human resource management functions. By simulating the special features of a job and organizational climate, the method can be adapted to fit many different personnel management philosophies. Attitude surveys have shown that employees and applicants believe that the assessment center approach gives them a fair chance to show their capabilities and is a good method for diagnosing training needs. Criticisms of the assessment center method have been raised and require careful consideration.

2

Case Studies of Assessment Centers in Operation

Key Concepts: Applying the assessment center method; designing exercises to fill HRM objectives.

This chapter presents case studies that show how three organizations have used assessment centers for very different purposes. In the first case, the organization used the assessment center to identify individual contributors with potential for success in middle management positions. In the second organization, the assessment center was used to diagnose strengths and weaknesses of current managers so that their development could be planned more effectively. The third case shows how an assessment center was used for the development of managerial skills and for broader organizational development.

In each of these examples, the organization, target jobs, and the specific features of the assessment program are described. The reader should note how each of the features of the assessment center has been designed to solve a particular human resource management problem.

Office Supplies Systems

OSS used an assessment center to help decide whom to promote from the ranks of sales representatives and technicians into the position of district manager. Over the years, OSS had not been pleased with the management talent of employees promoted into higher levels of the organization. Often the sales representative with the best sales record or the technician who was most technically astute was promoted into supervision. These candidates may have been excellent performers on an individual level, but that did not necessarily mean that they made good managers. Thus, the organization decided to set up an assessment center to help identify those top-performing sales and service people who also had the talent to be developed into effective managers. This is the most common use of assessment centers: a recent survey (Gaugler, Bentson, & Pohley, 1990) of over 200 organizations revealed that over 68 percent developed the program for promotion and early identification of managerial talent.

The Organization

Office Supplies Systems (OSS) sells office supplies and equipment to retail stores and businesses throughout the United States. OSS manufactures some of its own products, but most items are purchased from other manufacturers and resold to customers. The company has a catalog that customers can use for mail or telephone orders. The emphasis of the organization has been on direct contact with its customers through the sales people and the technicians in the field. The company policy is that every customer, no matter how small, is contacted at least once a month. Even though much of the business comes from direct orders, the sales people and technicians are largely responsible for developing good relations with the customers and dealing with defective products and shipping problems. As a result, the sales force and technicians are highly esteemed throughout the organization.

Target Jobs

The assessment center was designed to identify sales representatives and technicians who possessed the attributes needed to be effective middle-level managers. Figure 2.1 shows a simplified organization chart of the company. The first level of management is the district manager, who is responsible for twenty to twenty-five sales representatives and eight to ten service technicians. A district might cover a large part of a sparsely populated state or a small section of a large metropolitan area. The next level of management is a regional manager, who supervises several district managers. Finally, there are several area managers. In some areas of the country there are also section managers. An area

Figure 2.1
Simplified Organization Chart of OSS

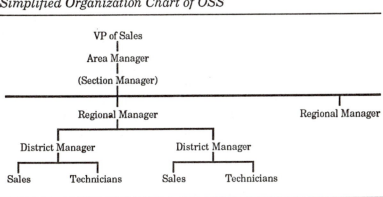

manager is responsible for several regions and reports directly to the vice-president of sales.

The organization had been concerned for some time that people moving into the district manager position did not have the potential to move up in the organization. It wanted people who could be successful not only at first-level supervision where day-to-day operations are important, but also at middle levels of management where skills such as coordinating with other units in the organization, deciding whether to open new markets, making financial decisions, and selecting new product lines are important. Thus, in setting up the assessment center, the organization decided to analyze carefully the attributes important for success in lower and middle levels of management. (Above the middle levels of management, the nature of the job changes again and broader executive talent becomes important.) The assessment center program was then designed to identify long-range potential for success in middle-level management positions. Most assessment centers are used for this purpose: the survey of over 200 organizations (Gaugler et al., 1990) revealed that 61 percent of assessment centers are used to help make the decision about whom to promote from nonsupervisory positions into management.

Dimensions

OSS decided to assess characteristics that would contribute to success over a long period of time in both lower and middle management positions. These characteristics were identified by analyzing the job requirements of OSS management positions, by examining the results of job analyses from other similar organizations, and by consulting the literature on leadership and management.

The following dimensions were identified as important for successful lower and middle managers and thus were evaluated in the assessment center: leadership, impact on others, decision making, motivation to manage, and communication effectiveness.

Assessment Exercises

The job analysis identified several types of situations that managers must deal with on a regular basis, as well as the types of problems encountered in those situations. The job analysis information was used to build several assessment exercises that simulated important elements of the lower and middle management jobs at OSS.

An in-basket exercise was developed to present typical administrative problems encountered in the paper work of managers and to assess decision-making skill, motivation to manage, and communication effectiveness. Two group discussion exercises were built to simulate situations in which managers must work together. In one exercise, participants must work cooperatively to set up new policies for reimbursement of travel expenses. In the other they must decide which district will receive extra resources to conduct a trial release of a new product line that may be very profitable. In another exercise, individual participants talk first with a person playing the role of a subordinate who is having difficulty getting his staff to complete projects on time, and then with a customer who calls with several complaints about service. There is also an analysis exercise in which the participant reads complex information about several geographic areas and writes recommendations for new marketing strategies based on that information.

OSS also gave a set of mental ability tests and personality tests to assess whether candidates for promotion had the basic intellectual skills and personality traits necessary for effective managers. The three mental ability tests covered verbal and quantitative reasoning, reading skills, and a measure of general intelligence. The two personality tests covered interpersonal styles and personality attributes, such as dominance, sociability, and aggressiveness. Psychological testing was under the supervision of an industrial/organizational psychologist.

Participants

The participants in each assessment center consisted of a total of six sales representatives and service technicians who either were self-nominated or had been nominated by their district managers as highly successful and potentially promotable. Self-nominees had to have gotten approval from the corporate human resource director in order to participate.

Assessors

Three managers from the ranks of regional, section, or area management served as the primary assessors in the program. This practice is typical: assessors usually come from management positions at least two levels above the participants (Gaugler et al., 1990). The assessors were trained and coordinated by a member of the corporate human resource management staff, usually some-one trained as a clinical or industrial/organizational psychologist. The managers observed the exercises and evaluated performance; the HRM staff member administered the exercises, led the integration discussion, presented the mental ability and personality test results, wrote reports, and gave oral and written feedback to participants and management.

Program

Administration of the exercises was completed in one and one-half days. The assessors then took an additional one and one-half days to prepare their evaluations and to integrate the information they had collected. During this time, the assessors compared their observations with checklists for effective performance in the exercises. Assessors made ratings on the performance dimensions compiled by the administrator. Where discrepancies occurred, the assessors discussed differences and came to agreement. Once a consensus was reached, the administrator used a statistical formula to combine dimension ratings into an overall assessment rating showing the predicted level of success in the organization. If assessors disagreed with this prediction, they discussed the evidence more thoroughly. Statistical methods of integrating assessment results are employed in only about 15 percent of the assessment centers in Gaugler et al.'s (1990) survey, but the practice seems to be spreading. Assessors spent approximately two hours discussing each candidate. While the assessors were conducting these discussions, the candidates received a day of training in corporate business practices, then returned to their job sites.

Feedback

Within a month, the HRM staff member gave each participant feedback about his or her performance in the assessment center. Feedback consisted of a verbal review of the findings and the recommendation regarding promotability. Soon thereafter the participant received a brief written report of the assessment results. A more detailed report of each individual's assessment was presented to the regional and area managers responsible for making promotion decisions. This report also included a summary of the findings for the group who attended the program together, as well as a summary of all participants who had been assessed for the same target jobs in the past.

Other Elements of the Program

The results of the OSS assessment center, including the overall assessment rating of promotability, were only one set of information the regional managers had for making a promotion decision. The organization's policy called for regional managers to seek out and use other information—performance ratings and sales performance records of each sales representative, for example. This information and a recommendation from the candidate's supervisor ensured that performance on the current job was carefully considered. Any regional manager who had an opening for a district manager reviewed all information in the personnel file, then interviewed three finalists.

Results

Eight years after the assessment center was set up, OSS evaluated the effectiveness of the program. Most regional and area managers believed the assessment center had been providing valuable information about sales staff and technicians that had not been available previously. They reported that they had been using the assessment center results to help them decide on promotions into the district manager position. Upper management was pleased that the new district managers had better skills to run their individual offices and to carry out the roles they played in the broader organization. Enough time had passed that some of these district managers had even been promoted into second- and third-level positions because of the competencies they demonstrated on the job. It appeared that a much better pool of managerial talent was being promoted from the ranks of the sales and technical staff and was then available for further advancement into middle-management levels.

Some problems with the assessment program were revealed by the evaluation study. In some regions, the assessment results were given too much weight in the decision to promote people. In these areas, candidates believed their job performance over the years was not given enough consideration, and they feared that the assessment center was a "make or break" event. In addition, other results showed that some candidates who performed poorly in the assessment center became discouraged about their futures because they suspected the low assessment rating was "a kiss of death." To allay some of these concerns, the vice-president of sales made several statements in memos and speeches to reconfirm the company's policy that the assessment center results were only one piece of relevant information to be used in promotion decisions.

Summary

The OSS assessment center was designed to provide information for making promotion decisions. The dimensions and exercises were appropriate for identifying people with potential for long-range success in lower-level and middle-level positions in this organization. The result of the assessment center was an evaluation of several managerial dimensions and a single overall assessment rating. Aside from feedback to participants, the findings were given only to the managers who made promotion decisions. The results were used in conjunction with other information relevant to the promotion decision.

Kimberly Brothers Manufacturing

The Organization

The Kimberly Brothers Manufacturing Company makes a variety of test equipment used by scientific institutions, research laboratories, schools and universities, and research and development units of other industrial organizations. The equipment is used for precision measurement and calculation and must meet high technical standards.

Kimberly Brothers Manufacturing used an assessment center for several years to assess the developmental needs of its personnel at several levels. The first assessment center, developed for first-level supervisors, was so successful that additional assessment centers were developed for second-level managers and for professionals, i.e., individual contributors such as scientists, engineers, and cost accountants. This chapter describes only the program for first-level supervisors, called the Supervisory Development Program.

The impetus for the program was the recognition by the new director of training and development that training resources were not being used effectively. Often there was not a good match between the training needs of employees and the actual training they received. On one hand, individuals were sometimes enrolled in courses and short programs that they did not need, while on the other hand, some individuals did not receive training in areas in which they were weak.

Thus the new training director called a halt to all training until he could have some assurance that there was a better correlation between the training needs of the individual and the training opportunities provided by the Training and Development department. He decided the organization needed a systematic procedure for assessing employees' training needs. For this purpose, he decided to set up a diagnostic assessment center. Diagnosis of training needs is the purpose of about one-third of the assessment centers covered in Gaugler et al.'s (1990) survey, and the practice seems to be growing.

Target Jobs

The Supervisory Development Program was designed for first-level supervisors throughout the organization. In the manufacturing areas these people are called foremen, lead operators, or supervisors; in the office areas, they are called supervisors or office managers; in the technical/professional areas they are called chief engineers or lead accountants. Supervisors in these different positions often had different training needs due to the type of work performed, the types of workers being supervised, and prior preparation for management. For this reason, generalized training in supervision and management was often inadequate.

Therefore, in setting up the program, the organizers identified a set of supervisory and management skills that were relevant to all types of supervisors. The results of the assessment would then be helpful to any first-level supervisor trying to improve his or her skills. Identification of individual strengths and weaknesses could then lead to developmental planning and training activities that would help each individual fulfill the job requirements.

It should be emphasized that the assessment center was designed to assess skills required for the jobs the supervisors already held. The assumption was that the assessment center could provide a valuable diagnosis of training needs beyond what was available from an on-the-job performance evaluation. We will see later that the assessment center evaluation must be combined with other information obtained from the supervisor's immediate manager.

Dimensions

Job analysis for the Supervisory Development Program led to the identification of dimensions that were quite different from those in OSS. For this diagnostic program, the dimensions were skills and competencies individuals needed in order to work successfully as first-level supervisors. Administrative skills included dimensions such as planning and organizing, delegation, and management control. In the area of decision making, the program assessed problem analysis and decision-making skills; oral and written communication skills were also assessed. Each of these dimensions was defined in terms of behaviors and in such a way that assessors could make meaningful distinctions among them. For example, problem analysis involves understanding the facts about a situation and detecting the true cause of poor performance, whereas decision making involves a careful evaluation of alternative solutions and making a good choice among them. Even though there may be some relationship between effective performance in these dimensions, the dimensions were defined so that it would be possible for a participant to perform well on one dimension and poorly on another dimension.

It should be apparent that these dimensions are quite different from the dimensions described in the OSS assessment center. These dimensions are skills that supervisors must display in their present jobs, not aptitudes that are predictive of long-range success. More importantly, in this diagnostic program, the dimensions are skills that the participant can improve on, given the appropriate training.

Assessment Exercises

The exercises were similar to the ones used in the selection program at OSS, but they were more complicated and there were also more of them. More importantly, they required demonstration of specific skills rather than general aptitudes. The in-basket exercise for the Kimberly program was twice as long as OSS's and required the participant to delegate effectively and employ management control skills. Whereas OSS used only two simulations of interpersonal situations on the job, Kimberly used four. The participant was expected to show the ability to deal with two different problems related to poor employee work habits and poor performance.

In addition, different *types* of exercises were used. A fact-finding exercise provided the participant with a small amount of information and a decision to make. A resource person, usually one of the assessors, had a large amount of relevant information that the participant could obtain by asking the right questions. Following the question-and-answer period, the participant had to make a recommendation and provide a rationale in support of his or her decision. The resource person challenged the decision and tried to get the participant to change his or her mind after further information was provided. This exercise measured the individual's ability to analyze a problem, ask probing questions, listen carefully, and maintain poise under stress. Finally, an oral presentation was required in which the participant presented recommendations for a new product line after studying marketing and financial data. Financial analysis ability and presentation skills were assessed in this exercise.

Participants

The participants in the program were first-level supervisors from throughout the organization. The program was designed for new supervisors who had been in their jobs about one year. During that period they would have received some basic training in supervision and gained experience on the job. The assessment center was then helpful in formulating a development plan to overcome weaknesses in their supervisory and management skills. In the initial months of the program, even experienced supervisors were assessed, and they, too, benefited from the diagnosis of training needs.

Assessors

The assessors for the program were second- and third-level managers, called department heads and superintendents. In all cases, the assessors were matched with assessees who were not in the same department so they could give impartial evaluations. The primary assessor, who gave feedback, was someone who had not worked closely with the participant in the past. This arrangement allowed the assessor to be objective in reviewing the observations and kept the assessment information separate from the information about job performance, which was discussed with the immediate supervisor.

Program

The program lasted five days. The first two and a half days were devoted to individual and group exercises. The schedule was planned so that each assessor saw a given participant in at least two different types of exercises. In addition to participating in the exercises, the participants completed self-assessments on each of the dimensions. The assessment exercises were followed by two days of management training. On the last day, the first steps of developmental planning were carried out; the participants started to lay out plans for ways to improve the management skills important for their work areas.

While the participants were going through the training and the initial developmental planning, the assessors were integrating their observations. This integration discussion was somewhat different from the discussion in the assessment center program at OSS, where only about an hour was needed to derive an overall evaluation of promotability using statistical aids designed to predict success. At Kimberly there was no overall assessment rating; what was important was a careful evaluation of each individual's strengths and weaknesses on the dimensions. Assessors needed two or more hours to discuss performance on the dimensions and arrive at a consensus about the diagnosis for each participant. The process of discussion to the point of consensus is used by the vast majority (85 percent) of assessment centers in Gaugler et al.'s (1990) survey.

The assessors gave a detailed evaluation of each dimension, including what aspects of the dimensions were problematic for the participant. For example, "poor delegation" could be a function of vague requests, few instructions, or inadequate methods of checking assignments. The assessors also described the circumstances under which the problem occurred. Using the example of poor delegation, the participant might readily delegate administrative tasks, yet not allow subordinates any choice in technical aspects of the work to be done.

The assessors then gave each participant suggestions for follow-up actions that might be beneficial. For example, they might suggest that the supervisor discuss with his own manager the assignments he plans to make to subordinates. Or, they might suggest outside reading on topics where the assessment showed a weakness.

Feedback

Reports prepared in this assessment program were more detailed than those in the OSS program. For each dimension, the assessors provided a detailed description of how the participant did on each exercise, including comparisons of effective and ineffective behavior in each case. In addition, suggestions for developmental follow-up actions were offered.

Approximately two weeks after the assessment, there were two feedback sessions scheduled with the participant and conducted by the primary assessor. Remember that the primary assessor was a manager one or two levels higher in the organization, but not in the same department as the participant he or she observed. The first feedback session was held with the participant alone. At this time, the assessor gave a detailed description of the behavioral observations and the evaluation of the dimensions. The assessor described his or her reasons for the evaluation and solicited the participant's acceptance of it. In the second feedback session, the assessor met with the participant and his or her manager. The purpose of this meeting was to explain the individual's strengths and developmental needs as seen in the assessment center. The three people then compared this assessment with the participant's performance on the job and the preliminary development plan laid out by the participant on the last day of the assessment program. They then selected a few areas that the participant needed to work on in the developmental plan. The implementation of the plan then became the responsibility of the participant and his or her manager. The assessor remained available only for consultation. Having management assessors give feedback to participants is somewhat unusual. Only about thirty percent of the organizations in Gaugler et al.'s (1990) survey follow this practice. Having management assessors also give feedback to the participant and his or her manager is even less common, although no precise estimates are available.

Other Elements of the Program

For this type of assessment center to be successful, it must be a part of a larger human resource management system. The participant and his or her manager must carry out the specific steps set forth in the developmental plan. Programs for strengthening management skills must be available, and the manager must coach, encourage, and reinforce improvement on the job. One effect of the first year of assessment center activities at Kimberly was a review of all training programs: some unnecessary ones were dropped, and new programs were added to develop skills that frequently showed up as deficiencies among the participants.

Results

One year after the program was started, the Training and Development staff evaluated its effects. Interviews with participants and their managers revealed that the majority of the participants were pleased with the results. They believed that the assessment center gave them valuable insights into participants' developmental needs. The program had helped both parties initiate developmental planning, a concept previously endorsed but seldom carried out. The Training and Development staff noted that there were fewer complaints by people attending training courses: instances of redundant or unnecessary training were reduced, and people seeking training found the specific content they needed.

Some problems were noted in the program. A few participants did not get clear feedback about their specific strengths and weaknesses; they were told only that they were generally good or bad without helpful diagnostic information. The problems were addressed in subsequent assessor training sessions. Other participants said the feedback was accurate but that no follow-up actions had been taken by their managers. When the program was launched, managers said they would do on-the-job training to correct weaknesses. The evaluation study showed that little coaching was taking place, largely because managers did not know how to coach. They requested help in this area, and a program was designed to train managers how to coach subordinates on the job. In a few cases, participants worried that the assessment center findings had been misused—that management took advantage of the results when making decisions about promotions, for instance—when the announced purpose was individual development.

Summary

Kimberly's Supervisory Development Program has several special features that distinguish it from the OSS program. A diagnostic program such as Kimberly's must assess skills that can be developed in a reasonable amount of time. Those developing such a program must strike a balance between, on the one extreme, assessing skills that could easily be learned in a brief orientation to the job and, on the other, assessing ingrained personal traits that cannot be changed. The exercises must provide multiple opportunities to evaluate participants on each separate dimension. The resulting assessment and integration might take more time, but the result is a thorough analysis of each dimension. Recommendations for follow-up action must be initiated by the participant and overseen by the assessors and the participant's immediate manager.

The two assessment center programs discussed thus far have emphasized assessment and prediction of success for individuals. The next program emphasizes skill development and focuses on improving the effectiveness of the broader organization.

Federal Commercial Promotion Agency

The Organization

The Federal Commercial Promotion Agency (FCPA) is a large government agency that helps individual companies and trade associations promote their products and services in other countries. It was created to counter the effects of a huge national trade deficit. The agency provides information about trade markets, foreign regulations, and policies of the U.S. federal government. It suggests how U.S. companies can work with purchasing agents in other countries to overcome some of the barriers that make foreign cooperation difficult.

The agency maintains field offices in major cities throughout the United States in addition to its Washington, D.C., headquarters. The staff of the agency includes economists, lawyers, marketing analysts, political experts, and cross-cultural specialists. Until recently, the staff had been largely reactive in its approach, simply responding to requests from U.S. companies. It became apparent that the agency had to change its orientation and become more proactive. Many companies were not aware of the agency's services, so a more aggressive marketing approach was needed within the United States. More controversially, there was pressure from Congress to seek out opportunities in foreign countries and then find U.S firms to supply goods and services. Various people in the agency supported or argued against these new initiatives, but Congress, the president's office, and lobbying groups agreed that the agency should become more proactive. Therefore, the agency needed some method to change the values of its various staff members and to impart the managerial skills necessary to this new orientation.

Agency management decided to design an assessment center that would simulate the world market. In the various exercises, participants would have the opportunity to discuss the new values needed for operation, to practice the new skills, and to learn to work together more effectively.

FCPA used the assessment center to develop executive skills and to promote better teamwork among its high-level administrators throughout the United States. Only about 16 percent of the organizations in the survey by Gaugler et al. (1990) use assessment centers for this purpose. This may be an underestimate, though, because many organizations use complex behavioral simulations for training purposes, but do not call them assessment centers. The FCPA had a spotty history of providing services to individual companies in different regions of the country. The agency recognized that more coordination was needed to deal with new pressures on the United States' economy to more effectively sell its products in foreign locations. To increase foreign sales, departments that normally worked with only one segment of industry needed to work together to promote a wider range of products. In addition, changes in the world economic and political realm required new values and approaches, both in overseas promotion activities and in the way the various divisions worked together within the United States.

Target Jobs

For several reasons, agency management decided that traditional job analysis was not appropriate for identifying the dimensions to be developed in this program. First, virtually all professional and managerial jobs in the organization were involved in the new initiative. Second, current operations did not call for many of the skills and styles of interaction needed in the new environment. Thus, it was not feasible to study current practices with traditional observation and questionnaire methods. Instead, management used a more deductive approach called strategic job analysis (Schneider & Konz, 1989; Taylor, 1990). They held discussions about future job demands with a cross-section of personnel at all levels of the organization. In addition, they assembled panels of industry representatives to suggest the types of new job activities that would be helpful. Starting with the organization's new objectives, the panelists identified the skills and competencies needed by all personnel in the organization.

Dimensions

Management selected several types of dimensions. At the individual level, initiative, assertiveness, and impact were important. At the group level, cooperation and negotiation skills were important. At the organizational level, the staff had to have a broader perspective and a sensitivity to extraorganizational events in order to be aware of changes in the foreign markets.

Exercises

To simulate the world market, the HRM staff developed a series of coordinated and integrated exercises. Background information for the exercises included a large briefing book that contained material about the simulated world economy, information on several fictitious countries, and details about numerous companies in the United States. The administrator gave each participant an assignment in the simulated agency, usually different from one he or she had in real life. This simulated agency was similar to the FCPA, but different enough so that the participants could not rely on the rules and practices they used at FCPA.

After reading the briefing material, each participant was asked to identify the most pressing problem faced by the agency and to make a recommendation for the next action step that should be taken. The director of the agency then convened a meeting where these proposals were discussed. The facilitators, playing the roles of representatives of U.S companies and foreign businesses, then started to contact the participants with questions about services and opportunities for business. Participants could make contacts with assessors, set up meetings with other agency staff members, write letters, and so on. These various activities took place in several rooms of a government training facility. Periodically, the assessment center administrator sent memos to the group and requested information or made proposals that required group action.

In summary, there were a series of integrated exercises that built on each other. Information provided in one exercise was useful in subsequent exercises. Several discrete exercises were embedded in the ongoing overall simulation. Assessors observed reactions to the planned exercises and also to the activities generated by the group itself as it ran the agency over the course of the program. At least two exercises of each type were conducted so that participants had a chance to receive feedback and change their behavior. For example, after the first group discussion, feedback was given and participants were expected to practice in areas of weakness in subsequent segments of the simulation. Approximately 20 percent of the organizations in Gaugler et al.'s (1990) survey use some form of integrated exercises: this practice seems to be growing.

Participants

Each group of participants going through the program represented a diagonal slice of the organization, including staff members, lower-level supervisors, middle-level managers, and top-level administrators. At any one assessment center program, there was normally only one representative of a given region, office, or department in the agency. Therefore, people who were in a direct-report relationship with each other did not attend the assessment center at the same time. This arrangement was set up so that people would feel safer exploring new ways to behave on the job and be more willing to discuss sensitive matters, such as changing their professional style and their values.

Assessors/Facilitators

The assessors in this program took on very different roles from the assessors in the assessment programs described earlier in this chapter. Here they were called "facilitators," and they were responsible for making observations of effective behaviors and giving immediate feedback so that the participants could learn from the simulation itself. The facilitators observed individual behavior, group interaction, and the effectiveness of the total organization. They were considered trainers rather than evaluators or judges. The skills of process observation (Schein, 1969) were particularly important. Therefore, the facilitators were usually human resource staff members who worked in training and organizational development capacities. Consultants and university professors are often used as facilitators.

Feedback

Throughout the program, facilitators made observations and took notes about behavior relevant to the dimensions described earlier. The facilitators met periodically to share initial impressions. Subsequent observations were made on individuals who appeared to be faltering and needed special guidance. Since activities were taking place in several locations, it was sometimes hard to observe everyone systematically. After each major segment of the simulation, the total group of participants and facilitators met to review the exercises up to that point. Participants received feedback about their performance from the facilitators and from other participants. The assessment center administrator then introduced specific questions and feedback to encourage discussion about issues the agency was facing.

After hearing some feedback, the participants got a chance to try new ways of behaving in subsequent exercises. When facilitators saw improvements, they offered comments at discreet times to reinforce the changes in behavior that were in line with organizational objectives.

Program

The assessment center activities at FCPA were only part of the larger organizational development process. Before the participants came to the program, they took a series of self-evaluation tests, which were compiled and scored by human resource staff.

In addition, peers of each participant provided descriptions of each individual's on-the-job behavior using a standardized questionnaire that measured concepts related to the dimensions being assessed. After the simulation activities, the participants were given the results of the tests and questionnaires so they could compare them with the assessment center observations. These various sources of information provided multiple views of how each participant was functioning as a manager.

At the beginning of the assessment center program, the participants discussed the changes in direction of the agency and the new types of behaviors that were required for success. They were given a list of the dimensions, and they discussed these in relation to their own jobs. The dimensions were offered as a model of job effectiveness that participants used to guide their behavior in the assessment center activities. Thus, the subsequent feedback was more meaningful in light of this initial framework.

Results

The agency found that the assessment center experience was an effective management training and team-building experience. The program helped the agency clarify its new mission and showed staff members the management skills required to carry out this mission. The dimensions provided a means of translating vague objectives into specific behavioral actions they could take. Experiences in the simulations introduced new ways of working together and made it easier to change work patterns. After several groups had gone through the assessment center, people started to refer to those experiences when they discussed how to handle challenging problems in the organization.

Some participants found the assessment center simulations too far removed from their work situations and said they did not benefit from the experience. Others objected to having outside consultants give feedback about actions that were effective or ineffective, believing that only people who were familiar with the operations could make relevant comments. The agency was also worried about whether the insights gained in the assessment center were actually being transferred back to the job. They decided to set up a series of "refresher" meetings in which participants periodically met to discuss difficulties they experienced applying their new skills.

Summary

The FCPA assessment center had advantages and disadvantages in relation to the other programs described earlier in this chapter. The exercises more closely resembled the work setting than the exercises in the first two programs. They provided the opportunity to practice new skills in a safe environment and to get feedback from impartial observers. The assessment center information was integrated immediately with the information from the peer questionnaires and self-evaluation tests. On the negative side, because large numbers of participants were often engaging in exercises in different locations, facilitators found it difficult to make careful observations. Thus, this program did not provide assessments that were as detailed and diagnostic as those at either OSS or Kimberly Brothers Manufacturing.

Review of Cases

The three case studies described in this chapter illustrate the several common features of all assessment centers, as well as many variations. All assessment centers involve observation of behavior relevant to dimensions of managerial effectiveness in simulation exercises. Evaluations by multiple assessors are integrated and fed back to participants and others who need the information in order to make personnel decisions. On the other hand, assessment centers for different purposes—promotion, diagnosis, or training—are designed somewhat differently. Variables include the following:

- dimensions to be assessed
- types of exercises
- content of exercises
- observation and evaluation procedures
- types of feedback
- support activities

All of these variables are employed to ensure that the assessment center meets the specific objectives of a given human resource management function. This theme is explored in more depth in the next chapter.

3

Basic Requirements of an Assessment Center

Key Concepts: Distinguishing features of a true assessment center; using a single assessment center for more than one purpose.

The three case studies presented in Chapter 2 showed how assessment centers have been used to help organizations make promotion decisions, diagnose training needs, and develop managerial skills. These reports revealed that there are several common features among assessment centers, as well as several differences among them. When assessment centers are devised to meet other human resource management objectives, there are even more variations. This chapter describes the essential features that must be present for any set of personnel evaluation procedures to qualify as an assessment center. It then discusses the theoretical principles underlying the assessment procedures for the three different purposes illustrated in the last chapter. These principles are then translated into practical applications to show how the various elements of an assessment center are designed for a specific purpose. The chapter concludes with a discussion of the possibilities of using a given assessment center for multiple purposes.

Essential Features of an Assessment Center

The assessment center is just one of many alternative methods for accomplishing the various human resource management objectives discussed in the last two chapters. Other methods have their own strengths, but these will not be discussed here. A concise summary of alternative methods of personnel assessment is presented in Thornton and Byham (1982).

There are several basic requirements for an assessment process to legitimately be called an "assessment center" according to the *Guidelines and Ethical Considerations for Assessment Center Operations* (Task Force, 1989). The *Guidelines*, which are reproduced in the Appendix, were written by a task force of experienced practitioners and endorsed by nearly two hundred people at the 1989 International Congress on the Assessment Center Method. Over the years, proponents of the assessment center method have insisted that this term should be applied to only certain methods. The reason for this protectiveness is that there is considerable research supporting the consistency and accuracy of the method. Individuals developing other assessment methods sometimes wish to benefit from the good publicity given the assessment center method without establishing the same level of empirical support. Therefore, proponents of the assessment center method have insisted that the term be reserved for only those procedures that contain the following basic elements.

Job Analysis

Analysis of job requirements is the first step in developing any human resource management procedure; it is particularly important for ensuring that a selection procedure is fair to all candidates (Arvey & Faley, 1988). When applied to assessment centers, job analysis involves some systematic procedure to identify the dimensions—that is, the skills, qualities, attributes, motivation, knowledge, or tasks —that are required for success in the target job or jobs. These dimensions serve as the framework for building situational exercises, observing behaviors of candidates, evaluating effectiveness of performance, and giving feedback. If an adequate job analysis has not already been carried out, a new analysis may be necessary. If the job does not currently exist, parts of that new job may already exist and can be analyzed to discover the relevant dimensions. Procedures for performing a job analysis as a preliminary to assessment center operations are described in Chapter 4.

Multiple Assessment Techniques

A variety of assessment techniques can be used to evaluate participants in assessment centers. These include interviews, tests, questionnaires, and situational exercises. The techniques must be designed to provide multiple opportunities to observe complex behavior related to the dimensions identified in the job analysis.

Situational Exercises

One of the distinguishing features of the assessment center method is the situational exercise (Bray & Grant, 1966). Situational exercises are simulations that portray important aspects of the target job. Job analysis reveals the most common tasks, problems, and situations that job holders must face. Situational exercises are then created that closely resemble these important features of the job situation.

A situational exercise presents the participant with a complex set of stimuli to deal with. For example, the "test" materials may include a complicated written case describing the economic conditions in a small town and call for the participant to perform a financial analysis to decide whether to open a branch bank. In a group discussion, the participant might interact with other participants to formulate a set of recommendations for higher management. In a simulation of one-on-one interactions, the assessee might be required to talk with a person who is playing the role of a problem employee or an irate customer. The common feature of these exercises is that the participant is faced with a complex set of conditions representing a situation that may actually occur on the job. The advantage of situational exercises is that they require the participant to demonstrate complex behaviors.

Behavioral Responses

Situational exercises are performance tests (Anastasi, 1988) that require the participant to display complex behavior in a simulation of some critical scenario in the organization. To be successful, the participant must display some overt behavior consistent with the behaviors required on the job. For example, in a group discussion, the participant must offer suggestions about a new program or procedure; in a written case study, he or she must write a critical analysis, a recommendation, or a proposal. Such responses are quite different from the responses a person gives when taking a paper-and-pencil test, where he or she may have to make several complex covert responses (in other words, think), but the only overt response is the simple motion of making a mark on a piece of paper. The test interpreter is then required to make some inference about the covert responses. In contrast, participants in a group discussion must not only think, but also speak and act in ways that influence others. In exercises such as these, the assessor is not required to make such large inferences about the participant's skills or motivations.

Another distinguishing feature of situational exercises is that there is interaction: other people in the group discussion talk and the participant must respond; in a presentation, the audience may ask questions; and in a simulation involving the problem employee, the verbal exchange may be intense. These sets of complex and dynamic interactions elicit a rich source of behaviors that are indicative of more complex competencies than can be assessed by most paper-and-pencil tests.

Behavioral Observations

Behavior of the participants in situational exercises is observed by trained assessors. Assessors take detailed notes of what the participants say and do. An example of a behavioral observation during a group problem-solving discussion might be: "Tim pounded his fist on the table and said, 'That's too little, too late,' when Bob offered to raise the travel allowance." Behavioral observations give a specific statement of observable actions and even actual words. They do not contain inferences, such as "he was angry," or interpretations, such as "he made a bad impression on other participants."

Multiple Assessors

In the assessment center method, more than one individual is involved in evaluating the participant. Observations from multiple assessors help ensure that idiosyncratic biases from any one assessor will not unduly influence the final outcome of the assessment process. For example, one assessor may hold the false assumption that all written reports must follow a certain format. When we solicit several points of view, we are acknowledging that we must make judgments about professional competence and that judgments, per se, have some subjectivity in them. In order to minimize the adverse effect of biases of any one assessor, observations of more than one assessor are pooled.

Assessors with several different points of view can make valid contributions to the evaluation of professional competencies. Assessors bring different backgrounds and experiences to the assessment task and contribute a rich variety of perspectives. Such diversity means that assessors may not always agree on the evaluation of a participant. Each of the different evaluations may be accurate and include valuable information; in fact, such differences are expected and welcomed as a part of the principle of multiple assessment. The staff of an assessment center may consist of managers and/or human resource personnel from within the organization, outside consultants, or a variety of other individuals familiar with the target job. Research has indicated that a variety of different types of assessors can make valid contributions to assessment (Gaugler, Rosenthal, Thornton, & Bentson, 1987). There is no common agreement about how many assessors are necessary for adequate evaluations in the assessment center context. In a typical assessment center, three assessors make independent observations of each participant's performance, as we saw in the OSS promotion program in Chapter 2. Sometimes many more than three assessors are involved, as we saw in the development program at the FCPA.

Trained Assessors

Assessors are trained to carry out complex assessment functions. They must be able to observe behavior, record those observations in some manner, classify behavior into the dimensions being assessed, make judgments about the level of performance displayed by the candidate, describe these observations to other assessors, integrate behavioral observations from different sources and exercises, and in some cases, make an evaluation of overall success and give suggestions for development in the future (Byham, 1977). In order to carry out these functions, assessors must be trained thoroughly. Then it must be determined that they can carry out these functions accurately. Some of the elements of assessor training include discussion of the meaning of the dimensions to be assessed, practice in observing and evaluating behavior, integration of the information in the assessor team, and giving feedback to participants. The *Guidelines* strongly state that the organization should examine all assessors to certify that they are competent to observe, classify, and rate behavior. More details on assessor training can be found in several sources (e.g., Byham, 1977; Thornton & Byham, 1982).

Integration of Observations

Here we must begin to think about a very controversial aspect of the assessment center process and about psychological assessment procedures in general. Traditionally, assessment centers have relied on managerial judgments. The results of individual exercises are observed and classified in a judgmental way. In addition, when the assessors integrate their observations across exercises and then integrate evaluations of dimensions to derive an overall rating, they do so judgmentally. The judgmental integration process has been called the "clinical method" (Dawes, 1979; Sawyer, 1966) because it is the method often used by clinical psychologists to combine information from different sources in order to carry out a diagnosis of an individual's personality makeup or predict the success of various forms of therapy.

There is an alternative to the judgmental method of integrating information that many people favor and that may be more appropriate for some assessment situations, for instance, when large numbers of candidates are being screened for low-level jobs. This is the "statistical" or "mechanical" method of combining information (Sawyer, 1966). With this method, pieces of information are assigned predetermined weights and then combined in a formula. For example, to arrive at an overall assessment rating of promotability, the rating on the dimension "decision-making ability" may be given twice the weight as the rating on "leadership." These different weights are selected to show the relative importance of the dimensions for the success of individuals in the target position. The statistical formula is a substitute for the assessors' judgment about the relative importance of the dimensions.

There is an unresolved debate over the best integration method to use. There is empirical evidence to support each method; at this time there is no definitive answer as to which is the best method. A much more thorough review of this debate is presented in Chapters 6 and 7, where research from the assessment center domain and from the broader domain of psychological assessment is discussed. Traditionally, the assessment center method has used the judgmental integration process; that process is a legitimate part of an assessment center. The reader should be aware, though, that some assessment center proponents strongly advocate the statistical integration process and can marshal clear evidence to support their position (Feltham, 1988b; Sackett & Wilson, 1982).

The previous discussion might suggest that assessment centers use *either* a judgmental *or* a statistical method to integrate their results. In fact, the two methods can be used to complement each other. Chapter 7 explores how the two methods can be used jointly to improve assessor decision making.

Theoretical Foundations for Alternative Assessment Center Programs

Chapter 2 illustrated three very different ways of carrying out an assessment center program. The special features of these programs were designed to accomplish very different purposes. The objective of a long-range promotion program is to assess potential for managerial success and to predict the success of candidates for higher-level jobs. The objective of a diagnostic program is to identify the relative strengths and weaknesses in the individual's job-related competencies. The objective of a development program is to teach a new set of skills to the individual participants and to develop teamwork skills within the group. These are quite different objectives; accordingly, very different assessment centers should be designed to accomplish these objectives. In the past, some assessment centers have been designed for one purpose and used for another. The results are usually disappointing. For example, an assessment center designed to aid in long-range predictions of management potential may not yield a good diagnosis of training needs, since the dimensions may not be amenable to development and the feedback may not be helpful in giving direction for change.

This section explores the theoretical foundations and general principles underlying different uses of the assessment center. Why should the student and practitioner of human resource management care about these theoretical foundations? Because understanding them helps in very practical ways when the time comes to design an effective assessment center. As Kurt Lewin, a famous psychologist in the 1930s, so simply and eloquently stated, "There is nothing so practical as a good theory." Several practical examples of assessment center design will be given following our discussion of principles of prediction, diagnosis, and training.

Principles of Prediction

We can look to the principles of measurement in the field of psychometrics for the theoretical foundations of good prediction (Ghiselli, Campbell, & Zedeck, 1981; Nunnally, 1978). Some key measurement principles are *standardization, reliability,* and *validity.* Standardization refers to the uniformity of the procedures for evaluating participants. A procedure is standardized if every person is provided the same instructions, the same questions, the same rules and time limits, and the same chance to respond fully. Several potential threats to standardization can occur in the administration of an assessment center. Situational tests can be unstandardized: participants may be given different amounts of time to complete a written case analysis; role players depicting a problem employee may act with different degrees of cooperation; and participants in a group discussion may get quite excited or remain rather calm. Usually, the impact of these threats can be minimized by careful administration of the program. Uncontrolled variations should be documented and reported along with assessment results.

Reliability refers to the consistency of scores for two measurements taken on two equivalent samples of behavior, or for two measurements taken at two points in time. Reliability also refers to agreement among scores given by different examiners. A test is reliable if we get a similar score no matter which form of the test is used, when it is administered, or who administers or scores it. Unreliability in assessment center ratings may arise if different topics are assigned in a leaderless group discussion, if assessors differ in the behaviors they observe and record, or if the assessor team is somewhat lax in integrating the behavioral information. Fortunately, most of these potential sources of unreliability are controlled by thorough training of the assessors, the use of clear scoring standards, and the administrator's faithful adherence to the procedure of sharing and evaluating information in the integration discussion for each participant. In the end, the research evidence shows that assessment center ratings are highly consistent.

Validity refers to the ability of the test to achieve its aims and objectives. Establishing the validity of a test is a complex process (Binning & Barrett, 1989; Landy, 1986) that involves the accumulation of evidence that the assessment procedure is measuring the targeted concepts and will contribute relevant information to the decisions that must be made. For example, in the case of the promotional assessment center, the most relevant validity information is the accuracy with which assessors could predict long-range success in the jobs in question (Society for Industrial and Organizational Psychology, 1987). Validity comes when the jobs have been carefully analyzed and when critical components have been identified and measured carefully. Validity of the assessment center can actually be diminished if it includes components *not* critical to the job. There is much theoretical (Wernimont & Campbell, 1968) and empirical evidence (Asher & Scariano, 1974) to support the use of behavioral *samples,* as distinguished from *signs,* of effective performance on the job. Signs can be thought of as indicators of important behaviors. Examples of signs include paper-and-pencil tests of mental abilities and personality characteristics, interviews that cover a person's work experiences, and biographical information forms that cover background and educational experiences. Behavioral sampling procedures are quite different; they require that the person demonstrate complex behaviors that are very much like on-the-job behaviors. Behavioral sampling is provided by the situational exercises introduced in Chapters 1 and 2; it is explained in more depth in Chapter 5. Assessment centers have the potential for high accuracy in predicting future success because they provide samples of behavior that show the participants' ability to handle actual work situations.

Principles of Diagnosis

The theory of diagnosis of differential strengths and weaknesses is similar to the theory of prediction of long-range success but is based on some additional principles of good measurement. Diagnosis requires clear and discrete measurement of separate characteristics (Wiggins, 1973). By contrast, for prediction of long-range success, we evaluate the dimensions as a way to ensure representative coverage of important elements in job performance, but our real interest is in predicting overall potential. For diagnosis, the measurement must give accurate measures of each of the separate dimensions in and of themselves. More than that, the measurement procedure must give measures of these attributes that are not highly related to each other (Cascio, 1987). For example, if everyone who scored high on leadership also scored high on oral communication, the assessment process would not provide a diagnosis of different skill levels on these two dimensions.

The result we are seeking from a diagnostic assessment center is classification (Cascio, 1987; Wiggins, 1973). Classification is the process of matching the profile of an individual's strengths and weaknesses with situation requirements to maximize the effectiveness of the entire system. In a diagnostic assessment center, we are trying to place a person in the correct types of training activities so that he or she will improve in job-related skills.

To help with classification of managers, an assessment center must provide accurate assessment of separate dimensions of managerial competence. For example, it must evaluate decision-making ability independently of other dimensions, such as impact on other people. To accomplish this "nondependent" evaluation, the assessment center must be designed with certain features: the dimensions chosen must be conceptually distinct, the exercises must be set up so that assessors can detect variations in an individual's performance from one dimension to another, and assessors must be trained to make the appropriate distinctions among behaviors relevant to the dimensions.

Principles of Training Relevant to a Developmental Assessment Center

If an assessment center is to be used for training managerial skills, a very different set of principles is involved in the design. Whereas the emphasis in promotion or diagnostic programs is on evaluation and measurement of behavior, here the emphasis is on change in behavior. As illustrated in Chapter 2, the Federal Commercial Promotion Agency used the assessment center to enable participants to learn new skills and ways of interacting with each other. As with the FCPA program, the exercises should provide opportunities for each participant to develop in areas where he or she is weak.

Principles of learning and development provide guidance in the design of several aspects of the assessment center, including the selection of dimensions to be developed, the way exercises are run, how and when feedback is given, and the general climate of the program. We will review all of these points after we present some key principles of training and development.

For a long time, psychologists have known about the conditions that foster learning (Goldstein, 1986). Early studies of learning patterns showed that new responses become associated with more basic responses after repeated pairings. From other learning studies, we know that people learn new behaviors that are followed by reinforcements. In the management development arena, a manager will learn new skills if he or she gets positive feedback from the new behavior or if there is an indication that it leads to the effective completion of a project or to profitability for the organization.

More recently, two areas of theory and research have contributed to the development of management training programs: adult learning (Knowles, 1970, 1973) and social learning (Bandura, 1977, 1986; Goldstein & Sorcher, 1974). Adult learning theory (Knowles, 1970) is built on the premise that adults learn differently from children because they have a large amount of experience to draw on, are more ready to learn, and want to learn skills that will help them carry out important roles in life. In view of these particular characteristics of adults, Knowles (1973) derived several suggestions for how training programs should be set up. The training should be organized around real-life problems rather than abstract disciplines. Also, adults need a safe environment in which to unlearn old modes of behavior. In addition, adults learn better if they are provided an opportunity to be actively involved in the learning process.

Social learning theory gives many different and helpful insights into how a management training program should be set up. Bandura (1977) has shown that we learn many important behaviors vicariously, that is, by watching others learn. We ourselves need not engage in the behavior; when we can observe the behavior of others, we see which actions are effective and reinforced and which are ineffective and not reinforced. This principle is exemplified in the situational exercises of assessment centers that involve participation with other managers. Bandura has also shown that people become more self-confident in their skills when supportive conditions prevail: when there are multiple opportunities to be successful, when the learner can observe other people being successful, when credible people provide support, and when the situation does not produce so much anxiety that the person questions his or her own ability to succeed. These conditions give us many practical suggestions about how an assessment center should be set up to foster actual learning and real skill development.

Application of Principles to Assessment Center Design

Let's turn now to the application of these principles to the design of an assessment center. In what ways do the three organizations described in our case studies utilize the principles we have just described? Does OSS's promotion assessment center use good principles of measurement and prediction? Does Kimberly's diagnostic program use good principles of differential measurement? Does the FCPA's organizational development program use good principles of training and learning?

Table 3.1 summarizes the different ways that assessment centers have been implemented, as illustrated in Chapter 2. It shows how several features of the assessment center procedure are carried out in the specific case examples. What should be apparent is that there is no such thing as a typical assessment center. This same observation was made many years ago in a survey in 1973 by Bender and was confirmed by a much more extensive survey in 1990 by Gaugler, Bentson, and Pohley. Both studies demonstrated that there is wide variation in the way all facets of an assessment center are set up and administered. What is not so obvious, and what forms the basic theme of this book, is that the characteristics of the assessment center must be matched with the purpose of the program. All too often in the past, assessment centers for diagnosis looked just like assessment centers for prediction of long-range potential. This may not be surprising because, in the early years, when organizations initiated assessment centers, they often wished to follow the excellent example set by AT&T and the Bell operating companies (Bray, 1964; Bray & Grant, 1966). Those programs had been confirmed by extensive research to be accurate predictors of managerial success over many years (Thornton & Byham, 1982). What was often not recognized was that the features of a program like AT&T's might not be appropriate for a program in another organization, used for a completely different purpose.

The bigger lesson to be learned by human resource managers is that excellent programs should not just be copied. The faddish adoption of techniques that work for someone else has been the curse of the human resource management field.

To be clear about my position on imitation and innovation, I should emphasize that it is entirely appropriate to benefit from

Table 3.1
Comparison of Assessment Centers

	Promotion or Selection	Diagnosis of Training Needs	Development of Skills
Participants	High-potential employees or applicants	All interested employees	All interested employees
Position to be analyzed	Job to be filled now or in future	Current or future job	Current or future job
Number of dimensions	Fewer (e.g., 5–7), more global	Many (e.g., 8–10), more specific	Fewer (e.g., 5–7)
Nature of dimensions	Potentialities, traits	Developable, conceptually distinct	Trainable skills
Number of exercises	Few (e.g., 3–5)	Many (e.g., 6–8)	More than one of each type
Types of exercises	Generic	Moderate similarity to job	Work samples
Time required for assessment	Relatively short (e.g., .5–1 day)	Relatively long (e.g., 1.5–2 days)	Relatively long (e.g., 1.5–2 days)
Type of report	Short, descriptive	Long, diagnostic	Immediate verbal report
Who gets feedback	Participant, manager two levels up	Participant and supervisor	Participant, possibly supervisor
Who gives feedback	HRM staff	HRM staff or assessor	HRM staff, trainer, or facilitator
Important outcome	Overall assessment rating	Dimension ratings	Behavioral suggestions

the sound research and development done at AT&T and to use the same procedures they have used, provided the new program has similar purposes. In fact, I would argue strongly that the same procedures *should* be used so that the earlier research results are applicable in the new setting. There is no need to "reinvent the wheel." On the other hand, the wheel may not be the apparatus you need for the vehicle you are building. That is, you may need an assessment center that is very different from the ones designed previously. Sackett (1982) observed that in the early 1980s, few job analyses had been reported in the development of assessment centers; organizations often used the same dimensions and exercises as their predecessors. Fortunately, the present situation seems to be different: Gaugler et al. (1990) found that over 90 percent of the organizations conducted a job analysis as a basis for their assessment centers.

Table 3.1 makes it clear that any one feature can be implemented in different ways. The job or jobs being simulated can be either *current* jobs, as in the case of the KBM diagnostic program, jobs at the *next higher levels,* as in the OSS promotion program, or *a set of jobs* that a variety of participants hold, as in the development and team-building program at the FCPA. The dimensions being assessed also differ markedly from one program to another. For promotion purposes, the assessment should be done on dimensions that reflect potentialities to grow over a long period of time, whereas for diagnosis and development, the program should assess skills or competencies that can be developed either during the program itself (in the case of a development program) or in the future (in the case of a diagnostic program).

There are also differences in the exercises used for the three types of programs. The basic types of exercises need not differ; all programs might use in-baskets, group discussions, and simulations of one-on-one interviews. The differences are in the content of the exercises and the types of demands placed on the participants. For a selection or promotion program, we would assume that the participant had little experience with the problems being presented. Thus, we would not require any specific knowledge or technical skill to be displayed. By contrast, for a diagnostic or development program, we would assume the participants had relevant experience and we would be assessing the level of skills or trying to enhance those skills. Thus, in these latter programs the exercises can involve technical material relevant to the target job.

The process of observing, classifying, and evaluating behavior is quite different in the three programs also. Recall that the purpose of the promotion program is to predict potential for success in the future. This final overall assessment rating is based on the accumulated information about performance on several dimensions. There may be many paths to this result in terms of the types of behavior observed and the dimension ratings given. But in the end, the particular qualities of any one dimension rating are not as important as the predictive accuracy of the overall rating. In contrast, for a diagnostic program, each dimension rating must be quite accurate. Thus, the way that assessors are trained and the ways they are required to observe, record, and judge behavior must be designed specifically to provide accurate measures on the separate dimensions. In fact, an overall assessment rating may not even be given. Chapter 6 goes into more detail on the alternative ways that observation and judgment is carried out in various types of programs. For now, suffice it to say that the observation procedures must be designed to provide the types of information needed to fulfill the objectives of the program.

The results and feedback generated from the three types of programs certainly differ. In all programs, the participants should be given feedback about their performance. The *Guidelines and Ethical Considerations for Assessment Center Operations* (Task Force, 1989), provided in the Appendix, emphasize that participants should receive feedback on their performance and be informed about recommendations made by the assessment team. When psychologists are involved in designing and implementing assessment centers, which is frequently the case, they follow this practice because it is a part of their code of ethics (American Psychological Association, 1981), which states that a client has the right to know the results and interpretations from assessment techniques. Beyond feedback to the individual, the results of a promotion program should be presented to managers two levels above the participants, since in most organizations these are the people making final decisions about promotions. In order to preserve the privacy of the participants, the assessment results should not be given to other people, especially the supervisory level directly above the participants. These supervisors are in the target position being assessed, and they can give evaluations of current on-the-job performance of the participants, but they will probably not be making decisions about whether others will be promoted into a position like their own. What the higher-level decision makers need to receive is an unbiased prediction of the likelihood of success if the candidate is promoted.

By contrast, in a diagnostic program, detailed information about performance on separate dimensions must be provided to the assessee and to the immediate supervisor. The detailed feedback often includes specific behaviors illustrating components of a dimension, for example, the person's leadership skill was considered weak because he or she never asked subordinates for their help in solving problems. Such information forms the basis of developmental planning and subsequent training and development activities. Some of these follow-up activities can be initiated by the individual, but the immediate supervisor must be involved in many development activities. Therefore, the feedback must be much more thorough than the feedback in promotion programs.

Feedback in a training program is different still. Two features are crucial: first, the feedback must be specific and give guidance for alternative actions to improve performance; second, the feedback must be provided soon after the behavior has been performed. Whereas results of a promotion or diagnostic program may come days or weeks later, feedback in a training program must come immediately if the person is to learn and have the chance to improve in subsequent exercises. This is why there must be two or more exercises and the facilitators must record their observations quickly and provide feedback to the participants in a helpful manner.

Summary and Conclusions

Two issues were raised at the beginning of this chapter: Are there distinguishing features of an assessment center, and can a single assessment center be used for more than one purpose? After reading about assessment centers so far, you might conclude that this method is not really different from other personnel evaluation procedures. After all, each one of the features is used elsewhere: multiple interviewers are commonly used to select professionals and managers; situational interviews and in-baskets are used as stand-alone techniques; multiple sources of data are commonly combined to predict job success. What is unique about the assessment center is the way these procedures are used in *combination* with each other. Thus, we can look at an assessment procedure and say whether or not it is an assessment center.

To be called an assessment center, the process must have all the required elements of job analysis, multiple assessors, multiple situational exercises, behavioral reporting, and integration by a team of trained assessors or by some statistical method that has been properly developed. Each of those elements can be varied somewhat to fit the specific purpose of the assessment program set forth by the human resource manager. Theories of measurement, differential diagnosis, and learning provide valuable practical suggestions for how each type of assessment center should be constructed.

The issue of whether or not an assessment center can be used for multiple purposes is a bit more complex. As an example, let's first consider whether an assessment center program designed primarily for promotion purposes can also be used for diagnosis and development. On the one hand, one might argue that during the assessment process the assessors have gathered a wealth of information, and it would be a good idea to use that information to help the individual develop. It would take only a little more time during the feedback session to give the participant suggestions about things he or she could do to improve. Even if the organization does not plan to do any systematic training, the participants might benefit from personal insight into their weaknesses and engage in self-improvement. Finally, talking about how the person can improve just seems to be a good thing to do.

On the other hand, it may be difficult and misleading to talk about developing many of the dimensions typically assessed in selection and promotion programs. Characteristics such as energy level, impact on others, adaptability, motivation, and integrity are not easy to change in the context of organizational life. There are those who would argue that organizations do not have the obligation to provide follow-up training to everyone who is considered for promotion. If the candidate does not have the motivation to manage others or to move upward in the organization, it may be unethical for the organization to try to change those basic values, even if it could.

Next, let's consider whether a program designed primarily for diagnosis or development can be used for promotion decisions. On the one hand, the organization may see that much valuable information has been gathered in the course of diagnosis or training that would indicate whether the person should be promoted to a position of more responsibility. The argument is that if a participant shows faults that are not likely to be changed easily in the short run, it would be irresponsible to the organization as a whole to promote the person.

On the other hand, if participants know that the assessment information might be used for decision making, they may not be willing to reveal weaknesses (even if we call them "developmental needs"), to explore alternative managerial styles, and to take the risks that are often required for learning. In essence, the climate of a selection program is incompatible with the climate of a development program.

In summary, I believe that it is very difficult to use one program for multiple purposes. In my opinion, the many adaptations of the assessment center method that must be made to attain different goals imply that a program set up to accomplish one goal may be incompatible with the needs of another program. One final thought: participants in an assessment center should be told how the information will be used (Task Force, 1990). For example, if the program is publicized as developmental, but higher-level managers will have access to the results (and thus may use them for making promotion decisions), then the participants should be informed of this.

Now that we have reviewed the requirements of assessment centers and the principles underlying their design and implementation for different purposes, we can go into more detail about each of their critical elements and see specific examples of dimensions and exercises. In addition, we will review the principles that govern assessment center development and the research into their effectiveness.

4

Dimensions to Be Assessed

Key Concepts: Assessing current skills vs. potentialities; assessing tasks; determining the number of dimensions.

This chapter explores the various characteristics, or "dimensions," that can be evaluated in assessment centers designed for different purposes. It covers the principles that should guide the selection of dimensions to be assessed, introduces some methods of analyzing the target job, and then discusses the nature of dimensions to be assessed in selection, diagnostic, and development programs. Finally, I speculate on alternative categorization schemes (other than human attributes) for the observation and evaluation of behavior in assessment centers.

General Principles

The purpose of the assessment center should guide the selection of the dimensions to be assessed. This basic principle seems quite logical, but all too often it has not been followed in the design of assessment centers. The human resource manager or other administrator designing an assessment center should formulate a clear statement of the purpose of the assessment center and should specify the ways in which the information will be used. Then, when analyzing the target job, the designer should select only appropriate dimensions for assessment.

Theory and research on social cognition show that the *purpose* of the observation process affects the way in which behavior is observed, encoded, stored in memory, and retrieved (Fiske & Taylor, 1984; Wyler & Srull, 1986). For example, if the purpose is to form a general impression of an individual, the observer will notice different behaviors and store them in memory in a different manner than if he or she is observing specific behaviors. Thus, in the assessment center context, the *purpose of the program* and the *types of dimensions* must be made compatible so that the observation and judgment tasks of the assessor are guided properly.

We sometimes see mismatches between the purpose of the assessment center and the dimensions assessed. For example, some assessment centers used for selection or promotion decisions assess knowledge and skills that can be readily learned on the job. This practice is not only inefficient, but also inadvisable in light of the *Uniform Guidelines for Personnel Selection* published by the Equal Employment Opportunity Commission and other federal compliance agencies (1978). The *Uniform Guidelines* are a set of regulations that describe the way organizations should develop, evaluate, and use procedures for selecting and promoting people in organizations. They have served as the basis for many court cases where unfair discrimination against minorities and women has been charged. The *Uniform Guidelines* admonish organizations against making selection decisions based on the results of tests of characteristics that can be learned in the initial training for a job.

For selection and promotion programs, organizations are usually interested in using an assessment center to help higher-level managers identify candidates who have the potential to learn and grow in a new position. Therefore, they should assess attributes related to the person's potential to learn (for example, basic interpersonal and problem-solving skills). Thus, the job analysis effort should be designed to identify those attributes that the assessors should be focusing on in the exercises. These attributes must be clarified for all assessors so they have a common frame of reference for their observations.

In contrast to the above situation, there are some selection programs that are designed to assess current levels of skills and competencies. For example, a government agency may want to know if an applicant has knowledge of certain rules, regulations, and procedures, or a manufacturing company may want to know if a welder has the skill to use certain equipment and materials. In such cases, actual work-sample procedures are appropriate for assessing present knowledge and skills.

For diagnostic programs, the goals are much different. Here the assessment center should measure only "developable" skills. A developable skill is one that can be improved in a relatively short time with a reasonable amount of effort by the individual and the organization. Thus, the organization must think carefully about what feedback it can give to the participant, what training programs are available to improve weaknesses if they are diagnosed, and what support can be given to the participant's immediate supervisor to help overcome deficiencies. If the organization is unwilling or unable to provide follow-up resources to remediate weaknesses on a given dimension, then that dimension should not be assessed in a diagnostic program.

Sometimes the dimensions in a diagnostic program are not matched to its purpose. Some assessment centers designed to diagnose training needs make assessments of characteristics that cannot be developed in any reasonable amount of time through organizational training activities. An example of such a dimension is intellectual ability or intelligence. It makes little sense to assess this characteristic and to give someone feedback about a deficiency in this area when there is little that can be done in the short run to change it. It makes much more sense to assess and provide follow-up training for deficiencies in dimensions such as problem analysis and decision analysis, because these dimensions are more conducive to change.

Development programs should be built around a somewhat different set of dimensions. Like the dimensions in a diagnostic assessment center, the dimensions here should be developable, but more specifically, they should be trainable in the context of the current assessment center. It would make no sense to ask facilitators to try to observe and give feedback on "customer service orientation" if the exercises had no content that provided opportunity for behaviors in that dimension. It is also helpful if the dimensions are qualities that can be observed by the participant's supervisor, coworkers, and subordinates, since it is a common practice to ask these people to provide descriptions of on-the-job-behavior prior to the participant's attendance at the assessment center. Feedback from these other sources can then be combined with feedback from the assessment exercises. In addition, the dimensions should be clearly related to the functioning of a group or the organization as a whole. In the context of a team-building program, for instance, it would serve little purpose to assess and give feedback on the individual's written communication skills.

Assessor Training

The dimensions to be assessed are a critical component of assessor training. Assessor training is too complicated to be described in detail here, but we can note at this point that the meaning of the dimensions comes up repeatedly as the assessors practice observing and classifying behaviors in the exercises. One purpose of assessor training is to develop within all assessors a common frame of reference for the observation and evaluation of behaviors. Assessor training tries to create an accurate picture of the characteristics required for successful performance in the target jobs. In the field of social judgment, this picture is called a *schema* (Fiske & Taylor, 1984). A schema is a mental picture of features of some group of people. In everyday life, we all hold schemata about numerous social groups. For example, a person's schema of older people may include the features of wise, conservative, and friendly. In the assessment center context, assessors must develop accurate schemata of the successful candidate so that observations are guided properly. The process by which we identify features that combine to form a particular schema is job analysis.

Job Analysis Methods

A thorough analysis of the target job or jobs provides much valuable information for the development of an assessment center. The job analysis process usually entails several steps to ensure thorough understanding of the job requirements. All too often, the pressure to start an assessment center makes it difficult to adequately carry out these basic yet necessary steps. It is important to note that job analysis provides valuable information that will be used at several stages of assessment center development. The job analysis provides

- a list of the dimensions to be assessed
- examples of behaviors that clarify the dimensions (for assessor training)
- suggestions as to the types of exercises that resemble job situations
- suggestions for the content of problems to be put into the exercises
- an indication of the level of proficiency required on the dimensions
- standards for scoring assessee performance in the exercises
- documentation of job-relatedness of the assessment process (for use in the event of a lawsuit)

The effort required for a thorough job analysis, therefore, yields many payoffs.

Although many different job analysis methods can contribute valuable information, usually no single method will suffice. Valuable information can be obtained from reading an in-house job description, consulting trade journals, observing incumbents actually performing the job, interviewing incumbents and their subordinates and supervisors, and, in some cases, interviewing people who are served by the incumbents (O'Hare & Love, 1987). (For example, customers can provide valuable insights into the behaviors appropriate for effective customer service.) Gaugler et al.'s (1990) survey showed that the vast majority of assessment center developers used several of these job analysis techniques.

A thorough guide to job analysis procedures will not be presented in this book because excellent sources already exist. Examples of well-written resource books on job analysis include McCormick (1979) and Gael (1983). A thorough description of job analysis procedures for use in developing an assessment center is contained in Thornton and Byham (1982). A brief list of key points follows:

1. Plan the job analysis
2. Study information already available in the organization (job descriptions, training materials, etc.)

3. Observe incumbents performing the job
4. Conduct one-on-one interviews with incumbents
5. Develop a job activity questionnaire based on the interviews; administer the questionnaire to a representative sample of incumbents
6. Collect critical incidents, i.e., descriptions of effective and ineffective behaviors, from incumbents' supervisors (Flanagan, 1954)
7. Interview incumbents' subordinates (or others who interact with them)
8. Establish a preliminary list of dimensions
9. Obtain ratings of the importance of the dimensions from supervisors and, if possible, from other groups who interact with the incumbents
10. Select the final list of dimensions

Incumbents and their supervisors are the primary sources of information about job activities and job requirements. Other people can also provide insights into critical job behaviors and the dimensions that are important for job success. Customers, as well as in-house clients, have a unique perspective that can help us understand the components of job success. These sources can be particularly helpful for jobs that require skills, values, and motivations necessary for successful interaction with other people.

The general idea is to use a variety of sources of information about any job being studied. Quite different pictures of the job may be obtained from each source. This does not mean that a given source is not valid; in fact, all provide accurate information from different perspectives.

The procedures outlined above provide an excellent means for analyzing a job as it is currently being carried out by its incumbents. These procedures are effective in capturing existing behaviors, activities, important dimensions, and types of problems encountered. If the job remains stable, the analysis of existing behaviors may be adequate for the development of assessment procedures to select and develop new employees for that job. In fact, many jobs do remain stable over a period of time, and the basic attributes required for success also remain stable in the short term.

Strategic Job Analysis

Job requirements do change. Activities may be added, responsibilities may increase, new skills may become necessary, and expectations of performance may increase—all due to environmental pressures, technological innovations, organizational restructuring, or changes in management philosophy. For example, the recent emphasis on customer service as a means of increasing revenues has caused many organizations to ask employees to show more skills in such areas as listening, responding with empathy, and helping clients solve problems. A traditional job analysis that examines how current employees carry out their jobs may not capture the kinds of behaviors and dimensions that are expected in the future.

To understand future job requirements, *strategic job analysis* (Schneider & Konz, 1989; Taylor, 1990) may be helpful. Strategic job analysis is a process of thinking about the future goals of the organization and determining what implications these changes will have for performance on specific jobs. It is a process of looking into the future as opposed to looking into the past. It is a deductive process of inferring job requirements from broader organizational goals, rather than an inductive process of examining how people behave on the job in order to identify job requirements. For example, we might start the analysis by noting that a new organizational objective is entrepreneurship. For middle managers, this means that risk-taking and innovation are relevant dimensions. These attributes might go undetected if we analyzed how managers are currently doing their jobs. Murphy and Kroeker (1988) pointed out the several advantages of taking this approach when defining the criteria and skills needed for effective performance. The approach allows us to assess the adequacy of our measures of performance effectiveness, to avoid missing important determinants of performance effectiveness, and to consider a wide range of important dimensions unrestricted by how we might ultimately measure them. A deductive approach also helps to ensure that broad organizational goals are considered and that work on individual jobs is linked to these goals.

When developing assessment centers, we have traditionally translated job-analysis information into the attributes needed for job success. Now we need to look in more depth at the various types of human attributes we can assess.

Alternative Ways of Conceiving Human Attributes

When describing what assessment centers assess, I have stated that assessment center candidates should use different types of dimensions for different assessment purposes. This section offers a way to conceptualize types of dimensions. The term "dimension" has been used in the literature on assessment centers to refer to a cluster of behaviors that can be defined with specific behaviors and observed with some consistency (Thornton & Byham, 1982). A good definition of a dimension includes a statement of the behaviors that make up the dimension, the conditions under which the behaviors are demonstrated, and the level of effectiveness on the dimension expected of someone in the target job.

Examination of the dimensions that have been used in the past shows that this term usually refers to some form of human attribute. (As we will see later, there are different ways that behaviors can be classified and clustered together.) In this section, we present alternative ways of thinking about different types of human attributes.

Human attributes can be arranged along a continuum, as illustrated in Figure 4.1.

Potentialities

On the right-hand side of the chart are basic human attributes that are deeply ingrained in an individual. Two examples are intelligence and shyness. Attributes of this nature are characterized by stability, consistency, and generality. First, they are stable in the sense that they have taken a long time to develop in adult individuals and will likely take a long time to change. This

Figure 4.1
A Continuum of Human Attributes

Current skills		Potentialities
Present knowledge	Abilities	Aptitudes
Well-developed skills	Competencies	Traits
Clear preferences		Values
Opinions		

does not mean that attributes of this type are unchangeable, and it certainly does not mean that they are in-born and genetically determined. It does mean that these characteristics will not change over a period of a few weeks or months. Second, consistency means that the characteristic manifests itself in a wide variety of situations. A person who is shy in classroom situations tends to be shy in other group settings as well. The point is that there is considerable consistency in the behavior of people in these types of human attributes.

Third, attributes on the right end of the continuum are widely pervasive in their effect on many different tasks or human endeavors. A person's basic values serve as a guide or motivator for a variety of activities (Rokeach, 1973). Similarly, a person's level of intelligence allows him or her to solve a variety of different complex and abstract problems. Generality does not mean that the trait affects *all* other related activities. A person whose intelligence level is high may not be very good in solving abstract mathematical problems. A person who consistently values hard work and advancement may not be interested in working on a project for which he or she holds no interest.

Examples of basic human attributes commonly assessed in promotional assessment centers include

Decision-making ability

Impact on others

Motivation to work

Each of these attributes meets the criteria for potentialities and will affect a wide variety of managerial functions. A person with a high level of decision-making ability who has a positive effect on others and is highly motivated will probably have a high potential for success in a variety of managerial and professional positions.

Skills

At the left end of the continuum lies a set of human attributes that are specific, developed as a result of recent educational, work, or life experiences, and subject to change more quickly than potentialities. These attributes are specific in that they refer to a limited area of knowledge or a circumscribed skill. To cite two examples, knowledge of how to calculate a rate of return on an investment would be a technique learned in a course on financial analysis or in a bank job. Similarly, a person's opinion about an alternative way to dispose of nuclear waste might be a function of knowing the relative risks involved; as such, it might be subject to change over time with further information. Such opinions are not pervasive in that they may be unrelated to opinions about how the U.S. trade deficit should be handled.

In the assessment center context, examples of dimensions that fall on the left-hand side of the continuum include

> Knowledge of agency regulations
>
> Financial analysis skill
>
> Orientation to company values

These attributes would be relevant to a specific job in a specific organization.

Other Attributes

In the middle of the continuum lies a set of dimensions that varies between the two extremes. These dimensions vary in terms of the major characteristics defining the continuum, i.e., specificity and stability. Terminology is not uniform here, but we can refer to these dimensions as abilities, competencies (McClelland, 1987), or general skills (Fleishman & Quaintance, 1984). What these dimensions have in common is that they are attributes that are relevant to performance in a well-defined area of work. Also, although they are learned, they are relatively stable over time.

In the assessment center context, examples of dimensions that fall somewhere in the middle of the continuum include

> Planning and organizing
>
> Management control
>
> Sensitivity

These dimensions can be made more explicit in several different ways. One way might highlight the more generalized characteristic, while a second might highlight the specific skill. For example, "planning and organizing" can be conceptualized as a general ability to lay out work in a deductively logical manner showing the sequential relationship among a variety of activities; alternatively, it can be conceptualized as a specific set of techniques including charts, diagrams, and symbols for displaying a manufacturing process. The former is more similar to a general characteristic, while the latter is more similar to a developed skill.

It is instructive to note that a significant number of assessment centers use dimensions falling all along the continuum represented by Figure 4.1. Table 4.1 shows the percentage of assessment centers assessing various types of dimensions, as revealed in Gaugler et al.'s (1990) survey of over two hundred organizations. Unfortunately, the survey results do not tell what types of dimensions are used in what types of programs. That issue will be explored in the next section.

Selecting the Appropriate Dimensions

In summary, dimensions should be selected based on the job analysis information and on the purpose of the assessment center. In other words, we must be careful to select not only the *right* dimensions, discovered in the job analysis, but also the right *type* of dimension, suggested by the purpose of the assessment center. For example, for development programs, the dimensions must be easily observable and the assessors must be able to give immediate feedback on the dimensions. For diagnostic programs, the dimensions

Table 4.1
Percentage of Assessment Centers Assessing Various Dimensions

Dimensions Assessed	Percentage of centers using dimension
Current skills	
Sales ability	21
Development of subordinates	17
Abilities	
Planning and organizing	86
Oral communication	91
Potentialities	
Judgment	74
Creativity	18

Source: Gaugler et al. (1990).

must be developable. For selection, any sample of aptitudes representative of the job requirements will be helpful.

In this same line of thinking, Byham (1990) offered another useful way to organize dimensions. His arrangement includes four categories of dimensions, moving from general to specific: *classes* of dimensions, e.g., communications and decision making; *dimensions*, e.g., oral communication and problem analysis; *situational dimensions*, e.g., quantitative analysis and staffing analysis; and *subdimensions*, e.g., technical translation and fact finding. Byham suggested that the level of specificity employed in defining dimensions depends on how the information will be used. For general selection programs, classes of dimensions are appropriate; for selection or placement into a specific position, situational dimensions are often useful; for diagnostic programs, subdimensions help give direction to trainable components of a dimension.

Determining the Number of Dimensions

Historically, assessment centers have involved twelve, fifteen, or more dimensions. In their survey of over two hundred organizations, Gaugler et al. (1990) found that the average number of dimensions assessed was eleven, but 15 percent of the organizations assessed more than eighteen dimensions, and at least one organization assessed one hundred dimensions! The assumption has been that assessors can reliably observe and classify behaviors into the chosen dimensions. An argument for using several dimensions is that it forces assessors to note a wide variety of behaviors, all of which may be relevant to professional effectiveness. There is no assumption that the several dimensions are unrelated to each other, or even conceptually distinct. Proponents of the practice of assessing many dimensions argue that multiple dimensions yield a healthy redundancy in assessment. By contrast, recent research (summarized in Chapter 6) has shown that assessors may not be able to adequately distinguish among a large number of dimensions. With large numbers of indistinguishable dimensions, assessors often give ratings that are interdependent and thus not meaningfully different from each other. The research shows that assessors can seldom make meaningful distinctions among more than five to seven dimensions.

In my opinion, future assessment centers should not attempt to assess more than about seven dimensions unless the designers are willing to go to great lengths to assess a larger set of dimensions by including many exercises, giving extensive assessor training, and spending a long time in the integration discussion.

Tasks as Categories for Observation

Up to this point, when discussing the dimensions to be observed in an assessment center I have referred to them as human attributes of one type or another. In the language of most assessment center proponents, the term "dimensions" has become synonymous with characteristics describing human beings. But these are not the only categories that can be used to classify behaviors. We can also group behaviors into categories representing *tasks*. Tasks are activities that state what work has been accomplished (Fleishman & Quaintance, 1984). Examples of tasks include writing a report or solving a performance problem with an employee. Each of these tasks can be broken down into sub-tasks, which require several behaviors. A task can be thought of as a sequence of activities carried out to accomplish some goal.

Tasks comprising managerial work have been specified by many job analysts in the past (Campbell, Dunnette, Lawler, & Weick, 1970). A well-known analysis of management by Hemphill (1959) revealed ten tasks, including providing a staff service, supervising work, and providing internal business control. A more recent effort along these lines (Lozada-Larsen, 1990) provided a list of seven managerial tasks, including managing human resources, managing financial resources, and providing customer services.

What are the arguments in favor of using tasks as dimensions in an assessment center? Some researchers (Klimoski & Brickner, 1987) have suggested that because of evidence that brings into question the ability of assessors to consistently rate behavior related to the same attribute in different exercises, we should ask assessors to use tasks as the categories for observation rather than human attributes. Task statements tend to be more job-specific than general human attributes and thus may provide assessment categories that are more clearly related to any one job. Tasks also may provide categories that are more conducive to observation.

It remains to be determined whether task categories provide a better classification scheme for assessors and, more importantly, whether task categories overcome the problems noted when assessors rate human attributes. Along these lines, Adams (1991) has provided some preliminary laboratory data that shows that assessors can classify behaviors more accurately using task categories than attribute categories. Ultimately, the test of these new proposals is whether or not the purposes of the assessment center are achieved better using human attributes or tasks (or some other set of categories). A more thorough discussion of these issues is presented in Chapter 6. We will see that no assessment center has been operated using tasks as the only dimensions, so we are left to speculate about whether this method would really work. Certainly no comparative studies have been carried out to evaluate the relative effectiveness of these two approaches in field settings.

There are several arguments in favor of using human attributes as dimensions in an assessment center. There is some evidence to suggest that people naturally think in terms of human traits when evaluating others (Mischel, Jeffry, & Patterson, 1974). Attributes also provide meaningful information when assessors provide feedback to participants. In addition, feedback about attributes can be applied more generally to numerous job situations. Furthermore, job performance can be described with relatively few skills, whereas task lists tend to be relatively long and detailed. Worker-oriented job analysis systems using human attributes as the framework have been proven valuable in many other personnel assessment and training applications (McCormick, 1979). Finally, we have the long history of developing effective assessment centers using attribute dimensions. Since no assessment center has yet been conducted with an alternative set of dimensions, such as tasks, as the organizing principle, it remains to be seen whether an alternative framework would be effective. Until that evidence is provided, I recommend continuing to use human attributes as the dimensions in an assessment center.

Summary and Conclusions

The dimensions used for assessment centers should be carefully chosen on the basis of job analysis information. Different types of dimensions should be used for promotion, diagnostic, and training assessment centers: more trait-like attributes are appropriate for applications involving long-range prediction of success, whereas developmental applications should be built around specific skills. In most assessment centers, only about five to seven dimensions can be assessed with any great precision. In order to make finer distinctions, a much more extensive assessment program must be used. To facilitate the assessors' job, dimensions must be defined clearly, in specific behavioral terms that distinguish each dimension from the others. A wide variety of different human attributes can be assessed accurately in this manner, including knowledge, skills, abilities, motivations, interests, and interpersonal styles. In the future, tasks may provide meaningful categories for assessment observations, but evidence to support their usefulness has yet to be provided.

5

Situational Exercises

Key Concepts: Evaluating the effectiveness of situational exercises; gearing exercises to assess center objectives; determining levels of complexity and fidelity; integrating assessment center results.

An essential element of any assessment center is the observation of behavior in situational exercises. Situational exercises are performance tests that present participants with complex stimuli and call for complex responses. The complex stimuli may include any of the following:

- financial, demographic, and community data available to a bank executive considering a new branch in a suburb,
- a set of personnel problems including alleged safety violations, absenteeism, and thievery being reviewed by a disciplinary committee, or
- a set of letters and memos in a manager's in-basket.

The corresponding complex responses may be:

- financial analyses and written rationale in favor of and in opposition to opening the new branch bank,
- decision-making and leadership actions to help the committee find solutions, and

- written responses, assignments, and directions to subordinates or others.

Each situational exercise is a test simulating some important aspect of the job for which the participant is being considered or trained. Each situation affords assessors the opportunity to observe and evaluate the participant on a number of predetermined dimensions, such as written or oral communication, problem analysis, leadership, and initiative.

The purpose of this chapter is to present examples of several types of situational exercises that have been used frequently in assessment centers and to evaluate their effectiveness for different assessment purposes. The chapter explores several issues relevant to the design, selection, and implementation of assessment exercises, based on the thesis that each type of exercise can be used for different purposes (Thornton & Cleveland, 1990), but that the content, level of difficulty, and similarity of the exercises to the actual job must be chosen very carefully in order to achieve the goals of different assessment center programs.

Types of Assessment Exercises

Many different types of assessment techniques have been used in assessment centers, including mental ability tests, personality questionnaires, projective tests, and background interviews, but the mainstay of the assessment center method is the situational exercise. There is a wide variety of situational exercises, each of which has been described in detail elsewhere for the reader who wishes more information. Thornton and Byham (1982) provided a detailed summary of the research on various situational exercises used in assessment centers. This section emphasizes the special characteristics of the different types of exercises, their strengths and weaknesses, and various considerations in choosing among them.

Table 5.1 lists the most common situational exercises and the percentage of assessment centers that use each type (Gaugler et al., 1990). The sections following the table describe each type, from simple to complex, in terms of the problems confronting the participants. This order is somewhat arbitrary, since even the most simple type of exercise can be made quite complex with special instructions or content.

As you read about each type of exercise, keep in mind that (1) not all activities are relevant to all jobs—for instance, an

Table 5.1
Frequency of Use of Various Types of Situational Exercises

	Exercise	Percentage of Assessment Centers Using Exercise
More complex	Business games	25%
	In-basket	81%
	Group tasks	Not in survey

	Group discussion
	  Assigned positions
	  No assigned
	    positions
		44%
		
		59%

	Oral presentation	46%
	Case analysis	73%
	Fact finding	38%
Simpler	Interview simulation	47%

Source: Gaugler et al. (1990).

in-basket may be critical to an office supervisor, but relatively meaningless to an assembly-line foreman, and (2) the content of the exercise may or may not resemble the target job —for instance, in a case where the target job is supervisor in an insurance office, the contents of the in-basket may closely replicate that of an insurance office, or it may replicate the in-basket of a government organization or a research laboratory. Job analysis tells us what the target job is like, but we must choose the extent to which we replicate that situation in the assessment center.

Interview Simulations

An interview simulation is a situational exercise in which the participant talks one-on-one with someone playing the role of a subordinate, colleague, or customer. Interview simulations are adaptations of the role-playing technique developed in the 1950s to foster attitude change (Fishbein & Aijen, 1975). The examples in Table 5.2 show the variety of one-on-one situations that can be simulated for different types of jobs.

Table 5.2
Examples of Interview Simulations

Target Position	Interviewee	Situation Simulated
Middle-level executive	Television reporter	Investigation of environmental violations
First-level supervisor	Subordinate	Discussion of a performance problem
Telephone sales	Client	Selling a product or service
Customer service representative	Irate customer	Complaint about a faulty product
Financial supervisor	New financial planner	Soliciting a client on phone

The "interviewee" in all these situations is a role player trained to act in a standardized manner. The role player might ask questions, make suggestions, answer questions, and even act upset, depending on what the situation calls for. The participant must talk with the role player and resolve the problem while being observed by an assessor. The interview simulation is particularly effective in revealing behaviors on dimensions such as oral communication skill, empathy and tact, and problem-solving ability with people.

The advantage of this exercise is that it is relatively short, requiring 15 to 30 minutes to prepare and only 8 to 10 minutes to carry out. Thus, several different interview simulations can be incorporated in an assessment program. Interview simulations are particularly appropriate for assessment centers designed to train inexperienced supervisors, because they provide controlled situations for assessing and learning rudimentary communication and problem-solving skills (Thornton & Cleveland, 1990). One disadvantage of the interview simulation is the need for a role player, which increases staffing needs. A solution is to have the assessor play the role of the interviewee, but this in turn causes another problem for the assessor who must then carry out two difficult functions simultaneously. Another potential problem of one-on-one exercises is that the interviewee may not play his or her role consistently from one participant to the next. This problem can be controlled through proper training of role players and careful monitoring by assessors.

Fact Finding

In this exercise the participant reads a small amount of information about a problem and then is given the chance to acquire additional information by directing questions to a resource person. The resource person can be a trained role player or an assessor. The fact-finding exercise is a variation of the incident process (Pigors & Pigors, 1961) originally designed to train managers in analytical thinking, practical judgment, and social awareness (Pigors, 1976). Vague questions result in general answers; specific questions yield valuable information. After the question-and-answer period, the participant is asked to make a recommendation and provide a rationale. The resource person may then challenge the participant, supplying new information in an attempt to elicit a change of position.

Table 5.3 illustrates various examples of fact-finding exercises. The fact-finding exercise is particularly effective for assessing and training the skills involved in soliciting information from customers, peers, and other sources who might not be willing or able to provide complete information. Assessors can also use fact-finding exercises to evaluate decision-making skills and tolerance for stress. One disadvantage of fact-finding exercises is that they are somewhat difficult to construct and administer. In order to be challenging, the resource material must be very thorough, and the assessor must anticipate many questions from assertive participants. In addition, the resource person/assessor must be familiar with the material in order to provide responses in a timely fashion. Also, as in an interview simulation, the resource person might have difficulty providing a standardized situation to all participants.

Written Case Analysis

In a case analysis the participant is given material to read that describes an organizational problem and is then asked to prepare a set of recommendations about it for higher management. The

Table 5.3
Examples of Fact-Finding Exercises

Target Position	Situation Simulated
Middle-level executive	Budget proposal has been turned down
First-level supervisor	Faulty product coming off assembly line
Telephone sales representative	Customer seeking help in identifying appropriate product to order
Computer analyst or accountant	Request from client department for a new information system

problem may require financial, system, or process analysis. For example, in one case analysis, each participant was asked to review record-keeping procedures in a community blood bank.

One advantage of this exercise is that it is quite flexible and can be tailor-made to assess general attributes, such as the ability to organize an operation, or specific skills, such as calculating a rate of return on investment. The results of this exercise can be a written report or an oral presentation, as shown in the next section. When a written report is submitted, assessors can evaluate both its form and its substance. Poor written work may suggest the need for remedial training in business correspondence. Superficial or faulty analysis of the case material or unsystematic evaluation of alternative solutions may be indications of the need for training in decision-making skills. A difficulty in using written exercises is in developing objective scoring guidelines for the assessors. Jacobson and Sinclair (1990) have shown that methods can be developed to reliably assess the quality of written responses.

When multiple assessors use objective standards to evaluate written work, high levels of consistency and accuracy are attained.

Oral Presentation

In an oral presentation exercise, participants are asked to make a short, extemporaneous speech about a simple topic or a longer, more formal presentation about a case study like those described above. The presentation is usually given to an assessor who then asks questions intended to challenge the participant. Where it is relevant to the target job, the assessor may even put the participant under stress by opposing his or her conclusion and pointing out its limitations and flaws. In another format, several participants give their presentations, then discuss their recommendations and choose the best solution.

A presentation exercise is a relatively easy exercise to construct and administer. Participants can be asked to talk on virtually any topic. Administrators can have a list of topics and use this exercise to fill time when other exercises move ahead of schedule.

This exercise provides an excellent opportunity to assess a particular facet of oral communication skill—the ability to make formal or semiformal presentations. In some assessment centers, the participants are provided materials such as flip charts, marker pens, and transparencies to use with an overhead projector. Assessors can then see how participants use these devices to enhance the effectiveness of their communications.

Leaderless Group Discussion

In this exercise four to eight participants are given several problems to resolve in a fixed period of time, usually one hour. They are asked to discuss the problems and to prepare written recommendations that have been endorsed by all the participants. For example, the problems may involve a set of recommendations on how to handle personnel issues that have arisen in the organization. In one form of the group discussion exercise, there are no roles assigned, and everyone cooperates in developing the best solution for the organization as a whole. In contrast, a more competitive situation can be simulated in which each participant is assigned the role of a head of a department or special interest group trying to get a share of a federal grant or other source revenue.

The leaderless group discussion is particularly effective for assessing group leadership skills, such as the ability to contribute good ideas and guide the discussion process (Harris, 1949). Problem analysis and decision analysis abilities can also be assessed (Bass, 1950, 1954).

Several limitations of the leaderless group discussion should be mentioned. The climate and tone of the discussion can differ from one group to another, ranging from quite lively and challenging to quiet and subdued, depending on the composition and mood of the group. This potential lack of standardization across groups means that assessors sometimes have a difficult time knowing whether the behavior they observe in a particular individual is a function of the individual or the group dynamic. We also must consider whether this exercise is a valid simulation of job situations, because few organizational settings are truly "leaderless." In most situations, there is a designated supervisor, task leader, or project coordinator who has some formal leadership assignment. Ideally, we want to know how well the individual executes the leadership functions he or she has been given. It may be more appropriate to design an exercise that involves an assigned leader, as discussed in the next section.

Assigned-Leader Group Task

In this exercise, the administrator of the program assigns one participant to act as the leader of the group and then gives the group some task to accomplish. For middle-management positions, the person may be assigned to head a team of staff assistants and build a piece of equipment using Lego blocks. In assessment centers in fire or police departments and in the military, the assigned leader may be put in charge of a group faced with a physical challenge, such as using ropes and boards to move the team over a barrier.

The obvious advantage of this type of exercise is that it simulates the job of many managers—leading a group of subordinates. Like the group discussion, the group task provides a means to assess a variety of leadership skills. Its disadvantage is that it is time-consuming to give all participants a chance to act as the assigned leader; to be fair, the assessment center would have to have one such exercise for each participant. Because most programs assess six or more people at a time, there would need to be at least six of these exercises to give everyone a turn in the leader role. Some programs overcome this problem by changing the leadership assignment part way through the exercise. Other programs provide four role players who act as subordinates for one participant (Slivinski, Grant, Bourgeois, & Pederson, 1977). This arrangement provides more standardization, but requires several role players for an extended period of time.

In-basket

An in-basket is a simulation of the paperwork that arrives in the mailbox of the typical manager (Fredericksen, Saunders, & Wand, 1957; Lopez, 1966). It might include memos, letters, reports, announcements, requests, and irrelevant information that present personnel, financial, accounting, or procedural problems for the manager. The participant is given a calendar, background information, general instructions, and paper and pencil for response, but usually no access to a secretary or telephone. The participant must write out instructions, draft letters, make decisions, and set up meetings, all within a relatively short time period. The time pressures force the participant to set priorities and make decisions.

When adequate staff personnel are available, a secretary or "assistant" may be assigned to each participant to help with routine work, such as making phone calls or arranging meetings. This procedure is used in the Israeli Air Force assessment center, where each officer candidate is assigned a lower-level enlisted person to supervise during the exercise (S. Haboucha, personal communication, July 16, 1990). Assessors evaluate the resulting written work and also observe how the candidate uses the assistant; the assistant, in turn, later provides information to the assessor about the candidate's supervisory effectiveness.

The written responses to the in-basket materials can be scored separately to reveal various dimensions of administrative skill, but more frequently there is a follow-up interview in which the participant explains to an assessor the reasons for action taken. Whereas the written material provides recorded evidence of how the action will be seen by others, the verbal explanations provide valuable insight into the participant's thought processes. Assessors must be trained to be somewhat skeptical of the participants' ability to retrospectively describe their thinking during the exercise, because people tend not to have accurate insight into their own processes of judgment and decision making (Hammond,

McClelland, & Mumpower, 1980). The actual written records probably provide the most relevant assessment data.

The in-basket exercise allows the assessment of a wide variety of dimensions and has a high degree of face validity for many managerial jobs, features that may explain why the vast majority of assessment centers use an in-basket (Gaugler et al., 1990). Dimensions such as delegation, planning and organizing, management control, and judgment can be assessed with an in-basket. Many studies have been conducted to investigate the relationship of performance on in-basket exercises and success in management (Schippmann, Prien, & Katz, 1990; Thornton & Byham, 1982). The evidence shows that in-basket scores are related to ratings of actual managerial performance, progress in management rank, and on-the-job performance of tasks similar to those assessed in the in-basket. Both Schippman et al. (1990) and Thornton and Byham (1982) concluded that the research evidence supports the use of in-baskets for making promotion decisions, but Schippman et al. warned that in-basket content varies considerably and research evidence is quite fragmented. Human resource managers are cautioned to seek evidence of the effectiveness of any individual in-basket exercise they are considering for an assessment center. This is sound advice for all assessment techniques.

One limitation of the in-basket exercise is time: it usually requires 2 to 3 hours to complete and then almost that much time to score. Additional time is required for a follow-up interview and evaluation of interview performance. Scoring can be difficult because the assessor must consider the complex set of responses given to several items, as well as the person's rationale for these responses. Brannick, Michaels, and Baker (1989) have shown that if assessors are allowed to make inferences about several dimensions on the basis of one "red hot" item, there are likely to be artificially high relationships among dimension ratings. Problems such as this can be minimized by developing clearer scoring standards for assessors. Scoring can be standardized by providing assessors with examples of behavioral responses to each item and by showing the relevance of the behavior to a specific dimension. With adequate training, assessors appear to be able to rate in-basket performance with high levels of consistency (Schippmann et al., 1990; Thornton & Byham, 1982).

To reduce time requirements and to standardize scoring procedures, there is experimentation underway to administer and score in-baskets with a computer (Heine & Struth, 1989). Using this method, participants are presented the items on a monitor and asked to choose from several alternative courses of action. Each alternative has been predetermined to indicate effective or ineffective performance on the dimensions being assessed. The computer can then score the responses and give ratings on the dimensions. The time saving is indisputable, but the accuracy of such a method has not yet been demonstrated. Allowing the participant to pick from among several alternatives is quite different from requiring the participant to generate and execute the response in his or her own words. This sort of test may predict managerial success, but in my thinking does not qualify as an assessment center exercise because complex, overt behaviors are not required.

Business Games

Games come in various levels of complexity. The following are typical examples:

- a two-hour simulation of a manufacturing operation run by a team of six department heads
- a four-hour simulation of stock trading by three four-person teams
- an eight-hour computer-driven game for twenty managers running a large multidivision organization.

The common denominator of these games is the relatively unstructured nature of the interactions among the participants and the variety of actions that can be taken by any or all participants (Jones, 1972). As a complex game unfolds, it often resembles a sequence of situational exercises: a leaderless group discussion takes place, a number of one-on-one interactions occur, someone makes a presentation, others engage in fact finding, the group convenes again to make decisions, and so on.

The interactive nature of business games provides opportunities to assess dimensions such as strategic planning, teamwork, and leadership. The content of the game can be geared to the assessment of financial analysis, marketing, or production control skills.

The complexity of business games, even the simple ones, creates advantages and disadvantages. On the positive side, games come closer to representing "real life" in the organization. Games look more realistic to participants than less complex simulations, and they can help experienced managers learn skills. Games can also be exciting and fun for the participants. On the negative side, behavior of participants is often hard to observe as they move around to different rooms and huddle in small groups. When used for training purposes, the situation may be so complex that no one has the skills to function very well and, consequently, little learning may take place (Thornton & Cleveland, 1990). It is interesting to note that complex business games are used in only about 25 percent of the assessment centers covered in the survey by Gaugler et al. (1990), suggesting they may present some administrative difficulties.

Integrated Exercises

Up to this point, this chapter has presented the exercises as though they were separate and distinct from each other. An alternative arrangement is to relate two or more exercises to one another. This can be done in several ways. For example, one set of instructions about the company, its industry, and the environment in which it operates can be used for all exercises. The background information from the in-basket can provide some operational procedures and problems that are then discussed in more depth in a group discussion. Similarly, the results of one exercise can be used as the input for another. For instance, the recommendations that a candidate generates in the written report for a case study can be used as the starting point for a group discussion.

There is much that remains constant from one integrated exercise to the next: the description of the organization, the rules and regulations for operation, the people in various positions, job descriptions, and so on. What someone learns in the initial exercises may be useful in subsequent exercises.

When Gaugler et al. (1990) surveyed over two hundred assessment centers, they found that 20 percent used an integrated exercise, typically composed of four definable segments. Integrated exercises have been used quite successfully at different job levels. Adams and Thornton (1988) developed a set of three exercises to select instructors of pilots. Slivinski et al. (1977) developed an integrated set of exercises for first-level management in the Canadian Public Service Commission. Spangenberg et al. (1989) used a set of exercises for middle-level managers in a South African organization.

Advocates of integrated exercises argue that this arrangement is more realistic (Slivinski et al., 1977; Spangenberg et al., 1989). People in real-life organizations familiarize themselves with their environment over time; they gain information in one interaction that helps in the next. In fact, integrated exercises may actually test the candidate's ability to capitalize on this accumulation of information in ways that disjointed exercises do not. Integrated exercises may also test the individual's ability to bounce back if he or she does poorly in an early exercise; that skill may be very important on the job.

It could also be argued that integrated exercises have high *face validity*, that is, they closely resemble the actual job and the actual organization. This feature means that employees may be more willing to participate in the assessment center and have more confidence in the results and feedback.

What, then, are the arguments against integrated exercises in management assessment centers? One argument is that the manager's job is very fragmented and made up of short, disjointed interactions (Mintzberg, 1975). The manager may be talking on the telephone about a financial matter one minute, responding to a memo about a production problem the next minute, and advising a supervisor on a disciplinary problem a few minutes later. The relevant background information, the people involved, and the skills required may be very different from one task to the next. Thus, a set of disconnected and unrelated assessment exercises may actually resemble a very important part of the manager's life.

A second argument against integrated exercises has to do with motivation. When exercises are discrete, unrelated activities, participants are given a "fresh start" in each exercise. If an individual does poorly in the in-basket exercise, for example, he or she has a chance to start over in the group discussion. A lack of understanding of the information in one exercise will not penalize the person in the next exercise.

Related to this second argument is the idea that separate exercises give independent measurements of the dimensions being assessed. This is good, because measurement principles tell us that an evaluation is more consistent and accurate if it is based on several different observations that are not artificially related to each other (Nunnally, 1978). Integrated exercises may lead to some "contamination" of performance from one exercise to the next. For example, if a participant does poorly on the first exercise, he or she may not have the right information for the next exercise. Separate exercises eliminate this possibility.

I do not have a firm opinion about whether exercises should be integrated or not. If the program requires an accurate assessment of management skills, I would keep the exercise content separate in order to provide several independent measurements. If it is important to have a high level of acceptance of the program among participants and others in the organization, I would build an integrated set of exercises that resemble a day in the life of the organization.

Evaluation of Relative Contributions of Exercises

There are data (Thornton & Byham, 1982) to support the value of each of the types of exercises discussed so far in this chapter. As pointed out earlier, the content, difficulty, and similarity of the exercises to the actual job must be determined carefully to make them appropriate to different types of assessment centers. Although they have all been used successfully in a variety of assessment centers, there is little data to evaluate the *relative* merits of different exercises. It is not possible to say which one is "better" or "worse" than the others.

The question "Which is better?" is easy to ask, but very difficult to answer. The answer depends on the job being studied, the purpose of the assessment center, and the resources available to conduct the assessment activities. The question may be partially answered by a thorough job analysis, which shows not only the dimensions to be assessed but also the types of situations the participants face on a regular basis. For example, a first-level supervisor may spend considerable time in one-on-one discussions with subordinates solving work-related problems, but seldom meet with other supervisors in unstructured groups. Thus, in this situation, interview simulations are appropriate exercises, whereas leaderless group discussions are not. On the other hand, staff professionals, such as engineers and cost accountants, may work regularly on teams and task forces. These activities require leadership skills that readily emerge and can be assessed in leaderless group discussions.

The answer to the question is also a function of the willingness of the organization to properly carry out the exercise. In-baskets and business games require extra training for assessors and considerable time to properly observe, review, and evaluate the complex behavior they elicit. If the organization is willing to carry out these complex exercises properly, they are likely to be quite powerful; if not, the organization is better served by the simpler exercises.

Determining the Number of Exercises

The data regarding the appropriate *number* of exercises to use in an assessment center are somewhat clearer and provide some guidance. Assessment centers that use a larger number of exercises and a wider variety of exercises tend to show more accuracy (Gaugler et al., 1988). A recent survey of over two hundred assessment centers showed that the typical assessment center used approximately five exercises, but some centers used ten or eleven exercises (Gaugler et al., 1990). This first finding must be tempered with the seemingly contradictory finding that the length of the assessment center does not affect its predictive accuracy (Gaugler et al., 1988). These two findings are not unreconcilable. It is reasonable to conclude that a variety of *types* of exercises is needed, but little is gained from having more than two of the same type. For example, it would be better to use two group discussion exercises and an in-basket and interview simulation than to use four group discussions.

Research has not been conducted to investigate what mixture of types and numbers of exercises is optimal, but theoretical support for the use of multiple types of exercises comes from correspondent inference theory (Jones & Davis, 1965). This theory states that we explain other peoples' behavior by searching for stable qualities in them that are discernible across different situations. When we see that an individual behaves the same way in several different situations, we infer that the behavior is a function of stable attributes of the individual and not of the external situation. For example, if I observe that Tom gets confused and cannot explain his decisions when speaking to another individual, to a small group, and to a large group, I can reasonably conclude that Tom lacks oral communication skills.

The implication of this is that we should use several, shorter exercises of different types—some oral, some written, some individual, some group—rather than a few exercises of the same type. With a blend such as this, inferences we make about stable attributes of people allow us to understand and predict their behavior in the future. Multiple exercises give assessors a chance to make these interpretations about dimensions and predict future managerial success.

A Model of Assessment Exercises

This review of assessment exercises suggests that there are two features of the exercises that determine their complexity: (1) the standardization of the stimulus material and (2) the structure imposed on the responses required of the participant. *Standardization* refers to the formality and uniformity of the testing situation. In a highly standardized test, all participants are presented with exactly the same instructions and questions. For example, a written multiple-choice test is highly standardized. *Structure* refers to the latitude the participant has to respond in a unique or individualized way. In an unstructured test, the participant can decide how he or she will respond. For example, a leaderless group discussion is unstructured.

Often these two features are related, in other words, standardized tests require clear and structured responses, and unstandardized tests provide little structure for required responses. (Again, think of the typical multiple-choice test, as opposed to a leaderless group discussion.) However, the complexity of the test stimuli and that of the required response are not directly linked. For example, a simple written test may require complex decision-making processes and written responses, whereas a complex organizational game may require a relatively simple choice or action.

Table 5.4 depicts a wide variety of existing testing devices in terms of these two variables— standardization and structure. It provides suggestions for new devices that have not typically been used in assessment programs. The blank sections of the figure represent assessment procedures that could be constructed. For example, the upper right portion of the figure (i.e., structured

Table 5.4
Model of Assessment Center Exercises

Structure of the Response Mode	Standardized				Unstandardized				
					Role-players (subordinate, peer, supervisor, customer)		Other assessees in:		
	Written	Videotape	Administrator	Assessor	One role-player	Two or more	Assigned roles	Nonassigned roles	Other teams
Structured									
Completion of form	Ability test Personality questionnaire Background information form								
Handwriting	Case study In-basket		In-basket						
Verbal presentation Verbal response to questions	Case study			Fact finding Background interview Interview after in-basket or analysis	Problem employee Irate customer		Analysis/ Discussion		

Table 5.4 Continued
Model of Assessment Center Exercises

| Structure of the Response Mode | Standardized | | | | Role-players (subordinate, peer, supervisor, customer) | | Other assessees in: | | Unstandardized |
	Written	Videotape	Administrator	Assessor	One role-player	Two or more	Assigned roles	Nonassigned roles	Other teams
Participant-controlled interview		Interview simulation		Fact finding	Interview simulation				
Group discussion		Case study Leaderless group discussion				Staff meeting	Leaderless group discussion	Leaderless group discussion	Game
Multi-group discussion									Game
Combination of verbal, written, and physical behaviors									
Unstructured									Game

Source: Adapted from Thornton & Byham, *Assessment Centers and Managerial Performance,* © 1982, Figure 5.1. Reprinted with permission of Academic Press, Inc.

response, unstandardized stimulus) suggests an exercise in which the participants are asked to fill out a questionnaire about some complex social interaction in which they have participated. On the other hand, the lower left portion of the figure (unstructured response, standardized stimulus) suggests an exercise that might involve some verbal response to social stimuli presented on a video disk. Examples of preliminary efforts along these lines have been described by Frank (1990), who has developed computer simulations of interactions with subordinates and customers. An innovative exercise using video technology that fits in the upper left-hand corner (structured response, standardized stimulus) was developed by Cascio (1989) to simulate job learning among firefighters. An experienced firefighter is shown training on a piece of equipment, the tape is stopped, and participants are asked to indicate on paper whether or not they think the trainee took the correct action.

Comments on Computer Technology in Assessment Centers

With the advent of personal computers, there have been some creative innovations in assessment center exercises. In the typical computer-driven exercise, the computer presents a video display of an employee talking about a job situation. The video stops and a narrator asks the participant what he or she would say next. Four alternatives are presented on the screen, and the participant makes a choice by pressing a key on the keyboard. In some applications, a branching takes place so that choice A results in one response from the employee on the screen, whereas choice B results in a different response, and so on. After further comments by the employee, the participant makes more choices of actions. The choices have been determined to reflect more or less effective actions related to dimensions of managerial performance. The computer then computes scores for the participant's performance.

This mode of presentation is an example of a high level of both standardization and structure. The standardization of the video-taped employee's responses eliminates some of the problems live role-players can cause if they do not treat individual participants equally. But the way participants respond to computer-driven exercises is quite different from more typical assessment center exercises. One of the essential features of an assessment center is that participants display complex and overt behaviors.

In the computerized exercise, the response is just pressing a key. Computerized exercises might have very high predictive accuracy, and if they do, they might have a place in the total set of evaluation techniques available to human resource managers. To this point, there have been few empirical studies demonstrating their predictive accuracy in the professional literature.

There are three obvious limitations to computerized exercises. First, the participant is given multiple choices and does not have to generate his or her own response. Second, the participant does not have to actually demonstrate the behavior, thus the exercise may be more a measure of opinion or knowledge than a measure of skill. Third, the exercise is not truly interactive the way an interview simulation or group discussion is, in which participants interact with one another or with role-players.

In my opinion, computerized assessment techniques are exciting and can be efficient in assessing many applicants. Still, much more research needs to be done and published in the professional literature before the human resource manager can be confident in their ability to provide accurate predictions of managerial success. I do not believe computerized tests provide the rich behavioral information—so valuable for diagnostic and developmental assessment centers—that more typical exercises provide.

Using Exercises to Measure Ability or Motivation

Any given assessment exercise can be constructed to provide either a measure of ability or a measure of motivation (or preferred style of behavior). In order for an exercise to measure a participant's preferred style of behavior, the participant should be given a choice of taking action or refraining from action. For example, in most group discussions, a participant can make suggestions or remain silent, defend his or her position or let counterarguments go unchallenged, attack the positions of others or passively accept them. All these actions reveal some level of assertiveness. To make the exercise a measure of ability, the instructions should *not* give the participant a choice of taking action. For example, the instructions might specify that each participant must make an initial two- to three-minute presentation of recommended solutions, thus ensuring the opportunity to assess verbal presentation ability.

The in-basket provides another exercise where the participant can be given choices or where actions can be "forced." For example, the participant usually has the choice of whether or not to delegate work to an assistant, reflecting a willingness to give responsibility to others. By contrast, some items can be structured so the participant is required to take some action. This way, assessors have a chance to assess the quality of problem-analysis and decision-analysis abilities.

Thus, if we wish to use the assessment center as a standardized measure of abilities, the exercises should *not* give the participants many choices about whether or not to act. By giving clear instructions that each person is expected to take action, *motivation* to act is eliminated as an explanation of behavior, and inferences about *abilities* are then possible. For example, in an assessment center designed to select instructors for an industrial training program, role-players (pretending to be trainees) sought specific feedback from the instructor candidates. The objective was to find out if the participants had the skill to give the feedback, not whether they had the interest in doing so voluntarily. On the other hand, if we wish the assessors to evaluate motivation, interests, and styles, the participant *should* have many choices. Jones and Davis (1965) have provided an explanation of how we make inferences about other people's behavior. They say that we can infer less about a person if behavior is a required part of the person's social role. Voluntary behavior is more informative about the person's motivation than required or role-related behavior.

Fidelity of Exercises

The question of fidelity of assessment center exercises—that is, the extent to which exercises resemble actual job situations—is a complicated one. The first response seems to be that the exercises should be very detailed representations of the job. Taken to the extreme, this would mean that the exercises should be an exact duplication of part of the job: such exercises are often known as work samples (Anastasi, 1988) or job replicas (Cronbach, 1970). A work-sample test duplicates one small segment of the actual job performed. For example, a welder can be given actual equipment and materials and asked to weld together two pieces of metal; a typist can be given handwritten material and asked to type it on a computer like the one used on the job; or a managerial applicant might be given financial information relevant to a business deal and asked to perform some computation of return on investment.

Work samples are particularly appropriate when the purpose of the assessment center is to assess the current level of skill or the ability to perform a specific job. For example, a work sample would be appropriate for testing a mechanic's ability to repair the carburetor of an automobile. Work samples are more appropriate when the assessment is targeted at one specific job, rather than a range of jobs or job levels.

For certain assessment purposes, there are several disadvantages of having a high level of fidelity in the exercises. If the purpose of assessment is identification of potential rather than assessment of present skills, the exercises should measure the basic aptitudes necessary to acquire job skills and not those skills per se.

Job replicas often give inappropriate and unfair advantage to individuals with certain job experiences. People who know the specific practices of the organization usually perform better than outsiders on an in-basket that replicates their own office setting. At the same time, the outsider may have better basic decision-making and leadership skills.

A solution to this problem—and one that I favor—is to design exercises that depict the same type of industry or business but not the exact organization. For example, a fictitious government agency might be depicted for use in assessment of candidates for promotion in government positions. A generic supermarket depicted in an in-basket exercise and leaderless group tasks might be used to assess candidates for a wide variety of different grocery stores and other retail stores (Fogli, 1985).

The approach advocated here is a compromise between generalized exercises that have little fidelity and therefore appear to be unrelated to the job and close replicas of each different organization in each new assessment center. Fidelity (or "face validity," as it is sometimes called) is important and will affect not only people's reaction to the exercises but also the accuracy of the responses they give (Nevo, 1989; Nevo & Jager, 1986). On the other hand, there are strong arguments against using work samples that may in fact penalize those people who do not have certain organizational experiences.

Integrating Other Assessment Devices with Situational Exercises

In addition to situational exercises, other measurement techniques can be used to evaluate individuals in an assessment center. The most frequently used of these are aptitude tests, questionnaires measuring personality characteristics (motivation, social interaction preferences, values, etc.), biographical information forms, background interviews, and interviews in which the participant is asked to describe how he or she would handle job situations. Occasionally, projective tests of personality (sentence completion tests, picture interpretations, etc.), current affairs tests, or measures of reading ability are used.

There are at least three ways other measurement techniques can be used. First, tests and interviews can be administered before the assessment center process begins as screening devices to select from among potential candidates. For example, a test of reading ability would select only those individuals who have the skill to comprehend the complex material presented in written case studies and in-basket exercises. Similarly, an interview might be conducted by a member of the human resource staff to assess the individual's commitment to and interest in a management career, especially since some people may feel pressured by their supervisors into attending the assessment center.

When tests and interviews are used within the framework of the assessment center, either of two procedures can be followed: these other methods can be used in *parallel* with or in *series* with the situational tests. In the parallel processing method, tests and interviews are used in the same way as situational exercises to provide information that the assessors consider simultaneously when formulating their overall dimension ratings. This process is depicted in Figure 5.1. In this approach, the assessors learn about behavior in exercises and information from the tests and interviews, then give an evaluation on the dimensions. The rationale is that the score on an aptitude test, along with observed reasoning behaviors in situational exercises, is relevant to the evaluation of dimensions such as problem solving and decision analysis. Assessors can gain a better understanding of success or failure in these dimensions if they have information about a participant's general reasoning ability as indicated by paper-and-pencil tests. A similar argument can be made for personality tests. The assertive behaviors

Figure 5.1
Parallel Processing of Assessment Center Results

Situational exercises
Paper-and-pencil tests ⟶ Dimension Ratings ⟶ Overall Assessment Rating
Background interview

shown in group discussion exercises might be understood more completely if the assessors have test scores measuring related characteristics. The tests may show that the individual describes him- or herself as quite assertive, but in actual group situations, that individual may be reticent because he or she lacks the skills to interact effectively or because he or she is not as outgoing as the personality test indicated.

The other way to use tests in an assessment center is to put them in series with the situational exercises, as depicted in Figure 5.2. First, the assessors evaluate all the information from the situational tests and derive dimension ratings. Then the test scores and interview information are introduced. The assessors then integrate all this information to arrive at an overall assessment rating.

A variant of this process is to have someone other than an assessor integrate all the information (i.e., dimension ratings from the assessment center, tests, interviews) at a later time. This might be done by a human resource staff member, a committee reviewing candidates for promotion, or a department manager examining the personnel file of people nominated for promotion. This process is commonly used by police and military review panels (Caspy, Ben-Ari, & Margalit, 1990).

There are advantages and disadvantages associated with each of these procedures. An advantage of parallel processing is that all information is used to formulate ratings on dimensions, and comparisons and contrasts can be made between the results of very different types of measurement. A disadvantage of parallel processing is that managers may rely too heavily on test scores,

Figure 5.2
Serial Processing of Assessment Center Results

which can be deceptively "objective" in comparison with the sometimes conflicting reports of several assessors watching several exercises.

An advantage of serial processing is that the major sources of information are kept separate in the early stages of assessment: the "here-and-now" behaviors of situational exercises are integrated before the information about "past" behavior from the interview and "test" behavior is examined. The disadvantage of serial processing is that it takes two separate integration meetings: one by the observers of situational exercises and one by people who review all available data. If someone else integrates the final set of information, the assessors may feel loss of control. Of course, assessors can perform both steps, as we see in some long-standing and successful assessment centers, such as SOHIO (Finkle, 1976; Finkle & Jones, 1970), but this is time-consuming.

It should be emphasized that assessors do not have access to test or interview data in either of these methods before they observe behaviors in the situational exercises. There is too much potential for this other information to influence the behavioral observations. For an interesting counterargument, the reader may wish to refer to the classic book, *Assessment of Men*, which describes the program of the Office of Strategic Services (1948) for selecting espionage agents in World War II. This account of the first assessment center in the United States shows how a very holistic assessment can be carried out by mixing together all sorts of information at all stages of the assessment process.

I favor the serial processing approach, in which assessments on the dimensions are based only on the behavioral observations from the exercises. Later, information from tests and interviews can be introduced by psychologists or other professionals trained to gather and interpret these data. Assessors can then modify dimension ratings or, more commonly, use the dimension ratings along with the other information to derive an overall assessment rating. I advocate this procedure because it keeps the different sources of data separate from each other for as long as possible.

Focusing on the Purpose of the Assessment

Throughout this book I have emphasized that the design of an assessment center should be based on the purpose of the assessment activity. Anyone involved in designing an assessment center should focus on this principle when considering the type and level of exercises appropriate for observation. The purposes of exercises in selection/promotion programs, diagnostic programs, and training programs are very different, as well. Just as the assessment center itself must be designed according to its purpose, so should each individual exercise be designed to meet a specific objective.

Table 5.5 provides a summary of considerations for selecting exercises for different assessment purposes. In programs designed to identify people with long-range potential, the purpose of the exercises is to assess potentialities, as described in Chapter 4. This behavioral information provides the basis for predicting success in a range of higher-level positions. In these cases, exercises can be thought of as aptitude tests (Anastasi, 1988). As such, the exercises should be designed to tap basic attributes that will allow the person to benefit from enriched experiences provided by the organization over the course of many months and years. These exercises can be more general in nature, in other words, not models of any specific job or organization. Fidelity, in this case, is unimportant because the purpose is to predict success in a wide variety of jobs, some of which may not even be known at time of assessment.

In most selection programs, the participants are relatively inexperienced and thus do not have a basis for engaging in exercises that require specific knowledge of a particular organization. By necessity, therefore, the exercises cannot be replicas with a high level of fidelity. Work samples are not appropriate for this type of program. Instead, exercises that enable the person with the basic set of attributes to perform well without penalty due to some lack of experience are most appropriate. At the same time, the exercises

Table 5.5
Comparison of Exercises for Various Assessment Purposes

	Purpose of Assessment Center			
Exercise Characteristic	Identification of Potential	Selection	Diagnosis	Training
Target job(s)	range of jobs	specific job	current job	current or higher-level job
Number of exercises	3–6	3–6	7–10	7–10
Level of fidelity	low	moderate	high	high
Complexity	simple	moderate	complex	depends on skill of participant

should have a moderate degree of fidelity, so that candidates see their relevance to the job they are applying for.

For some selection programs, the organization must single out people who have fully developed skills. In those cases, work sample exercises are appropriate.

For diagnostic assessment centers, the exercises serve a very different function. Here the exercises must be designed to provide accurate assessment of several distinct attributes. Whereas in most selection programs the dimensions serve as intermediate steps in the process of evaluating overall potential, in a diagnostic program the dimensions are the end-products of assessment. Therefore, the exercises must provide detailed evaluation of each separate dimension. This means that the assessment must be thorough for each and every dimension and that low correlation among the dimensions should be possible.

To be effective, a diagnostic center needs a relatively large number of exercises. For instance, in assessing participants' ability to lead groups, the assessors need to make more than one observation of group interactions. Unlike the selection program, in which group leadership is just one of many attributes needed for successful performance, a diagnostic program must pinpoint deficiencies in the various facets of the individual's group leadership skills. For example, we would like to know if an individual is unable to clearly state ideas or if he or she lacks the assertiveness to make contributions heard.

The exercises in diagnostic programs must have a much higher level of fidelity than selection programs. The exercises should be more like work-sample tests and measure present levels of skills.

For a developmental assessment center, considerations are different still. To ensure transfer of training from an assessment center to the job situation—a perennial problem for any training program—the exercises must have several special features. They must be highly relevant to the job to bring out the best efforts of the participants. They must provide opportunities for successful practice in a nonthreatening environment, and they must provide situations that can be observed by assessors or facilitators who can later provide feedback and guidance for continued improvement. There must be enough exercises so that participants can solidify their new skills in the program before having to use them on the job.

Summary

Situational exercises provide a rich source of data for the evaluation of candidates' potential for long-range success, for diagnosing current skill levels, and as vehicles for training managerial skills. A variety of different types of exercises should be used, ranging from simple one-on-one simulations to written case analyses and complex organizational games. A large number of shorter simulations provides better diagnostic information than a small number of complex simulations for most assessment and developmental programs. Information from interviews and paper-and-pencil tests can provide valuable information in an assessment center. Such information can be combined with assessments of behavior observed in the exercises in different ways. Any given exercise can be used for a variety of purposes. Table 5.5 provides a detailed comparison of the characteristics of exercises for different assessment purposes.

6

Observing and Classifying Behavior

Key Concepts: Contrasting theories of social judgment; methods for gathering and evaluating observations; empirical evidence for and against various methods of observing and judging behavior in an assessment center.

In the last two chapters, we discussed two main elements of the assessment center method: the types of dimensions that are appropriate for different assessment centers and the types of exercises that elicit behaviors relevant to those dimensions. In this chapter and the next we will discuss the process of evaluating behaviors to assess managerial competence. This chapter describes the steps that *individual* assessors take to observe, classify, and evaluate behavior in separate exercises. Chapter 7 describes the steps the *group* of assessors take to share their evaluations, determine final dimension ratings, and derive overall assessment ratings.

This chapter opens with a brief introduction to two contrasting theories of social judgment. These theories provide a framework for understanding the steps carried out in the assessment center method. The discussion of each step includes a description of assessment center practice for that step, the philosophical contributions of each of the two theories of social judgment, and relevant assessment center research.

The second major section of this chapter discusses alternative methods of gathering and evaluating assessment center observations. The most common variation of the traditional assessment center, called the "within-exercise dimension rating method," is described and evaluated in some detail, since this procedure is used frequently and is somewhat controversial. This section also covers alternative methods of observing and recording behavioral observations, such as behavior checklists and behaviorally anchored rating scales.

Finally, and most importantly, we will examine whether research evidence supports or refutes the rationale underlying the assessment center method.

Introduction to Two Theories of Social Cognition

Before we describe the steps in the traditional assessment center process, it will be helpful to compare two general descriptions of social judgment. *Social judgment* refers to the process of perceiving and evaluating the behavior of others and forming impressions about their strengths and weaknesses. One point of view describes social judgment as an objective process in which we accumulate many specific pieces of factual information, then integrate this information in a logical and systematic way to form accurate judgments about people. The second point of view states that our observation of behavior is influenced by subjective biases, that we selectively store and use only certain information, and that we have very limited and flawed capacities to remember prior events and to make accurate interpersonal judgments.

As illustrated in Table 6.1, the first point of view—referred to in this book as the "behavior-driven" approach—has also been called a data-driven approach (Abelson, 1981), a bottom-up approach (Fiske & Taylor, 1984), and a behavior model (Borman, 1977, 1978) of human judgment. These terms convey the idea that we are capable of attending to detailed behavior of other people, storing memories of specific events, and forming objective judgments based on what actually takes place. The alternative point of view—called the "schema-driven" approach (Fiske & Taylor, 1984)— has also been termed a top-down approach and a cognitive categorization model (Nisbitt & Ross, 1980). These terms convey the idea that what we think about other people's behavior is influenced by

Table 6.1
Comparison of Two Theories of Social Judgment

	Behavior-driven Theory	Schema-driven Theory
Alternate terms	Bottom-up approach Behavioral model Data-driven approach	Top-down approach Cognitive categorization model
Basis of evaluation	Behavior displayed by person	Prior beliefs and stereotypes about person
Memory storage	Specific actions	General impressions
Quality of judgment	Objective	Subjective

our prior perceptions, memory, and inferences about these people; that we fail to objectively see many detailed behaviors that take place; and that our memory consists largely of general impressions and broad evaluations of people.

Table 6.1 highlights the differences between the two theories, but we should keep in mind that there are similarities as well. For example, behavior-driven theories allow for some loss of memory detail over time, and schema-driven theories recognize that we store specific information along with our general impressions of other people.

The assessment center method is based on a mixed theory about perception and memory of social observations (Ebbeson, 1981). In this mixed theory, both specific instances of events and general categories of events are recorded in memory. In line with a behavior-driven approach, the assessment center method is based on the assumption that assessors can systematically observe and use behavioral information generated by the exercises. In fact, many of the techniques and procedures used in an assessment center are designed to help the assessors make and remember detailed observations. In line with a schema-driven approach, assessors are taught to use meaningful dimensions of managerial performance (prior beliefs) to help focus their attention during the complex exercises, and to make systematic judgments about the level of skill demonstrated. In addition, procedures are designed to minimize the negative influences of prior impressions and at the same time to benefit from the positive influences that meaningful dimension categories can provide. For example, assessors are trained to have a common understanding of a dimension such as "skill in delegation" and are given examples of specific behaviors of good delegation to watch for.

As we describe the assessment center process, keep in mind that each procedure is designed to help the assessors carefully observe, record, remember, share, and use objective behavioral information.

Steps in the Behavior Reporting Method

The traditional assessment center method has its origins in the method devised by AT&T (Bray & Grant, 1966) and adopted widely through the years. This method is called the "behavior reporting method" because the emphasis is on recording and sharing behaviors observed in each situational exercise. (No ratings of exercise performance are given.) The traditional assessment center method involves the following steps:

- observation and recording of behavior
- classification of behavior into managerial attributes
- presentation of exercise reports by one assessor to others
- preliminary ratings of overall dimension performance
- discussion of preliminary ratings to achieve consensus
- preliminary overall assessment ratings (optional)
- discussion of overall assessment ratings to achieve consensus (optional)

The first four steps are discussed in this chapter; the last three steps are discussed in Chapter 7.

There have been many modifications of each step in the traditional method. A few of these modifications are covered in this chapter, but many other variations will not be described.

Observation and Recording of Behavior

Assessment Center Practice. Figure 6.1 shows a simplified model of the elements of the assessment center method. The left-hand side of the model shows the methods for evaluating each participant as he or she participates in several exercises. The assessor observes and records behaviors—shown here with numbers 1 to 18. Behavior 1 in the group discussion might entail the participant suggesting that the group spend 15 minutes on each of the four problems they have been given, followed by the fact that the suggestion is accepted and followed. Behavior 3 might entail the participant saying that the suggestions thus far have not dealt with the central problem described in the case materials, followed by the fact that the conversation shifts direction. Each of these behaviors would be classified into the dimension called leadership. In like fashion, behaviors are observed and classified into other dimensions, such as decision making and assertiveness. The same process is carried out for each of the other exercises. Of course, some dimensions may not be observable in certain exercises.

Assessors record behaviors while participants engage in group discussions, interview simulations, or other exercises. Assessors usually use a blank form, similar to the one shown in Figure 6.2, to write down details of what they observe. Usually the assessor has only one chance to observe the behavior as it unfolds in the exercise. Sometimes assessors are not present and the exercises are videotaped (Byham, 1989). This practice allows the assessors to watch the tape at a convenient time and even to replay it in order to pick up subtle details. Videotaping also enables an assessor to view an exercise in which he or she was also a role-player or resource person. Under normal circumstances, videotaping is not recommended for most organizations because some participants feel increased stress or may even "play act" for the camera. In addition, reviewing the tape increases the time required by the assessors. Furthermore, I believe there is little to be gained by repeated observations; the assessors can grasp the vast majority of behaviors with one viewing, if adequately trained (McIntyre & Vanetti, 1988). Virtually all (95 percent) assessment centers follow the practice of having assessors take notes during exercises (Gaugler et al., 1990).

In the case of written exercises, such as the in-basket or a case study analysis, there is a permanent record of the overt

Figure 6.1
Summary of Exercises, Dimensions, and Ratings in an Assessment Center

Exercises	Within-Exercise Dimension Observations	Overall Dimension Ratings		Overall Assessment Ratings	
		Prelim	Final	Prelim	Final
Group Discussion					
Behaviors 1 2 3 4 5 6	Leadership Decision Making Assertiveness				
One-on-one		Leadership			
Behaviors 7 8 9 10 11 12	Leadership Decision Making Assertiveness	Decision Making		Overall Assessment Rating	
In-Basket		Assertiveness			
Behaviors 13 14 15 16 17 18	Leadership Decision Making Assertiveness				
5 or 6 Exercises	8 to 15 Dimensions				

behaviors of the participant that can be scrutinized for evidence of dimension-related behaviors. In such exercises, the assessor can easily reexamine the written work to confirm what action was taken. Still, there is no substantiated difference in the reliability of assessments of written exercises and overt behavior.

Figure 6.2
Example of Behavioral Observation Notes

Briefing Exercise
Assessor Report Form

Assessor's Name___I. Sharpe_____Date:___10-20-87_____

Participant's Name___Bob_____Assessor's Name_____

Greeted Bob warmly and shook his hand
Asked if housing arrangements were satisfactory
+Sen Said he could understand Bob missing his family
    during training
+Lead Being alone will help you concentrate on training
    where high performance is required
    Clearly stated objectives of this briefing session
    Asked if Bob had questions
-Sen did not answer question about second objective
    Stated "practice makes perfect"
+Lead Said I want to reinforce your good skills
    and correct your weaknesses
-OC Fumbled with words when describing first
    objective in some detail
-OC Had poor eye contact—looked across the room
    Stated that Bob had to over-learn so as
    to handle emergencies
    Asked if there were questions
    Described second objective in more detail
    Asked if there were questions
+Lead Stated that he would expect Bob to learn
    exact procedures
-OC Looked down at table most of time
    Stated he had confidence in Bob
    Said "let's get on with it"
    Didn't ask for Bob's cooperation

Schema-driven Theory. Schema-driven theories suggest that we have limited capacities to attend to the vast array of environmental stimuli around us all the time (Fiske & Taylor, 1984), and thus, we must selectively attend to only some events (Alba & Hasher, 1983). According to schema theory, this selective perception operates in a predictable way: we tend to undersample relevant observations (Cooper, 1981; Major, 1980), that is, we make relatively few observations that are pertinent to the judgments we must make. More specifically, according to schema-driven theory, our prior knowledge of an individual influences our subsequent observations. The prior knowledge might be information about the person's lack of education or poor job performance, or it might be an initial impression formed in the first few minutes of interaction. According to this view, the observer has a difficult time withholding judgment until all the evidence is in. In other words, he or she may make judgments before much relevant information has been gathered. In particular, the initial schema held by an assessor about a participant might direct subsequent observations so as to provide support for the initial impression. Thus, there may be a process of selective perception that filters out details not consistent with the existing knowledge (Cooper, 1981).

Behavior-driven Theory. A very different view is provided by behavior-driven theories, which emphasize that observers are able to observe and remember specific behaviors (Hintzman, 1986, 1988). Research has shown that when observing others, people perceive and remember most of the social interactions that take place (Hastie & Kumar, 1979; Locksley, Borgida, Brekka, & Hepburn, 1980). Each observation becomes represented in memory by several different features (Kintsch & vanDijk, 1978; Linville, Fischer, & Salovey, 1989); for example, a segment of a leaderless group discussion is stored in memory in terms of who was speaking, what was said, nonverbal gestures that accompanied the words, and what reactions were elicited from the audience. Summarizing much of the literature on social cognition, Higgins and Bargh (1987) concluded that "people apparently encode environmental information fairly accurately without supplementing the original information with previous knowledge" (p. 373).

There is much theoretical support for the assumption that observers can make and retain careful observations of the complex behavior that takes place in the exercises. Furthermore, there is both direct and indirect experimental evidence from studies in numerous areas of psychology that specific behavioral observations can be made and retained. Direct observation of behavior is widely used in behavioral assessment (Foster & Cone, 1986), behavior modification, and behavior therapy (Kazdin, 1984). There is a long history of these procedures (all based on the ability to observe and give feedback about specific behaviors) being used for the treatment of alcoholism, eating disorders, depression, and mental retardation (Leitenberg, 1976). All these examples illustrate that people can and do make objective observations of specific behaviors.

Hintzman (1986, 1988) has even argued that all experience is recorded in human perceptual processes. Likewise, Johnson and Raye (1981) argued that all perceptual events produce persistent memory traces. Such claims may seem exaggerated, and few would claim that humans perceive and store in long-term memory literally all of the stimuli hitting our senses. But, the primary issue is whether we can record details of observations if we are asked to do so. Theory and research suggest we can.

These two different views of social perception may both be true under certain circumstances. The question then is when, and under what conditions, one or the other is likely to operate. Fiske and Taylor (1984) maintain that more detailed records of experiences will be stored in memory and can be remembered if the observer takes the task seriously. In addition, Nathan and Lord (1983) have shown that when observers can see how behaviors fit into meaningful mental patterns, there will be a direct record of specific details stored in long-term memory. Other research shows that the *purpose* of observation determines what is observed and selected (Higgins & Bargh, 1987). In most everyday social interactions, individuals need to form only general impressions of other people. Thus, we tend to extract and retain overall impressions, a fact that supports the schema-driven approach. On the other hand, when people are told that the purpose of observation is to note details in what they observe, they can in fact do so. Furthermore, if *accuracy* is stressed, details are noted, selected, and retained quite thoroughly (Alba & Hasher, 1983). These are the very conditions that exist in assessment centers: assessors take the task seriously, dimensions provide meaningful categories, assessors are responsible for reporting behaviors, and accuracy is stressed.

Assessment Center Research. Few studies have directly examined the observation process of assessors. McIntyre and Vanetti (1988) found that behavior observation training (in comparison with no training) led to greater accuracy. Furthermore, warnings that the candidate was generally "good" or "bad" did not interfere with observation accuracy. The most thorough study was conducted by Gaugler and Thornton (1989) who investigated the accuracy of assessors' observations of videotaped exercises. Observational accuracy was measured by calculating (1) the ratio of "good" observations (i.e., specific and behavioral records) to the total number of dimension-relevant behaviors actually displayed by participants (determined by experts after a careful review of the tapes) and (2) the ratio of good observations to the total number of observations made. Results showed that assessors recorded approximately 50 percent of the observations made by the experts and that approximately 75 percent of the assessors' observations were actual behaviors rather than inferences or impressions. Assessors observed a smaller percentage of the behaviors when asked to look for nine, as opposed to six or three, dimensions. This research suggests that although assessors can and do make many good observations, they do not record all of the dimension-relevant behaviors that participants exhibit. Because the assessors in this study were trained for a limited amount of time, we can assume that experienced assessors would observe a larger percentage of the behavioral events. The results also show that assessors have trouble making behavioral observations when asked to observe larger numbers of dimensions.

Classification of Behavior

Assessment Center Practice. While the assessors are observing behaviors they may actually start the classification process by making notes that signify the dimension in which a particular behavior belongs. Figure 6.2 shows a few examples: "+OC" means effective oral communication; "-Sen" means poor sensitivity. The thorough classification process takes place very soon after the exercise is completed. Assessors look back over their notes and identify all the oral communication behaviors they observed. They then record these behaviors on a separate form, as shown in Figure 6.3, to facilitate reporting to the other assessors in the integration discussion, which takes place after all the exercises have been completed.

Figure 6.3
Example of Classification of Behaviors

Briefing Exercise

Oral Communication

Effective expression in individual and group situations.

+ Clearly stated objectives
+ Said "practice makes perfect" to make his point emphatically
− Fumbled with words when describing first objective in detail
− Had poor eye contact
− Looked down at table

Leadership

Ability to influence others, through direction and personal guidance, to achieve goals.

+ Stated being alone will help Bob concentrate on good performance in training
+ Said "I want to reinforce your good skills"
+ Stated he expected Bob to learn exact procedures
− Failed to ask for Bob's cooperation

Schema-driven Theory. Schema theories of interpersonal perception emphasize that the classification schemes we use are often just devices to help us simplify our observations and may not be meaningful categories. The categories we use, the associations we make among specific behaviors within categories, and the associations we make among categories may be artificially created by the implicit personality theories we hold about people (Cooper, 1981). An implicit personality theory is the set of beliefs and assumptions we have about which traits go together. For example, I may believe that people who speak fluently are intelligent. According to schema theory, these systems of beliefs may be artificially created and not based on real behavior.

Behavior-driven Theories. In contrast to the notion that attribute dimensions may be artificial categories, other theory and research suggest that these dimensions are meaningful and "real" categories. Support for the idea of meaningful categories comes from work by Rosch, Mervis, Gray, Johnson, & Boyes-Braem (1976) on physical objects, and by Hampson, John, and Goldberg (1986) on social activities. According to these researchers, natural categories exist in various areas of our thinking, and these categories are perceived quite generally across samples of people. Furthermore, we are able to perceive information about objects that allows us to categorize objects and behaviors into the natural categories. In the assessment center context, these ideas support the notion that there are meaningful categories, such as " leadership" behaviors and "decision-making" behaviors. Furthermore, it implies that assessors can observe behaviors such as "the participant suggested that the group spend fifteen minutes on each of four problems and the suggestion was followed by the group" and distinguish it from the behavior "participant stated three reasons why he would not put sales representatives on commission." The first is an example of leadership, and the second is an example of decision making.

The theory underlying the development of behaviorally anchored rating scales (Smith & Kendall, 1963) provides another bit of support for the belief that observers can meaningfully classify behavior. This technique assumes that work behaviors can be sorted consistently into meaningful categories. Using this technique, supervisors observe work behaviors, classify these behaviors into categories, and over time accumulate evidence to support ratings of meaningful areas of work performance.

In the context of performance appraisal research, Nathan and Lord (1983) provided further evidence that observers can classify behaviors into separate categories and make ratings based on actual behaviors displayed. In an experiment, they found that poor behaviors of the "good performers" and good behaviors of the "poor performers" had a clear impact on the ratings. General impressions of overall effectiveness had some effect on the ratings of dimensions, but the subjects were clearly able to distinguish among the behaviors and dimensions they were rating.

As we saw in Chapter 3, job performance dimensions can be defined quite broadly or narrowly. But at what level of abstraction should we operate? Hampson et al. (1986) have studied the appropriate level of abstraction of dimensions, and they present a three-level model. They found that for most purposes the top level, involving broad traits such as extraversion and conscientiousness, is too abstract, whereas the bottom level, involving traits such as musical or stingy, is too specific. The middle level, involving concepts such as energy level, sociability, reliability, and assertiveness, seems to be most useful. Assessment center dimensions generally fall into this middle level of abstraction.

Assessment Center Research. The classification process of assessors is a neglected area of research. Gaugler and Thornton's (1989) study is the only research that has been done to date. The authors calculated the ratio of good observations correctly classified by assessors to the total number of good observations classified by experts (28 percent) and the ratio of the total number of good observations the subject correctly classified to the total number of good observations the subject made (40 percent). Assessors were able to correctly classify far more behaviors when they had to deal with three dimensions than when they had to deal with six or nine dimensions. The relatively weak classification accuracy scores found in this study suggest that these subjects were not making "clean" distinctions among the dimensions, but they did better when they had a small number of clearly defined dimensions. Well-trained and experienced assessors may be more effective at this task.

Summary. At the end of this process of observation and classification, the assessors have detailed narrative reports of behaviors classified into the appropriate dimensions. Each of these reports is completed by the assessor soon after he or she views the candidates participating in the exercises. Scheduling time for assessors to complete these reports is difficult, but it must be done so that the notes and observations are fresh in assessors' minds. Research in the area of social perception shows that specific behavioral information fades quickly unless there is some record made immediately after the events take place (Fiske & Taylor, 1984; Wyler & Srull, 1986). Once all of this information is collected, the assessors are ready to meet and present their observations.

Presentation of Reports

Assessment Center Practice. When the assessors meet to integrate their observations, they discuss the performance of one participant at a time. Each assessor reads the narrative report of behaviors observed. Assessor A may report on the group discussion, Assessor B on the one-on-one simulation, Assessor C on the in-basket, then Assessor A on a fourth exercise, and so on. As illustrated in Figures 6.1 and 6.3, in each narrative report the assessor describes the behaviors he or she observed relative to the various dimensions. In their reports, assessors consider several points relevant to each dimension, for example, did the participant set a follow-up date to review performance improvements discussed in a performance appraisal simulation? While the reports are being read, the other assessors listen and take notes on a dimension summary form illustrated in Figure 6.4. There is usually one page for each dimension. This format provides a place to accumulate behavioral evidence relevant to a dimension across all exercises.

Schema-driven Theory. When presenting their reports, assessors rely heavily on the notes they have taken while observing the exercises. However, because they cannot write down every detail, assessors must frequently rely on their memory. To what extent can assessors recall the actual events that take place? According to the schema theory, memory is predominantly composed of abstract representations or interpretations of events we have witnessed (Cooper, 1981; Fiske & Taylor, 1984). This perspective

Figure 6.4
Example of Dimension Summary Form

Oral Communication Effective expression in individual and group situations (include gestures and nonverbal communications).

		Overall
1.	Briefing	<u>4</u>
2.	Training	
3.	Debriefing	

Notes

1. Briefing
+ greeted John with smile and handshake
+ "pleased to work with you" +warm, support
+ spoke firmly yet quietly
− fumbled for right words to state objective, then gave clear description
+ maintained good eye contact
+ slowed down his speech to make a point

2. Training
+ gave clear, brief description of objectives
+ made small jobs about an exchange in the briefing
+ gave overview of procedure
− stumbled over description of 2 steps John didn't understand
+ showed energy and enthusiasm
+ used hand gestures to get John involved
− didn't directly answer a question by John

3. Debriefing
+ stated that these were strengths & weaknesses in John's training performance
− didn't give clear example of poor performance
+ reviewed positive steps in performance
+ showed enthusiasm
+ summarized objectives, performance, & continuing strengths and weaknesses
+ ended on up-beat note—confidence in future

says that while *short-term* memory may consist of accurate details, *long-term* memory consists largely of general categories lacking in detail (Wyer & Srull, 1985). Furthermore, any detail transferred to long-term memory remains there only for a limited period of time. Decay takes place, and this decay is selective: according to this theory, we tend to retain only those bits of information that are consistent with the general impressions we hold.

An even more extreme process, called *reconstruction,* is proposed by other theorists (Cooper, 1981). In this process, we reconstruct events that never took place; in other words, we believe that events took place that are consistent with our initial impressions, when in fact those events never actually happened. In an assessment center we would be troubled if an assessor falsely recalled that his favored participant summarized the group's final conclusions when in fact another person had done so.

Behavior-driven Theory. A very different view of memory comes from other sources. Theory and research on interpersonal perception provides support for our ability to remember a vast amount of detail about observations we have made. Some memory theories (Hintzman, 1986, 1988; Smith & Medin, 1981) suggest that our memory consists of traces of all the perceptions we have ever experienced. These memory traces include records of detailed episodes we have observed. Furthermore, we can retrieve rich details about these events (Fiske & Taylor, 1984). Johnson and Raye (1981) even maintain that we can distinguish between the traces in memory that were created by actual external events (for example, we met someone who criticized his wife, the food in the cafeteria, and the president of the United States) and inferences that we have created internally (for example, "that new employee is a negative person"). They also argue that the externally generated memory traces (all those complaints) are actually more specific and fixed than the internally generated ones (the "negative person"). Locksley, Stangor, and Hepburn (1984) have shown that when properly aided and tested, memory is not distorted to match prior impressions contained in a schema.

Even if we accept that memory consists of extensive and detailed information, we must also recognize that people have difficulty locating and recalling the information. The retrieval of assessment observations is made easier by training assessors thoroughly in typical actions that participants may display in each exercise, relevant to each dimension. In addition, we can provide assessors with lists of "points to consider" when preparing exercise reports or delivering these reports in the integration discussion.

Preliminary Ratings of Overall Dimension Performance

Assessment Center Practice. When all the exercise reports have been read, each assessor takes a few minutes to review the accumulated behavioral evidence and determines a preliminary overall dimension rating for each of the dimensions. These preliminary ratings are made independently and written on the dimension summary form. The ratings are then posted on a large flip chart or chalk board. Table 6.2 illustrates the ratings determined for one participant by a group of three assessors over five dimensions.

Schema-driven Theory. According to this theory, people develop and use simple guiding principles for making judgments about others. The theory says we make judgments on the basis of

Table 6.2
Preliminary and Final Overall Dimension Ratings

Dimension	Preliminary Overall Dimension Ratings			Final Overall Dimension Rating
	Assessor A	Assessor B	Assessor C	
Leadership	4	4	4	4
Decision making	2	2	3	2
Assertiveness	2	3	3	3
Oral communication	3	4	4	3
Planning and organizing	2	2	4	4

very little information instead of the abundant information that is usually available. This process of simplification is one of two alternative theoretical explanations for the processes of integration and judgment that take place at this stage of assessment. Many people maintain that our interpersonal judgments are based on memory, which is fallible and selective. This position holds that because of selective memory decay, integration and judgment will depend more on information that is consistent with our general impression of the participant. For example, Cooper (1981) emphasized that there will be considerable "halo error" in ratings, that is, artificially high relationships among attribute ratings caused by the broad effect of a single bit of strong information on the evaluation of several characteristics. (As we will see in the next section, this view of halo error may be inaccurate. Recent analyses of halo error [Murphy, Jako, & Anhalt, 1991] suggest that many of the observed relationships among dimension ratings may be due to actual relationships among similar attributes.) Fiske and Taylor (1984) summarized much research that suggests that internal impressions, rather than detailed episodes in memory, are easier for people to recall and thus will dominate our evaluations. Feldman (1981) suggested further that we will "reconstruct" or invent events that will fill in empty spaces in memory in order to substantiate and support our judgment.

The most thorough criticism of human inferential processes is provided by Nisbett and Ross (1980). They claim that humans use several heuristic procedures, or "rules of thumb," which introduce errors in the decision process. Examples of these rules include

- "Representativeness"—Objects are assigned to categories after one observation, and we proceed to make judgments based on presumed category membership.
  Problem: The information about the category is not always accurate and is overused.
- "Availability"—Information that is readily available in memory is used to make judgments about frequency, probability, and causality.
  Problem: Available information may not be valid.
- "Salience and vividness"—We put more weight on readily visible and outstanding information.
  Problem: Vividness is not usually relevant to the value of the information to our decision.

These and other shortcomings in our judgment processes make it particularly difficult for us to make accurate predictions about future events. All hope is not lost, though, as we will see later. Nisbitt and Ross (1981) point out circumstances when human judgment is quite adequate to accomplish great feats, such as putting a man on the moon.

Behavior-driven Theory. According to behavior-driven theory, people use the objective and detailed information available to them and combine this information in a logical manner. Hintzman (1986, 1988) maintained that the judge will recall and use actual behaviors to form an evaluation. Anderson (1974, 1981) has shown that people use a simple mental algebra to combine information through adding or averaging to form an overall evaluation. Along these lines, we have reviewed how Nathan and Lord (1983) have shown that ratings of specific dimensions are based on performance demonstrated, not just general impressions the observer has formed. Alba and Hasher (1983) reviewed much research on human perception and concluded that the distortions in judgment emphasized by the schema-driven theories are actually quite infrequent. And finally, Murphy et al. (1991) have argued that the supposedly pervasive "halo error" may not be all that pervasive, but rather a reflection of actual relationships among performance dimensions.

Summary. Given the discouraging point of view about social perception and human judgment held by the schema theorists, we might wonder if there is any hope for the accurate assessment of employee performance. The answer is clearly "yes," because the assessment center process is very different from most of the processes studied by social judgment researchers. Researchers in social judgment have dealt mostly with everyday experiences of human interaction. They have studied these phenomena in temporary groups of subjects in laboratory situations where people have limited information. As Bernardin and Beatty (1984) have observed in their review of performance appraisal research and practice, *performance* appraisal is different from *personal* appraisal. They see reason to be optimistic that many of the obstacles to good judgment that plague daily human judgments can be overcome in the controlled performance appraisal situation. Improvements in judgments about job performance can be expected when managers are systematically trained to rate performance using clear standards for judgment, when behaviorally anchored rating scales are used as originally intended, when diaries are kept, and when managers are properly motivated to provide accurate ratings. Whether or not this is overly optimistic is debatable. However, in the case of assessment center evaluations, where many of the everyday pressures to distort appraisals (Murphy & Cleveland, 1990) are absent, there is even more reason to be optimistic. Is there data to support this optimism?

Assessment Center Research. After they have heard the preliminary reports of other assessors, but prior to any discussion, do the assessors agree on the overall dimension ratings? One way to answer this question is to compare the ratings given by two or more assessors. These comparisons are called reliability estimates and can range from .00 to 1.00. For this kind of study, reliability figures of .80 to 1.00 are considered high, .60 to .80 are moderate, and .60 or below are low. Table 6.3 shows that in past assessment center studies, the level of agreement among assessors on preliminary overall dimension ratings has been found to range from

Table 6.3

Studies of Agreement among Assessors on Preliminary Overall Dimension Ratings

Authors	Estimates of Agreement among Assessors (average reliability)
Konz, 1988	.81
Tziner & Dolan, 1982	.50
Schmitt, 1977	.67
Borman, 1982	.76
Keho et al., 1985	.82
McConnel & Parker, 1972	.83
Neidig & Martin, 1979	.94
Sackett & Hakel, 1979	.69

relatively low (.50), to moderate (.67), to quite high (.94). Thomson (1970) found high levels of agreement for both psychologist assessors and management assessors. As we will see in Chapter 7, the levels of agreement are even higher after the integration discussion, but it should be clear that agreement can be fairly high from the start.

Integration Procedures

Up to this point we have discussed the processes underlying assessors' observations and judgments. The following brief description of the last three steps in the assessment center method completes this sequence. A more complete analysis of the group processes of the assessor discussion will be presented in the next chapter. After the preliminary overall dimension ratings are posted (see Table 6.2), the assessors discuss any discrepancies in ratings and come to agreement on the final overall dimension ratings. This process is one of arriving at a consensus and involves more than just averaging the preliminary ratings. Of course, when there is agreement from the beginning, as there was for leadership in our example, the final rating is usually that score. On the other hand, a minority opinion may prevail in the discussion as the behavioral evidence is reviewed more carefully. In our example, the group ended up giving the participant a 4 on planning and organizing, even though only Assessor C rated it that high on the preliminary ratings.

After agreement has been reached on the dimension ratings, each assessor may give a preliminary overall assessment rating. An overall rating is appropriate if the purpose of the program is to make a recommendation for hiring or promotion. On the other hand, if the purpose of the program is diagnosis of training needs or development of managerial skills, there is no need for an overall rating: the most important outcome of the assessment is the information about the dimensions themselves. In fact, deriving an overall assessment rating may be dysfunctional, that is, it may undermine the process of identifying strengths and weaknesses in a supportive fashion and create anxiety that the results will be used for making organizational decisions instead. Assuming that an overall assessment rating is appropriate, each assessor independently reviews the final dimension ratings and uses his or her best judgment on how to combine the information. These preliminary overall assessment ratings are posted on the flip chart and discussed until consensus is reached on a final overall assessment rating.

Comparison of Schema-driven and Behavior-driven Theories

We have seen two clear and well-developed points of view about how interpersonal perception and judgment unfolds: the schema-driven and behavior-driven theories. We have seen theoretical and research support for each one. Which one is most accurate? It is probably inappropriate to seek a definitive answer to this question. Neither of these approaches explains what happens in all instances of interpersonal judgment. A better approach is to try to understand *when* each process occurs, *what conditions* foster behavior-based or schema-based evaluation, and *what can be learned* from each theoretical position that will foster better assessment. A review of the literature on this subject provides several clues about when and where the two approaches operate, but one gets the impression that few theoreticians have attempted to integrate the two positions. It appears that if a researcher is in one camp, he or she sees little of value in the other camp.

The approach of this book has been to convey the value of each explanation of social judgment. The research contains some hints about the conditions governing the two opposing approaches. If people are simply forming general impressions of others, then schema are more likely to affect observations, memory, and judgments (Fiske & Taylor, 1984). On the other hand, if people are told to observe details, they can and do perceive and retain a vast amount of specific information (Sherman, Judd, & Park, 1989). If observers must rely on memory, implicit personality theories may come to mind, and artificially high relationships among the dimensions may result (Cooper, 1981). But if some device—such as a diary—is used to record observations, halo error in the form of artificially high relationships among rated dimensions is reduced (Bernardin & Walter, 1977). Nathan and Lord (1983) have shown that if behaviors fit into clear cognitive dimensions, observers are able to put observations directly into long-term memory, but if observers do not have a clear understanding of the categories, they will not recall real behaviors and may in fact reconstruct events to fit the general schemata they hold (Alba & Hasher, 1983). Nisbett and Ross (1980) contend that when individuals are given instructions to engage in careful problem solving, they use more systematic, scientific strategies for making inferences. Swann (1984) suggested that accuracy in human perception is greater when the judge is making situation-specific predictions than when he or she is making global or trans-situational predictions. Accuracy is greater because the observer is examining only a limited set of behaviors and can be more familiar with the specific situation and with the surrounding situations to which inferences are being made.

All of these bits of evidence suggest there is good reason to have confidence that assessors can make effective judgments about managerial competencies if the conditions are right. We have seen how many of these conditions are built into the assessment center method:

- assessors are given time to make specific observations and take notes
- assessors make ratings soon after observations and do not have to rely on long-term memory
- dimensions for effective managerial performance are clearly defined
- assessors often have no vested interest in the outcome and can look at behavioral evidence objectively
- assessors are making predictions about success in specific jobs that are familiar to them

Alternative Methods of Recording and Integrating Observations

Over the years, human resource experts have designed many variations on the original "behavior reporting method." If the assessment center method has been so successful, why do we see these variations? The answer to this question is based on some speculation, but we can reasonably suggest a few explanations. There have been many developments in parallel areas of personnel evaluation, such as performance appraisal and selection interviewing, that have been tried out in the assessment center context. For example, the use of behaviorally anchored rating scales (Smith & Kendall, 1963) and behavioral observations scales (Bernardin & Beatty, 1984) suggest new ways of rating behavior in situational exercises. In addition, developments in theories of social judgment (some of which have been reviewed earlier in this chapter) have suggested changes in assessment center methods. In addition, research evidence on assessments has raised certain questions about the accuracy of the assessment center method that may be improved with new procedures.

Probably the most influential push for change has been pressure to streamline the assessment center method. An assessment center takes a great deal of the participants' time, and even more of the assessors' time. In view of the high cost of running an assessment center, compared to the cost of a simple test or background interview, it is altogether reasonable that assessment center designers would try to cut down on time and expense. There have been innovations in almost all phases of behavior processing, including the recording of behavior, classification of behavior, rating effectiveness, reporting accuracy, and integration of data in an overall assessment rating.

Within-Exercise Dimension Rating Method

The traditional observation and classification process described earlier in this chapter is called the behavior reporting method. A major variation on this method is the "within-exercise dimension rating method." This term is long and somewhat awkward, but we will continue to use it because it precisely conveys the way many assessment centers are operated. More importantly, it appears that whatever method is used has important effects on how assessors observe behavior, interact with each other, and rate performance. In the within-exercise dimension rating method, assessors are asked to provide a rating on each dimension that can be observed in an exercise. After they have observed and classified behaviors, they typically use a 1 to 5 rating scale to evaluate the participant's performance on each of the appropriate dimensions. These ratings may affect individual judgments and the group dynamics in the assessor discussion, a topic pursued more fully in the next chapter.

Our interest now is in the quality of these within-exercise dimension ratings. What evidence is there that they are adequate measures of the attributes they supposedly measure? A detailed review of the research on within-exercise dimension ratings is presented here for two reasons. First, many assessment centers use the within-exercise rating method, and we need to know how effective it is. Second, some of this research raises serious questions about the accuracy of the traditional assessment center method, and we need to answer these questions.

Assessor Reliability. Three studies have examined assessor agreement for within-exercise dimension ratings. It should be recognized that data addressing this issue are seldom available in operational assessment centers because usually only one assessor observes a candidate in each exercise. Borman (1982) reported estimates of assessor reliability that ranged from .44 to .92 with an average of .76. Kehoe, Weinberg, and Lawrence (1985) found that assessors differentiated among participants' skills with a high degree of consistency, with reliability estimates ranging from .66 to .94. Last, Konz (1988) reported an assessor reliability of .75 for the dimension ratings made in one exercise. Although there is some variability in these figures, the results suggest that different assessors rate a given dimension within an exercise with an acceptable level of agreement.

Relationship of Within-Exercise Dimension Ratings to Other Measures. Russell (1987) studied the relationship of within-exercise dimension ratings from an in-basket and an interview simulation with *self-ratings* of interpersonal behaviors, which were seen as important to effective managers. He found that self-ratings were not related to the dimension ratings from the in-basket but were related to several of the dimension ratings from the interview simulation. Russell concluded that assessors' ratings do not reflect underlying personal characteristics, but instead reflect the degree to which candidates' behavior is congruent with managerial role expectations within a given exercise. The results might also suggest that people see themselves more accurately in some situations than others.

No studies examined the ability of within-exercise dimension ratings to predict measures of the same attributes in work settings. However, three studies examined the relationship of within-exercise dimension ratings and across-exercise dimension ratings. Hinrichs and Haanpera (1976) found that the ratings from an in-basket and a written job report were only slightly related to overall dimension ratings, but ratings from the group discussion exercise were related more strongly. Thus, the assessors were putting more weight on the group discussion than the other exercises when forming their overall dimension ratings, possibly because they saw that this exercise was most job-relevant.

However, Neidig, Martin, and Yates (1979) found that all of their exercises contributed to the dimensions they were designed to measure, with the in-basket contributing the most unique and the background interview the least unique information. Kehoe et al. (1985) found that ratings from the last exercise candidates participated in contributed substantially more to the across-exercise dimension ratings than the first two exercises. However, because exercise order was not varied, it is not known whether this finding was due to a recency effect or real differences in the exercises.

Construct Validity. Construct validity is a technical term used by experts in psychological measurement. Construct validation is a complex process of forming hypotheses about an assessment procedure and then examining empirical evidence to support or refute those hypotheses. Construct validity is established by examining a wide variety of evidence about the internal structure of an assessment procedure and discovering how that procedure relates to other tests and measures of effectiveness. One type of construct validity evidence is the relationship among various parts of the assessment procedure. We can get some insight into what an assessment center measures by looking at the relationships of the ratings on several dimensions within several exercises. There are two statistical procedures that have been carried out on within-exercise dimension ratings: factor analysis (Gorsuch, 1983) and convergent/discriminant validity analysis (Campbell & Fiske, 1959).

A technical note may help here. Many research investigations use statistical methods to study the relationship among variables of interest. The most common method is *correlation*, which gives an index of how the scores on one variable are related to scores on a second variable. The index is called the *correlation coefficient* and it ranges from -1.00 to .00 to +1.00. A positive correlation means that as one variable gets larger, the other variable also gets larger. A negative correlation means that as one variable increases, the other decreases. The size of the correlation tells how strongly the two variables are related. For research in this area, correlations of .60 or greater are considered high, .40 to

.60 moderately high, .20 to .40 meaningful, and less than .20 too low to be useful in most situations.

Factor analysis is a statistical procedure that examines the correlations of a large set of variables with each other. If a group of variables tends to be correlated with each other, they form a "cluster" or "factor." Discovery of these factors within a test can help us understand the composition of that test. When applied to assessment center ratings, factor analysis has been used to examine the correlations among all within-exercise dimension ratings across all the exercises to identify groups of ratings that "go together." Two types of factors or clusters might exist: *dimension factors* consisting of the ratings on a given dimension across all exercises, and *exercise factors* consisting of the ratings on all the dimensions within a given exercise. An example of a dimension factor would be ratings of leadership in the group discussion, in the one-on-one exercise, and in the business game; an example of an exercise factor would be leadership, decision making, and sensitivity within the group discussion.

Using data from three organizations, Sackett and Dreher (1982) found that within-exercise dimension ratings fell into exercise factors and not dimension factors. Borman (1982) found many within-exercise dimension ratings were highly related suggesting that assessors were making global judgments of candidates' performance. Bycio, Alvares, & Hahn (1987) used factor analyses to test three hypotheses about assessors' within-exercise dimension ratings. One hypothesis included both dimension and exercise factors, another hypothesis included exercise factors but only one dimension factor, and the third hypothesis included only exercise factors. Although the data did not clearly support one hypothesis over the others, the authors concluded that exercise factors were present. In contrast, using similar analyses, Louiselle (1986) found that the best explanation of correlations among a set of within-exercise dimension ratings was provided by both exercises and dimensions.

Another kind of construct validity evidence is the *pattern* of relationships among within-exercise dimension ratings. Evidence for *convergent validity* is present when we see high correlations between the ratings for the same dimension observed in two or more different exercises, for example, problem solving in the interview simulation and problem solving in the case study. *Discriminant validity* is present when we see (1) relatively *low* correlations among all the dimensions within each single exercise, for example, problem solving, sensitivity, and leadership within the group discussion, and (2) *very low* correlations between ratings on one dimension in the first exercise and another dimension in a second exercise, for example, leadership in the group discussion and sensitivity in the interview simulation.

Table 6.4 shows the results of a representative sample of studies of convergent and discriminant validity. Hinrichs and Haanpera (1976) found that correlations between the same dimension in different exercises averaged .49 for 14 dimensions. In Sackett and Dreher's (1984) study the ratings converged on some dimensions (e.g., oral communication, analytical ability), but showed no correlations across exercises for other dimensions.

Studies that allow the most meaningful comparisons report both convergent and discriminant validities. While the convergent validities in a study by Archambeau (1979) were fairly high, the average correlation of different dimensions within the same exercise was much higher indicating a lack of discriminant validity. The same pattern of higher correlations within an exercise than correlations of the same dimension across exercises was found in a study by Russell (1987). Similar results have been found in other studies (Baker, 1986; Bycio et al., 1987; Konz, 1988; Neidig et al., 1979; Outcalt, 1988; Robertson, Gratten, & Sharpley, 1987; Sackett & Dreher, 1982).

Thus, the research on the within-exercise dimension ratings indicates that although a reasonable level of convergent validity has been found in some assessment centers, a lack of discriminant validity (as indicated by high correlations among dimensions within an exercise) has also characterized the ratings in these centers.

Summary. The results of these studies of within-exercise dimension ratings have raised serious questions about the ability of assessors to make meaningful judgments about dimensions of managerial performance. They suggest to some researchers that assessors do not have a clear and common understanding of distinct attributes, but rather tend to make overall judgments of performance in each situational exercise. Such results have led several critics to argue that the traditional explanation of the assessment center method (i.e., assessors can make judgments about managerial attributes) is ill-founded.

Table 6.4
Average Correlations from Validity Studies of Within-Exercise Dimension Ratings

Authors	Convergent Validity[a]	Discriminant Validity[b]
Hinrichs & Haanpera (1976)	.49	not reported
Sackett & Dreher (1984)	.09	not reported
Archambeau (1979)	.61	.89
Russell (1987)	.25	.52
Baker (1986)	.26	.58
Bycio et al. (1987)	.36	.75
Adler & Margolin (1989)	.32	.82

[a]Correlations of same dimension measured in different exercises
[b]Correlations of different dimensions within an exercise

Three counterarguments can be presented. First, only some of the results of these studies of within-exercise dimension ratings are damaging to the traditional explanation in that, even though the exercise factors exist and suggest general evaluations of performance, reliabilities of the judgments and convergent validities are acceptably high in these studies.

Second, the method used in the assessment center may determine the results. It is possible that the method of observing and evaluating behavior in an assessment center influences the pattern of ratings observed in these construct validity studies. Support for this idea comes from studies of human perception that show that the perceiver's goals in the observation (e.g., to form an impression or to remember behaviors) influence the way information is interpreted, stored, and retrieved from memory (Hastie & Carlston, 1980; Jeffery & Mischel, 1979; Wyer & Srull, 1981). In the assessment center context, the purpose of observation in the behavior reporting method is to classify behaviors into dimensions; whereas in the within-exercise method, it is to evaluate performance on several dimensions within a particular exercise. These differing goals may have different impacts on assessors' judgments.

Support for this reasoning was found in a study by Silverman, Dalessio, Woods, & Johnson (1986) that investigated how the two assessment center methods affected the way assessors organize and process information and how they rate performance. The results showed that higher convergent and discriminant validity existed for the within-dimension method (a modification of the behavioral reporting method in which assessors made within-exercise dimension ratings after they had made the across-exercise dimension ratings) than for the within-exercise method. Further statistical analyses indicated that a stronger exercise effect was present for the within-exercise method. Factor analyses indicated that for the within-exercise method, very clear exercise factors were present, but with the within-dimension method the assessors were thinking about candidate performance more in terms of similarities in behavior across exercises. The implication of this study is that the assessment center method has an impact on how assessors organize information: the within-exercise dimension rating method may be causing the assessors to show more halo error in their ratings and to show little differentiation among the dimensions. More research is needed before we can conclude much about the effect of the assessment center method on dimension ratings, but the results suggest the behavior reporting method produces ratings that are more accurate than the within-exercise dimension ratings.

Recording Behavioral Observations

The traditional assessment center method calls for assessors to make a narrative record of the behaviors they observe in an exercise. As illustrated in Figure 6.2, assessors take notes on specific behaviors they observe. An alternative procedure provides assessors with a checklist of behaviors that could possibly take place; the assessor marks which behaviors occur. Figure 6.5 shows an example of some items on a behavioral checklist for a leaderless group discussion. If the assessor sees the participant start the discussion and direct its course, he or she can simply make a mark by the entry "Effectively leads the discussion."

The supposed advantages of this method are that it reduces the assessors' writing time, allows the assessors freedom to watch

Figure 6.5
Example of Behavioral Checklist

Leaderless Group Discussion Exercise

Initiative

_____ Proposes a viable method to organize the meeting

_____ Proposes to the members that an opinion be ruled out if all agree

_____ Proposes that the options initially chosen be discussed later

_____ Proposes various methods of organizing the discussion

_____ Proposes to the members that they begin by eliminating options

_____ Proposes that each member identify their priorities

_____ Proposes that each member choose one option they most prefer

_____ Keeps the discussion active by moving on to other options

_____ Proposes revisions of an option

_____ Introduces a vote before discussion has ended

_____ Proposes that if the members cannot decide between two options, they can choose the third option

_____ Introduces points that have already been mentioned

_____ Introduces the voting procedures

_____ Effectively leads the discussion

_____ Controls the discussion by speaking frequently

more carefully, and can reduce the number of judgments the assessor must make. The potential disadvantages of checklists are that assessors have to look through lists of behaviors to find the correct entry and may miss subsequent behaviors. Assessors still have to make judgments as to whether the listed behavior actually matches the behavior demonstrated. Furthermore, the entries on the list must be, to some extent, abstractions of specific behaviors rather than what the person actually does. Finally, it is not feasible for the list to be long enough to include all behaviors that might be displayed, and thus the assessor is faced with making additional narrative notes anyway.

There is some evidence that behavioral checklists improve assessment center ratings. Reilly, Henry, and Smither (1990) found that a behavior checklist (in comparison with the conventional 1 to 5 rating scale) led to greater agreement in ratings of the same dimensions across exercises, although there was no reduction in correlations of dimensions within exercises. More research needs to be done with behavioral checklists before we can conclude whether they are superior to the traditional method of note taking.

Classifying Behavior

Given a list of behaviors that might take place in an exercise, the process of designating which dimensions they reflect is a fairly logical one. Hypothetical behaviors (or behaviors observed in prior assessment centers) can be "preclassified" into the appropriate dimensions. In instances where such preclassification has taken place, computer programs in which the assesssor indicates which behaviors have been displayed generate dimension scores automatically. The advantages are obvious—the assessors' task is immensely simplified. Once the behavior is checked off, it is automatically classified and the dimension score produced instantaneously.

Some caution is needed, though, because this process may compound the problems noted above at the observation stage. Assessors must still make inferences about the similarity of the demonstrated behavior to the available entries on the list. Any deficiencies in the list will be compounded in the classification process.

An even stronger argument against using preclassified behaviors comes from research by Murphy and Constans (1987,

1988). Their research and analysis, from an information-processing perspective, demonstrated that behavioral anchors on rating scales may affect the way assessors observe, store, and use information. The results showed that assessors' memory for participants' behavior was distorted in such a way that ratings may be too high or too low, depending on the anchors used.

Comparative Studies: Narrative Reports vs. Alternative Rating Formats.

Borman (1978) identified the rating form or format as one of the four potential reasons why performance ratings are not more consistent and accurate. (The other three reasons are lack of opportunity to observe behavior, lack of understanding of rating errors, and organizational constraints.) Ideally, the rating form should be compatible with the mental processes of assessors and should not require them to make judgments they are incapable of making. Several researchers (Baker, 1986; Campbell, 1986; Louiselle, 1986) have suggested that rating formats other than the traditional narrative report may improve the accuracy of assessment center ratings by simplifying the information-processing requirements of assessors. Louiselle (1986) compared the impact of a traditional narrative report form and a preclassified behavioral checklist on the relationship among dimension ratings made after each exercise. For ratings obtained with the narrative report form, results of a factor analysis showed that the solution that best explained the assessors' ratings included both dimension and exercise information. However, for the behavioral checklist ratings, no acceptable solution was found for the data. Thus, the narrative report form demonstrated some evidence of convergent and discriminant validity of dimension ratings, whereas the behavioral checklist did not. The lack of effectiveness of the checklists in this instance may be a result of failure to adequately construct the checklist on sound theoretical or empirical bases.

Baker (1986) and Campbell (1986) each compared the construct validity of within-exercise dimension ratings obtained from the use of a behavioral checklist to those obtained from the use of behaviorally anchored rating scales (BARS). A behaviorally anchored rating scale is a format in which the numerical levels are illustrated with specific behaviors representing high, moderate, and low performance. Baker (1986) found that the within-exercise dimension ratings obtained with the behavioral checklist had greater discriminant validity for the nonassigned-role leaderless group discussions, whereas the within-exercise dimension ratings resulting from the BARS format had greater discriminant validity for the assigned-role leaderless group discussions. In addition, the checklist had lower correlations among the dimensions within an exercise for both types of leaderless group discussions than the BARS format. Campbell (1986) found that the BARS format demonstrated superior discriminant validity, but neither format exhibited superior convergent validity.

Taken together, these three studies point to the differential effect various rating formats may have on subsequent judgments. Unfortunately, the data lack consistency and are too limited to determine if there is one "superior" rating format. This same conclusion, that is, no single format is superior to the others, has been drawn from research on performance appraisal (Bernardin & Beatty, 1984; Murphy & Cleveland, 1991).

Exercise Ratings

In view of the problems that some researchers have seen in the within-exercise dimension ratings, there have been proposals to abandon dimension ratings and substitute ratings of overall exercise performance. An alternative step in which the assessors make a rating of *overall exercise performance* has been added to some assessment centers. Before such a change is recommended widely, the qualities of overall exercise ratings should be analyzed, and their value discussed.

Assessor Agreement. Table 6.5 lists a representative sample of studies in which the agreement among several assessors on overall exercise performance has been studied. Studies have reported mixed levels of assessor agreement for leaderless group discussions and business games, high levels of agreement for the in-basket exercise and role-play exercise, and marginal agreement for the oral presentation. Borman (1982) reported an average assessor agreement of .76 across six different types of exercises. These studies suggest different assessors are rating overall exercise performance similarly. Assessors seem to agree on ratings for some exercises more than others, but no explanation for this pattern is discernible.

Assessor agreement between two different types of assessors has also been measured. Greenwood and McNamara (1967) found that the intergroup agreement between professional

Table 6.5
Studies of Assessor Agreement on Overall Exercise Evaluations

Exercise	Author	Average level of Agreement
Leaderless group discussion	Bray & Grant (1966)	.75
	Gatewood et al. (1990)	.93
	Greenwood & McNamara (1967)	.64
	Tziner & Dolan (1982)	.83
Business game	Bray & Grant (1966)	.60
	Greenwood & McNamara (1967)	.74
	Tziner & Dolan (1982)	.92
In-basket	Bray & Grant (1966)	.92
	Tziner & Dolan (1982)	.84
Oral presentation	Tziner & Dolan (1982)	.69
Role-play	Tziner & Dolan (1982)	.82

and nonprofessional observers ranged from .12 to .81. Although some reliabilities were quite low, there were no significant differences in reliabilities between the two types of assessors. Gatewood et al. (1990) studied the level of agreement between a group of experienced assessors and three different groups of less experienced assessors. Agreement among groups ranged from .66 to .84. Both of these studies suggest that "experts" and "nonexperts" agree on their ratings of overall exercise performance, but the level of agreement in some comparisons is rather low.

Predictive Accuracy. Bray and Grant (1966) found that assessor ratings of overall performance in a leaderless group discussion, in a business game, and in an in-basket exercise correlated with more general evaluations of assessment center performance (correlations ranging from .30 to over .50) and with assessors' overall evaluation of management potential for both college and noncollege participants. Konz (1988) found all nine exercise ratings correlated with the overall assessment rating.

Along these lines, other studies (Borman, 1982; Tziner & Dolan, 1982) have also found that exercise ratings were related to the overall assessment ratings. In addition, Borman (1982) and Tziner and Dolan (1982) found significant correlations between exercise ratings and training performance, but Borman, Eaton, Bryan, and Rosse (1987) did not.

The relationship of exercise ratings to behavior on the job is less supportive. Wollowick and McNamara (1969) found that two group exercises and an in-basket exercise correlated significantly with change in management level, but Outcalt (1988) found that five exercises correlated only slightly with job level and salary level. Three studies found no or very low relationships between exercise ratings and job performance (Hinrichs & Haanpera, 1976b; Konz, 1988; Outcalt, 1988).

Thus, exercise ratings appear to predict subsequent assessment ratings quite well and appear to be relatively accurate indicators of training performance. However, the relationship between exercise ratings and the overall assessment ratings is only minimally relevant, and their relation to subsequent advancement and performance is too low to warrant practical application at this time.

Other Evidence of Accuracy. Five studies examined the relationships among ratings on several exercises to determine the extent to which individual exercises were measuring similar or different concepts. Konz (1988) studied the ratings on nine exercises and found an average correlation of .21. Borman (1982) found that ratings on four exercises involving face-to-face role-playing were the most highly related to each other (average correlation of .48), while ratings on a structured interview and an in-basket were related less highly with the other exercise ratings (average correlation with the other four exercises was .26). In another study (Tziner & Dolan, 1982), the correlations of five different assessment exercises ranged from .38 to .63, with the leaderless group discussion and the role-play exercise being the most similar. Bray and Grant (1966) found that ratings (and rankings) on a business game and ratings (and rankings) on a group discussion were moderately related. Finally, Moses (1973) reported moderate correlations of a competitive group exercise in one assessment center with a competitive group exercise and a cooperative group exercise in a second assessment center.

In summary, it appears that the ratings of performance in different exercises are related to each other to a moderate degree, and ratings in similar exercises (e.g., group exercises) are more highly related than ratings in dissimilar exercises (e.g., a group exercise and an individual exercise). The similarity in exercise ratings may be due to actual similarity of performance or to some biases that artificially raise the correlations. These biases may be similar to the ones that some critics believe lead to high relationships among within-exercise dimension ratings.

The accuracy of exercise ratings can also be investigated by examining their relationship with other variables. Borman (1982) found low correlations between assessor ratings of exercise performance and ratings of first impression, physical attractiveness, and likability. These findings should be interpreted favorably, because they show that the overall exercise ratings are not measuring irrelevant variables. Tziner and Dolan (1982) found an average correlation of .30 between ratings of five assessment exercises and scores on three intelligence tests. These results suggest that more intelligent individuals receive higher exercise ratings than less intelligent individuals.

Thus, whereas exercise ratings may be reflecting something more than superficial characteristics (e.g., personal appearance), intelligence may be an underlying factor in exercise ratings. Such research findings lend support to one of Klimoski and Brickner's (1987) hypotheses that assessment centers measure managerial intelligence. However, more studies of this type need to be conducted in order to be able to make firm conclusions regarding the underlying nature of exercise ratings.

Comments on Alternative Methods

It should be obvious that I do not support the modifications of the traditional assessment center process. The innovations that have been attempted have not yet been adequately researched to allow endorsement at this time. Further research may prove their effectiveness and would be greatly welcomed. Until that time, variations on the traditional method should be undertaken with great care and viewed with skepticism. This is not to say that we cannot provide assessors with a number of aids to help with their training, processes of judgment, and final evaluations. In fact, many of these aids are mentioned throughout this book.

Summary and Conclusions

This chapter has presented a large amount of information dealing with the practice, theory, and research related to the processes individual assessors carry out in observing, classifying, and evaluating behavior in an assessment center. There is mixed support for each step in the assessment process: some theory and research supports the accuracy of these processes, and other theory and research does not. The nonsupportive evidence suggests a need to improve the assessment center method, and many innovations have been proposed.

A trend in the results can be detected, which suggests that there is more consistency and accuracy in later steps in the assessment center process, where more aggregation of data has taken place. In other words, the consistency and accuracy of any one individual assessor evaluating a *small* amount of behavior on *one* dimension in *one* exercise are not very great. By contrast, the consistency and accuracy of judgments improves when judgments are made about *larger samples* of behavior across *several* exercises. For example, the consistency and accuracy of overall dimension ratings is greater than these qualities for within-exercise dimension ratings.

We will note this trend again in the next chapter, where we examine the process of combining judgments of several assessors. The evidence will show even more clearly that final dimension ratings and the overall assessment rating have even higher levels of consistency and accuracy.

The review of theory and research in this chapter leads to the conclusion that assessors can and do follow a behaviorally oriented approach in assessing participants' performance. The assessment center method is consistent with theories of human judgment that emphasize (1) the influence of specific behavioral events on human perception, (2) the ability to remember detailed information about human events, and (3) the ability of observers to use specific behavioral information to evaluate performance on defined dimensions.

While there is not much research on observation and classification in operational assessment centers, the research on ratings derived from assessors' judgment shows both support and nonsupport for their ability to make reliable ratings. On the positive side, assessors' final dimension ratings show considerable agreement and validity in relation to comparable measures on tests and subsequent job performance. On the other hand, within-exercise dimension ratings show varying levels of reliability and convergent validity and consistently fail to show accuracy in measuring separate managerial attributes. The main reason for this seems to be that ratings of dimensions within an exercise correlate more highly with each other than do the ratings of the same dimension measured in different exercises. This pattern of relationships among within-exercise dimension ratings is not as damaging as it may first appear, as research suggests these findings may be due to the assessment center method used. If the behavior reporting method is used (as opposed to the within-exercise rating method), the assessors seem to be able to organize the observations more consistently into the dimensions. But there is a limit to the number of dimensions assessors can handle. Assessors probably cannot make meaningful distinctions among more than six or seven dimensions when they are observing and classifying behaviors.

The evidence that shows a failure of within-exercise dimension ratings to yield accurate measures of separate managerial attributes may or may not be important, depending on the purpose of the assessment center. If the purpose of the assessment center is to make a single overall prediction of success, then the accuracy of the separate dimension ratings is of secondary importance: the dimension ratings are only a means to structure judgment before making the summary assessment. If the purpose of the assessment center is to provide a diagnosis of strengths and developmental needs on separate abilities, then we need measures of these separate dimensions that have high accuracy. In that case, the assessment center must be designed to provide distinct assessment of separate dimensions: there must be conceptually distinct dimensions, assessors must be thoroughly trained, there must be enough exercises to provide a range of information on each separate dimension, and the behavioral reporting method would be preferred.

The recommendation to use the behavioral reporting method for some assessment center purposes is based partially on evidence that this procedure influences the processes of the assessors discussing and integrating the information. The next chapter deals specifically with the assessor discussion process.

7

Group Discussion of Assessment Information

Key Concepts: Comparing the statistical and judgmental data integration methods; examining the impact of group dynamics on the integration discussion; evaluating final dimension ratings and overall assessment ratings.

Chapter 6 covered the process each *individual* assessor goes through to observe and classify behaviors, recall information from memory, and make judgments about the level of performance on assessment dimensions. It described how the individual assessors then report their observations in the integration discussion and then form preliminary overall dimension ratings. Up to this point, the process is essentially one of individual judgment. We now turn to the *group* process, where the assessors integrate their individual judgments.

Assessment Center Practice

The last steps in the assessment center process involve *group* decision making. Assessors meet to discuss the preliminary overall dimension ratings and form final overall dimension ratings. Then, in some assessment centers, these dimension ratings are integrated to form an overall assessment rating.

Deriving Final Overall Dimension Ratings

The assessors share their preliminary overall dimension ratings, usually by posting them on a flip chart, and discuss them in order to resolve differences. There are several possible patterns of ratings that might be generated. When there is total agreement, for example, all three assessors give a "4," then the integration is straightforward and the participant gets a "4." On the other hand, if there are differences among the ratings, discussion takes place. One might think that agreement at this stage of the integration process is desirable. After all, wouldn't that be an indication of consistency? Some research on the group judgment process shows that disagreement at this stage can be beneficial and can lead to increased levels of accuracy in the final group decision (Libby, Trotman, & Zimmer, 1987; Rohrbaugh, 1979; Sniezek & Henry, 1989). Disagreement may reflect a diversity of valid opinions that leads to better decisions in groups (Wanous & Yountz, 1986).

The traditional assessment center method calls for group consensus. In this context, consensus means that each assessor can accept the rating as an adequate representation of the performance. Consensus does *not* mean that there is total agreement by each assessor that the rating is exact.

Overall Assessment Rating

After the assessors have agreed on the final overall dimension ratings, they may derive an overall assessment rating for each participant. An overall assessment rating is appropriate if the purpose of the assessment center is to provide a recommendation for selection or promotion. If this is the case, decision makers in the organization want a clear indication of the final conclusion of the assessment: a prediction of success or failure in the new job. An overall assessment rating is usually not warranted in assessment centers used for diagnosis of training needs or those used for training and organizational development. In such programs, the end products are the dimension ratings or the feedback on areas for improvement. The next discussion, then, is relevant only to programs where an overall assessment rating is warranted.

To arrive at an overall assessment rating, each assessor looks over the final dimension ratings and makes an individual judgment on whether the participant is likely to be successful in the target job. This overall assessment rating is a combination of all information presented to this point. The assessor must use his or her judgment on how to combine the dimension ratings. No formal equation is used for weighting the several dimensions, but, of course, job analysis information has shown the relative importance of the several dimensions being assessed. In addition, during assessor training, the assessors have thoroughly discussed the importance of the dimensions and have developed some common frame of reference for combining the dimension ratings into an overall assessment rating. It is expected that each assessor will consider the job requirements and the accuracy of the information regarding the participant, and will combine the dimension ratings based on that knowledge and on training received in the assessment center process.

The overall assessment rating can take several forms. For a selection program, the rating might be "probability of success." For a promotion program, the rating might be "probability of success in the next level" or "probability of success in middle management." In the Management Progress Study launched twenty-five years ago (Bray & Grant, 1966) the assessors made two predictions: "probability of promotion" and "whether the person should be promoted." The first was a prediction of whether the person had the qualities the organization was currently seeking for promotion, whereas the second was an evaluation of whether the person had the qualities that *should* be recognized and rewarded in the organization.

After the assessors independently give their overall assessment rating, the ratings are posted on a flip chart and compared. If there is total agreement, that rating is final. If there is disagreement, the assessors discuss their differences and come to a consensus, much the way they do in deriving overall dimension ratings. By this point, there is seldom need for extensive discussion. In the majority of cases, disagreement is minimal, and this part of the integration discussion goes very quickly. There have been suggestions that this part of the integration process be eliminated (Feltham, 1988b; Sackett, & Wilson, 1982), but little time would be gained. In addition, assessors wish to see closure in the process; elimination of the integration discussion would deprive them of a meaningful final step. The vast majority of assessment centers currently in operation use consensus discussion to derive final ratings. Gaugler et al. (1991) found that 84 percent of the two hundred organizations they surveyed followed this procedure. On the other hand, alternatives have been proposed, and we must ask whether some other method of combining the data would improve predictive accuracy. In the Gaugler survey, 14 percent of the organizations surveyed used some statistical method of integrating the data.

Alternative Methods of Data Integration

There are two ways that quantitative data such as assessment ratings can be integrated: judgmental and statistical. Judgmental methods involve some subjective process in which people combine the information according to their evaluation of the emphasis that should be given to each piece of information. The process of arriving at a consensus during the integration discussion is an example of the judgmental method of decision making. Statistical methods involve the use of a mathematical formula to "add up" the information. In such a formula, the relative importance of the dimension ratings are specified ahead of time. For example:

$$\text{Overall Assessment Rating} = (4 \times \text{Decision Making}) \\ + (2 \times \text{Leadership}) \\ + \text{Sensitivity} \\ + \text{Company Orientation}$$

In this example, decision making is four times as important, and leadership is two times as important as sensitivity and company orientation. These "weights" are determined by statistical methods, such as multiple regression. To carry out a statistical study like this, the investigator needs data from a large sample—at least one hundred to one hundred fifty people. The data from such a study would include the scores on the "predictors," which in this case would be the ratings on the several dimensions, and scores on some "criterion," such as progress in managerial ranks or evidence of successful performance on the job. Statistical analyses of the relationship between the criterion scores and the predictor scores reveal the weights. Once these weights are determined a formula is used to combine the dimension ratings and predict success.

There is much theoretical and empirical evidence from other areas of psychology to support the statistical method of information integration. Early reviews of studies comparing statistical and judgmental methods in clinical psychology (Meehl, 1954; Sawyer,

1966) and other fields (Dawes, 1979) showed that statistical methods provide more consistent and accurate predictions. Judgmental methods can be faulty when judges do not consistently use subjective weights to combine several pieces of information. In addition, accuracy is reduced when assessors do not have a clear understanding of what variables are most important. There is even some support in the assessment center literature that supports the statistical combination of dimension ratings.

There are at least two places where group discussion is typically used to integrate assessment center data: first, when assessors formulate final dimension ratings, and second, when they arrive at an overall assessment rating. Assessors experience typical problems during group discussions at each of these stages. The next section explores the process of group decision making. Does the empirical data from the assessment center literature justify statistical integration during these stages? The evidence follows.

Deriving Final Dimension Ratings Statistically

To date, no assessment center research study has investigated the best procedure for deriving final dimension ratings. To the best of my knowledge, no study has compared the traditional, judgmental method of reaching consensus on final dimension ratings to a statistical method. The simplest approach would be to average the preliminary dimension ratings, with each rating carrying equal weight. Conceivably, ratings from certain assessors could be weighted more heavily, although it would be difficult to establish before the assessment center which assessors are more accurate. Even if it were possible to determine *during* the discussion who was more accurate, the procedure would not be socially acceptable. We are left, therefore, with little more than speculation about any procedure other than the traditional one of achieving consensus on final dimension ratings.

Deriving Overall Assessment Ratings Statistically

The statistical method of data integration could be useful at two points in the assessment center process: (1) in combining final overall dimension ratings into the overall assessment ratings, and (2) in combining preliminary overall assessment ratings into the overall assessment rating.

Combining Final Overall Dimension Ratings. Arguments for statistically derived overall assessment ratings are based on the premise that individuals can take only a very limited number of factors into account at any one time, and assessors are not able simultaneously to consider and integrate a large number of dimensions in reaching an overall rating. With the statistical method, assessors' duties would end after they reached consensus on final dimension ratings. Proponents of the judgmental method of integrating assessment data argue that it is difficult to empirically derive the appropriate weights for a statistical combination of information; that assessors prefer the judgmental approach; and that unique insights into the candidate's strengths and weaknesses can be gained through the integration discussion (Thornton & Byham, 1982).

A fair amount of assessment center research has been conducted that compares the two data integration techniques at this stage. Unfortunately, however, the research produced equivocal results. Feltham (1988b), Moses (1972), and Huck (1974) found no significant difference in predictive accuracy for the judgmentally derived overall assessment rating and the statistically derived overall assessment rating. Mitchel (1975) also found virtually no difference between the two data integration techniques in three samples over one-, three-, and five-year periods. A strength of Mitchel's study is that he conducted cross-validation, that is, he used a method of checking the stability of statistical results in separate, independent samples.

Conversely, results from three studies support the statistical method of data integration. (Although it should be noted that these studies did not involve cross-validation with new samples of subjects.) Wollowick and McNamara (1969) found that the judgmentally derived overall assessment ratings correlated less with a measure of management success than the statistically derived overall assessment ratings correlated with the same criterion. In addition, the accuracy of the judgmentally derived overall assessment rating was lower than the accuracy of a summing of the overall exercise ratings, a summing of the across-exercise dimension ratings, and objective test scores. Higher correlations for the statistical method were also reported in Borman's (1982) study, which compared the ability of the two data combination techniques to predict three criterion measures. Lastly, Tziner and Dolan (1982) found the statistical combination of assessment ratings to be superior to the judgmental combination in predicting training performance. Again, we must be cautious about these results, since the studies were not cross-validated in independent samples. The results of Mitchel's (1975) cross-validation are quite revealing. Initially, the statistical method provided more accurate predictions of success than the judgmental rating. But, when the statistical formula was used on different samples over different time periods, the accuracy of the statistical method dropped considerably.

Silzer and Louisville (1990) questioned the necessity of holding the discussion about dimension ratings at all. They compared the predictive validity of preconsensus and postconsensus discussion ratings and found mixed evidence for which was more predictive of managerial performance two years later: the ratings of two dimensions *before* discussions were more predictive, but the ratings on two other dimensions *after* discussion were more predictive. More studies along these lines are needed.

Another way that dimensions can be combined statistically to form an overall rating is to weight them all equally. This means that the scores are simply added up into a combined score. For example, if there are five dimensions and a participant was rated 3 on three dimensions and 4 on two dimensions, his or her overall assessment rating would be 17. Arguments in favor of equal weighting are that it is a consistent process and that it prevents assessors from inappropriately emphasizing one piece of information. For example, in the selection of a police chief in a medium-sized city, it was revealed that a finalist was having financial problems. This information was relevant to some dimension ratings, such as judgment and community sensitivity, but it was overemphasized by the assessors. The ratings of judgment and sensitivity were given too much weight in the final decision. A second person was chosen, but quickly resigned. The first person then got the job and was quite successful. He had resolved the financial problem and became a fine manager. Unit weighting may have prevented the one bit of information from coloring the other ratings. Of course, new pieces of information may be relevant in certain situations, and there may be a place for special considerations in the judgmental process that are not accommodated in the statistical process.

The process of equal weighting is known as "unit weighting" because all the dimensions are given a weight of 1. Feltham (1988b) has shown in one study that unit weights produce an overall rating that is more accurate in predicting success than an overall consensus rating, but there was no confirmation of the prediction in a second independent sample.

No firm conclusions about the superiority of one data integration technique over the other can be made on the basis of these studies. Until the data are more conclusive, I recommend retaining the process of having assessors combine assessment center data in the way it has been done in studies showing long-range accuracy. Furthermore, although a statistical method may be appropriate when the purpose of an assessment center is to arrive at one final "select/don't select" decision for each candidate, this type of data integration technique is not appropriate when the purpose of an assessment center is to generate developmental feedback or to identify training needs.

Combining Preliminary Overall Ratings. What about the stage where assessors have posted their preliminary overall assessment ratings? Some researchers have questioned the usefulness of the integration discussion at this point (e.g., Sackett & Wilson, 1982; Wingrove, Jones, & Herriot, 1985). Specifically, they have argued that if integrated ratings can be predicted by individual ratings, then instead of the integration process, a statistical method can be used to arrive at a final overall assessment rating. Two equally logical points of view can be taken. According to Sackett and Wilson (1982), using a statistical method would have several benefits, including the savings in time and money and the elimination of social influences that may adversely affect the final rating. (Many of these social influences are discussed later in this chapter.) On the other hand, Thornton and Byham (1982) argued that the integration discussion is a critical part in an assessment center, because it holds individual biases and stereotypes in check. An integration discussion ensures that individuals support their ratings with behavioral evidence; it also ensures that individuals have a chance to change their ratings after hearing alternative interpretations of a candidate's performance. Whether the integration discussion actually leads to better or poorer decisions depends on the nature of the discussion: that issue is discussed later in this chapter.

Some studies that have compared preliminary and final overall assessment ratings suggest that the integration process adds very little to this stage of assessment. Sackett and Wilson (1982) found that for a group of 719 participants, assessors' preliminary overall assessment ratings disagreed with the final ratings for only 1 percent of the participants. In addition, the final assessment ratings could be accurately predicted by a simple rule based on final dimension ratings. In addition, Wingrove et al. (1985) found that final assessment ratings were no more predictive of training performance than preliminary assessment ratings.

In ascertaining whether the integration discussion might result in poorer decisions, Herriot, Chalmers, and Wingrove (1985) examined what group dynamics characterized the integration discussion. They identified 2,640 cases where three of four assessors agreed on their preliminary ratings, then checked to see what the fourth assessor did with his or her final rating. In two-thirds of the cases, the dissenting assessor did not move to the majority's position, but in one-third of the cases, he or she did. Among the shifts from preliminary to final ratings, Herriot et al. found some predominant patterns. For example, they found that an individual was more likely to shift from a *high* preliminary rating to the majority position than to shift from a *low* preliminary rating. In addition, the individual was more likely to shift to the majority's *low* position, in comparison with shifting to a *high* position. In combination, these patterns of shifts suggest a negative bias in the group's decision process, that is, the group seemed to be trying to avoid giving high ratings, which in this assessment center led to a recommendation for officer training. This and other group dynamics will be explored in more depth later in this chapter.

One conclusion we might draw from these studies is that the integration discussion is unnecessary because assessors' final ratings typically do not differ from their preliminary ratings and, in fact, can be predicted from their dimension ratings. We might further conclude that these studies even suggest that the integration discussion may be harmful, since group dynamics may have a negative effect on discussions and since gains in predictive accuracy as a result of these discussions have not been shown.

Before such conclusions are warranted and the traditional assessment center method is modified in practice, far more research is needed. Studies must be done to establish that overall assessment ratings derived from a data integration method that does *not* include discussions about dimension ratings and preliminary overall assessment ratings have the same predictive accuracy already proven for the same ratings derived in the traditional manner. If assessors do not anticipate the integration discussion, their observations, categorizations, and ratings may be carried out quite differently. It is not appropriate to *assume* that the new data integration method will yield highly accurate overall assessment ratings.

Summary

As a result of the findings stated above, some have advocated the discontinuance of the integration discussion at this stage of the assessment center process (Herriot et al., 1985; Wingrove et al., 1985). There are several problems with this recommendation. The statistical procedures used to develop a formula for combining dimension ratings have several features that may impose limitations on the application of the results: (1) they give an *optimal* solution for a set of data and may overstate the typical relationships of the variables; (2) they are developed from *one sample* of subjects, which is usually small and may not be representative of the entire range of applicants; and (3) they investigate the *linear* combination of dimension scores. In considering the statistical method as an alternative, we must recognize that (1) the formula for one sample may not be appropriate for an independent sample, (2) statistics derived from small samples are unstable, and (3) special combinations of dimensions, which allow for the possibility that patterns of high and low dimension scores may be meaningful, may be important. Dugan (1988) argued that these statistical procedures may not capture the rich ways that assessors use information. She noted that prior research and informal discussions with assessors reveal the special combinations of assessment observations not captured with the statistical formulae.

Given the controversial issues surrounding the statistical integration method, the group discussion process continues to be used in many organizations. Thus, we need to analyze this process.

The Process of Group Decision Making

Anyone who has participated in a group discussion, either to solve a problem or to accomplish a task, has probably noted that either the group can be the source of valuable ideas and a vehicle for progress or it can suppress creativity and progress and lead to erroneous conclusions. Even the most brief reading of the theoretical and research literature on group decision making reveals the same two sharply contrasting views. One view, which we might call pessimistic, notes that the group discussion process interferes with good decision making and results in "process losses" (Steiner, 1972). The more optimistic view holds that groups have the potential for "process gains" (Steiner, 1972), that is, to generate good ideas and provide better solutions (Argyris & Schon, 1974; Hill, 1982).

Disadvantages of Group Decision Making

There are many potential problems with group decision making (Moscovici, 1988). For one, the final decision of the group may not be better than the decision of the best individual in the group (Einhorn, Hogarth, & Klempner 1977). Similarly, the group discussion process may dilute the good information contributed by the most accurate person. This problem may arise because one person, for example someone with poorer judgment, unduly dominates the discussion and leads others to focus on poor information. Processes of conformity may operate such that a more passive member of the group, yet one who could make a valuable contribution, simply follows the suggestions of the other group members.

On the strength of the research that has found that the best member of a group makes a better decision than the group itself, some have advocated identifying the best member and dismissing the others (Libby et al., 1987). This is usually not practical though, because even if the researcher can identify the best member after the experiment, the group itself cannot identify the best person during the discussion (Miner, 1984). Another reason the rest of the group cannot usually be dismissed is that this practice meets with great resistance in practical situations.

Another dynamic that may distort group decisions is the group polarization process (Lamm & Myers, 1978; Myers & Lamm, 1976). Group polarization means that the initial position of the majority of the group is strengthened following group discussion. Members may move toward the dominant position in the group for any number of reasons. Ideally, this would only happen when the substance of the majority's position is sound, and this often happens (Lamm & Myers, 1978; Myers & Lamm, 1976). Unfortunately, other less desirable processes occur also. For example, group members may adopt the majority position because of some artificial rule (such as "the majority rules") or because members want to be seen as agreeable to other group members. One form of group polarization is the "risky shift" phenomenon (Kogan & Wallach, 1964), in which the final group position is more risky than the initial position of some individual members. For example, it has been found that under certain conditions, the group will endorse a stronger statement of opinion on an issue after the discussion process. One interpretation of this dynamic is that there has been a diffusion of responsibility to all members of the group in comparison with the responsibility that might fall on any one individual (Latané & Darley, 1970). This interpretation makes sense when there is some negative effect of the group's decision on another person (Lamm & Myers, 1978), a situation that often exists in assessment centers when the results will be used in promotion or hiring decisions. As reported earlier, Herriot et al. (1985) found a negative bias operating in judgments about candidates for officer training school. Individual assessors tended to lower their preliminary ratings to match the majority's rating, especially if the majority was already giving a low rating. In this assessment center, a low rating resulted in the rejection of the candidate's application for an officer training school. Thus, movement toward the majority position in this group represented a shift toward a risky position.

"Groupthink" (Janis, 1982) is another potentially dangerous process that may undermine the quality of group decisions. Cohesive groups may inhibit differences of opinion and promote conformity to informal, unspoken norms of agreeableness. Members in a cohesive group may strive for unanimity at the expense of appraising alternative actions and positions. Groupthink becomes "a deterioration of mental efficiency, reality testing, and moral judgment from in-group pressures" (Janis, 1982, p. 9). There may be a tendency for this dynamic to operate in assessor groups. Assessors who work together in the organization or serve together in an assessment center for a long time may feel pressure to be "nice" and agree with each other. The assessment center integration method has been designed to protect against these dynamics because it follows some of the prescriptions Janis (1982) offered to combat groupthink: assessors are taught to be critical thinkers and to challenge the ratings of other assessors; everyone is assigned the role of devil's advocate and asked to challenge ratings; and assessors are given a chance to review all data and change their minds as the integration discussion unfolds. In addition, assessor groups are usually not stable groups that work together over time. Thus the negative dynamics of a cohesive group may not operate in assessor integration discussions.

Advantages of Group Decision Making

The other view of group decision making emphasizes evidence that groups can work effectively together and produce decisions quite superior to those of any one individual (Argyris & Schon, 1974; Hill, 1982). Moscovici (1988) observed that the historical emphasis on conformity in groups has been replaced with a recognition that the individual influences the group. In fact, Nisbitt and Ross (1980) assert that "assembly bonuses," that is, the gains that come from individuals working in groups, are the best hope for overcoming many deficiencies inherent in individual human judgment.

What support is there for the group judgmental process of combining information? McGrath and Kravitz (1982) concluded that one of the most robust findings in the literature is that groups tend to follow the pattern of "truth supported wins." This means that even though there may be some group process losses—in which the group decision is less effective than that of the best individual—if the good solution has support, the group will accept it. Laughlin and his associates (Laughlin, 1980; Laughlin & Ellis, 1986; Laughlin & McGynn, 1986) have shown that the "truth supported wins" pattern is an accurate description of how groups operate when solving inductive reasoning problems. In addition, many of the arguments that groups do not adequately process information are based on one of two reasons: either the group is not motivated properly, that is, members do not put forth effort, or they have limited information-processing capabilities (McGrath & Kravitz, 1982). Neither of these two conditions seem to be present in the assessment center context: assessors are typically hand-picked for their interpersonal skills and interest in human resource issues, and they are trained in and certified to have the required assessment skills.

Benefits come from group decision making when several individuals with heterogeneous skills and experience contribute to the decision. Of course, assessors must bring unique information to bear on the evaluation of participants. Here again, an assessor team is usually composed of managers with different organizational experience, and each has the opportunity to observe different exercises. For these reasons it is not surprising when there is a lack of agreement on dimension ratings across exercises. The advantage of this arrangement is that individuals can then pool their expertise to provide a wider variety of information. In addition, the assessors provide "checks and balances" that prevent misinformation or poor judgment by any one individual.

Sniezek and Henry (1990) have proposed and tested a decision-making procedure that parallels the one followed in the integration discussion of an assessment center. In this procedure, individuals make judgments that are then revised in the process of interaction with the group. These revised individual judgments are then evaluated and combined by the group in a discussion that requires group consensus. Two studies (Sniezek & Henry, 1989, 1990) provide support for the efficacy of this procedure. The group judgments were found to be superior to numerically averaged judgments of the individuals, when compared to judgments of experts. Furthermore, in the group process, the change in the group's judgment and the judgments of most of the individuals was in the direction of the more accurate judgment. The correction of the initial judgment was considerable. In fact, an improvement of over 32 percent was demonstrated using Sniezek's decision-making approach. That improvement is far greater than the average of 12 percent improvement found by Hastie (1986) in his review of earlier group decision-making models.

Miner (1984) conducted research that clarified that the *process* used by the group in deriving the decision determines whether the group produces quality decisions. He found that if the individual group members make independent decisions before the group discussion, the group decision is better than when the decision is made *without* initial individual judgments. This finding implies that at any stage of the integration session, assessors should report behaviors, perform independent ratings, and then proceed with discussions. Miner (1984) found that after the experiment, he could identify a "best individual" who outperformed the group, but the group itself could not identify the best individual at any better than chance rates.

Thus, even though there was some process loss in comparison with the best individual, there was no way for the group to identify the "best" or most accurate member during the decision process. In a practical sense, there was process gain in comparison with the decision that resulted from a statistical average of the individual decisions. The process Miner found most effective in this research is exactly the procedure used in the assessment center method: preliminary independent ratings are made by each assessor, then the group makes the final overall assessment rating.

Summary

Which view of group discussion is more accurate, the one of process losses or of process gains? Both contain elements of truth; the challenge is to understand under what circumstances groups work well together. While there is less definitive research in identifying the variables that determine group effectiveness, many clues exist to show what makes a difference. As this literature is reviewed, it will be apparent that the assessment center method creates many of the conditions that have been shown to lead to effective group decision processes. In fact, the assessment center integration discussion is an elaborate case study of how human behavior can be evaluated and predicted; it also shows the value of many of the principles that have emerged in lab and field research on group decision making over the past three decades.

Factors Affecting Group Effectiveness

Piecing together the fragments of research and theory provides some indication of the factors that make a difference in whether group processes improve or undermine the quality of decision making. Some of these factors include: knowledge and skills of group members, effort applied to the decision-making task, group accountability for decisions, consistent use of an effective decision-making strategy, use of techniques to minimize the forces of conformity, and careful information processing.

Knowledge and Skills in the Group

When group members have a high level of knowledge and skills relevant to the task at hand, they are more effective than if these skills are absent (Chaiken & Stangor, 1987). Desired levels of knowledge and skill can be assured by selecting competent group members and by training them properly. These conditions are standard practice in the development of an assessment center. Higher-level managers are frequently selected to be assessors because they are familiar with the target job or jobs. Further screening is done to select managers who have demonstrated judgmental and interpersonal skills relevant to the assessment tasks they must carry out. But that is only the beginning. Assessor training is then conducted to enhance the specific skills assessors need for the assessment center they are part of. The *Guidelines and Ethical Considerations for Assessment Center Operations* further specify that assessors should be tested and certified competent to carry out the assessment tasks.

Effort

For a group to be effective, its members must be motivated to carry out the necessary judgment and decision making; ideally, the effort of the group must be at a high level and well coordinated. Barker, Wahlers, Cegala, and Kibler (1983) concluded that when a group is asked to achieve a high level of performance in terms of sound judgment and fast responses, it performs better than it would under less pressing conditions. Hackman and Morris (1978a,b) suggested that the effort of group members can be improved by redesigning the group task to include the following features, all of which will elicit effort from workers: utilization of a variety of skills, the opportunity to accomplish a specific task, work on a significant task, autonomy, and feedback about group effectiveness.

Virtually all of these factors are present in an assessor integration discussion. Assessors are certainly under pressure to produce a lot of accurate work. Working as an assessor also requires a wide variety of skills: administering and evaluating exercises, preparing evaluations and suggestions for placement or development, and, in some cases, writing feedback reports and giving oral feedback to participants and their immediate supervisors. Clear and identifiable tasks are accomplished in the assessment in the form of recommendations for hiring, promotion, or development, and these tasks are significant in the professional lives of the participants as well as in the life of the organization itself. Autonomy is experienced because there is no one else to overrule the judgments made by the assessor team. On the other hand, feedback on the effectiveness of the assessment center is often lacking: assessors often do not know how their recommendations are used in the organization. Feedback of this kind might do much to improve assessor motivation, which is already at a high level.

All these conditions seem to minimize the possibility of "social loafing," a phenomenon in which people in groups "slack off" or reduce their effort. Social loafing seems to occur more frequently when the individual's effort within the group is not readily identifiable and people are not accountable for their individual contributions (Weldon & Gargano, 1985; Weldon & Mustari, 1988). The importance of accountability for decisions is explored further in the next section.

Accountability

Tetlock (1983, 1985) has argued that individuals will engage in complex decision strategies, rather than simplified thinking, when there is a norm of structured, balanced debate within a group. If the social context makes the decision-maker accountable to others whose positions are not known ahead of time, then individuals will use more thorough and vigilant information processing. According to Tetlock, complex decision making requires the willingness to be inconsistent in our thinking (i.e., to recognize good features in a rejected position and bad features in a preferred position), to engage in self-criticism, and to have more insight into the decision strategy we use.

Accountability is fostered in the assessor discussion as a result of several facets of the traditional assessment center method: the structured method of recording and reporting behaviors; the requirement to back up any evaluations with behavioral evidence; the detailed reporting of both positive and negative observations related to each dimension; the lack of personal connection between assessor and participant; and the separation and independence of the multiple assessments. All these features of the group decision process perpetuate a climate of accountability in the assessor discussion.

Consistent Use of Strategies for Decision Making

Groups work most effectively when they utilize existing strategies that each individual has learned previously (Hackman & Morris, 1978a,b). Any one of a number of decision-making strategies may work in a given situation. The point here is that group norms supporting the use of a strategy must be maintained or the strategy may be abandoned. The task of maintaining the proper strategy in assessment center discussions usually falls to the administrator leading the discussions. Experienced assessors sometimes need reminders because they may try to take shortcuts, and new assessors or assessors who assemble for only one or two programs often need careful guidance because they have not practiced the techniques often enough. One challenge organizations face is the maintenance of quality and integrity of the assessment center process when it is carried out in different departments and divisions (Schmitt, Schneider, Cohen, 1990). Maintaining the "operational validity" (Byham & Temlock, 1972) of an assessment center includes careful scrutiny to ensure that decision-making strategies are being applied consistently. Assessment center administrators make it a practice to observe a sample of assessor discussions to see if the proper integration procedures, described earlier in this chapter, are being followed.

Group Dynamics

Groups must guard against the detrimental processes noted earlier in this chapter. Hoffman (1978a, b) pointed out many of the factors that can inhibit effective problem solving in groups, including pressures toward uniformity, pressures toward conformity, and an informal structure that has no leader. Most assessor teams are temporary groups who meet only for the duration of a particular assessment center. Thus, there is little concern that ill feelings created in the discussion will carry over to the job. Furthermore, the assessor discussion process follows a procedure that Hoffman suggested actually promotes effective group problem solving: all ideas are laid out for consideration and evaluated, and conflict is exploited, that is, the group uses differences of opinion to better understand the participant.

The assessor discussion process also follows many of the suggestions offered by others about how to foster effective group dynamics in the decision process, such as assigning people the role of devil's advocate (Schweiger, Sandberg, & Rediner, 1989) and focusing on the data and not personal credentials of the person proposing the idea (Janis, 1982). It is heartening to know that research has shown that certain characteristics of the assessors do not effect the influence they have on the other assessors: for example, holding a line or a staff position (Neidig & Martin, 1979), being male or female, or being chair of the team (Sackett & Wilson, 1982).

Message-relevant Thinking

Theories of persuasion also help us understand the conditions under which groups process information. According to Petty and Cacioppo (1986), the messages that come to us may be processed systematically (i.e., very carefully and thoroughly) or only peripherally (i.e, very quickly, using simple rules). Systematic processing will take place if people are motivated and able to engage in careful thinking about the relevance of the message to the problem at hand. Several factors motivate and enable individuals to engage in systematic thinking: relevance of the material, repeated exposure to the message, adequate prior knowledge about the topic, prior learning of ways to organize material, and concern for truth seeking, that is, a goal to seek a correct solution versus one that is accepted by others (Chaiken & Stangor, 1987). These are the very conditions present in the assessor discussion. Assessors are experienced managers, they have a clear understanding of the dimensions as mental frameworks, behavioral data are available for their consideration, and the goal is to derive an accurate evaluation of each participant without external pressures. In addition, assessors have the time to devote their full attention to the assessment effort.

Furthermore, when using the systematic style of thinking, people are less likely to be influenced by another person's status or appearance. This point is supported by the assessment center research cited earlier, which shows that the sex and status of assessors do not determine influence in the integration discussion.

Summary

There is much theoretical and research evidence to support the proposition that the decision process used in the assessor integration discussion can foster good decisions. Many of the factors that lead to process gains are present in the process, but that is not a guarantee that they will actually be followed. A poorly run integration discussion could succumb to the many conditions that lead to poor decision making. We must now look to the research evidence to examine the quality of final dimension ratings and the overall assessment ratings that result from the integration discussion.

Assessment Center Research

We have seen that the assessment center method sets up conditions that benefit group discussion in decision making. This section summarizes research on the consistency and accuracy of assessors' consensus judgments. The results show that final dimension ratings have a high level of consistency and accuracy, and the overall assessment ratings predict a wide variety of measures of managerial effectiveness and success. This section also presents other evidence supporting the accuracy of these ratings.

For most assessment centers, the most meaningful results are the final dimension ratings and the overall assessment rating. The dimension ratings are used for diagnosing strengths and weaknesses, for planning individual training programs, and for developing managerial skills. The overall assessment rating is used for making selection and promotion decisions. The following sections review the considerable research showing the quality of these ratings where assessors have used the traditional method of the consensus discussion.

Quality of Final Overall Dimension Ratings

In the last chapter, we noted a trend in the evaluation studies that suggested that assessment ratings are more consistent and accurate when judgments are based on an aggregation of a wide range of information. Within-exercise dimension ratings made by one assessor show lower levels of consistency and accuracy than dimension ratings based on observations from several exercises.

Similarly, the evidence we are about to examine shows that the final overall dimension ratings have a high level of consistency and are related to measures of managerial effectiveness taken concurrently with the assessments and criteria gathered sometime after assessment. We all see that, although assessors appear to use only a limited set of dimension ratings when deriving an overall assessment rating, they usually use more than one dimension. Statistical analyses show that only a few groups of dimensions are needed to support assessors' judgments, but here again, more than one single, general impression is being assessed. We will also see that the method of integration of the behavioral data may affect the quality of dimension ratings.

Consistency among Assessors. After hearing all the reports about performance in the exercises, assessors agree with each other on overall dimension ratings to a very high degree. Several studies (Kehoe et al., 1985; McConnel & Parker, 1972; Neidig & Martin, 1979; Sackett & Hakel, 1979; Schmitt, 1977) have reported estimates of assessor agreement for across-exercise dimension ratings, with average figures ranging from .69 to .94. Only Konz (1988) reported lower assessor agreement, in the range of .14 to .49 for ten dimensions. Thomson (1970) found no significant differences between the reliabilities of psychologist assessors and manager assessors, and the agreement within groups was quite high.

In a slightly different analysis, Smith (1988) investigated inter*team* agreement on dimension ratings for two types of assessment center methods (the behavioral reporting method and the within-exercise method) by examining the agreement of the dimension ratings across teams. Regardless of whether final dimension ratings were obtained via consensus discussion or by averaging individuals' preliminary ratings, the level of agreement was greater for the teams using the within-exercise method.

All these studies demonstrate that assessors are consistent in determining their across-exercise dimension ratings. Additionally, evidence suggests that some assessment center methods, such as those where assessors give and report within-exercise dimension ratings, may lead to greater assessor reliability and agreement than other methods, such as those where assessors report only behaviors before assigning their individual across-exercise dimension ratings.

Prediction of the Overall Assessment Rating. The correlations between various dimension ratings and the overall assessment rating have generally been fairly high. Hinrichs and Haanpera (1976) found that the average correlation between each across-exercise dimension rating and the overall assessment rating in eight countries ranged from .25 to .82. Hinrichs (1978) and Mitchel (1975) also reported high correlations between dimension ratings and the overall assessment rating. Lastly, Huck and Bray (1976) found correlations between scores on groups of dimension ratings and the overall assessment rating to be high for both white and black assessment center participants.

Studies have shown that three to seven dimensions typically contribute to the prediction of the overall assessment rating (e.g, Bray & Grant, 1966; Hinrichs & Haanpera, 1976; Kehoe et al., 1985; Konz, 1988; Russell, 1985; and Schmitt, 1977). Neidig, Martin, & Yates (1979) found that out of nineteen dimensions, five predicted unique aspects of the final assessment rating, but only two of the dimensions cross-validated. By contrast, Sackett and Hakel (1979) found that five to seven dimensions were needed to capture all of the predictable variation in the overall assessment rating, and the statistical formula worked with a second sample of participants.

The relatively small number of dimensions (i.e., three to seven) that assessors seem to use in formulating overall assessment ratings does not appear to be a function of the amount of training. Dugan (1988) compared the results of hundreds of assessments by assessors trained for two weeks with assessors trained for three weeks. Between three and seven dimensions were used by the former group and three to six dimensions were used by the latter group. Dugan suggested that a combination of factors may have caused the lack of a training effect, for example, limitations in abilities to process such complex information, overlap in the concepts measured by dimensions, and limitations of the statistical methods used in the study.

These studies suggest that even though assessors are often told to use all the dimension information, only a few dimensions, that is, three to seven, are needed to support assessors' overall assessment ratings. Because a large portion of variation in overall assessment ratings can be accounted for by a statistical combination of the final dimension ratings, some have suggested there is no need for the assessor discussion (Herriot et al., 1985; Wingrove et al., 1985). This suggestion is premature, though, because it is quite possible that the integration discussion yields an overall assessment rating that is more accurate than the statistical combination of dimension ratings. We will explore this issue later.

Prediction of Subsequent Performance. Moses and Boehm (1975) investigated whether across-exercise dimension ratings for men and women predicted the management level participants attained two to ten years after participating in an assessment center. The relationships were meaningful, but not very high; the correlations for the various dimensions ranged from .20 to .30 for female participants and from .25 to .38 for male participants. Similar levels of accuracy were found in a study by Ritchie and Moses (1983) that examined the predictive accuracy of dimension ratings for female participants seven years after assessment, and in a study by Wollowick and McNamara (1969) that investigated the predictive accuracy of dimension ratings three years after assessment. Using a similar criterion, Hinrichs (1978) found that for most dimensions the accuracy of prediction increased as time after assessment increased (average correlations one year after assessment were .28; average correlations eight years after assessment were .42). In the only exception, Outcalt (1988) reported an average correlation of only .15 in his study of the relationship between across-exercise dimension ratings and job level. Thus, there is fairly consistent evidence that final dimension ratings are meaningfully related to managerial progress years after the assessment center.

Three studies investigated the ability of across-exercise dimension ratings to predict salary progress. Bray and Grant (1966) examined the relationship between nine clusters of dimensions and salary progress and found that for four samples of men, correlations ranged from -.41 to +.57; and that twenty of the thirty-nine correlations were positive and significant. In the second study, the average correlation between across-exercise dimension ratings and salary progress was only .17 (Mitchel, 1975). Lastly, Outcalt (1988) reported significant correlations between eight dimension ratings and salary level, ranging from .13 to .17. It appears that dimension ratings predict salary progress less accurately than management level attained, although in at least one study these predictions are fairly accurate.

Job performance ratings were used as the criterion measures in five studies. The evidence is mixed. Thomson (1970) found that across-exercise dimension ratings made by both psychologist assessors and manager assessors correlated with supervisor ratings on the same thirteen dimensions obtained six months to two years after the assessment center. Outcalt (1988) found meaningful correlations with a special appraisal of on-the-job performance using newly developed scales (but not the regular corporate performance appraisal form). In another study, Huck and Bray (1976) found the average correlation between four assessment factors and six job performance dimensions was .28 for white participants and .18 for black participants. On the other hand, Hinrichs and Haanpera (1976) found that all of the correlations between dimension ratings and performance appraisal data were low. Finally, Konz (1988) found that only one of ten dimensions correlated with a measure of job performance.

Thus, results from the above studies suggest that across-exercise dimension ratings predict subsequent management level quite well, and increasingly so as time elapses. Across-exercise dimension ratings also were found to predict salary progress and job performance in some studies but not in others, and usually at a lower level of accuracy.

Other Studies of Final Dimension Ratings. The accuracy of final dimension ratings can be evaluated by examining a wide variety of evidence. Correlations among the dimensions, results of factor analysis studies, and correlations of final dimension ratings with other measures of the same attributes all provide evidence of what the final dimension ratings really measure.

Three studies examined the correlations among across-exercise dimension ratings for individual participants. Archambeau (1979), Outcalt (1988), and Konz (1988) found a high correlation among final dimension ratings. These results suggest that final dimension ratings are related to each other and do not typically reflect entirely distinct attributes. These studies also suggest that assessors' ratings of dimension performance may be influenced by some general impression of the candidates.

Factor analyses have been performed on the across-exercise dimension ratings in several studies, and the results have generally yielded two to four factors. For example, in a study by Schmitt (1977), analysis of seventeen dimensions resulted in three clusters: administrative skills, interpersonal skills, and activity/forcefulness. Similar results, in terms of type and number of factors, have been found in other studies (Archambeau, 1979; Bray & Grant, 1966; Hinrich & Haanpera, 1976; Huck & Bray, 1966).

Studies comparing the structure of dimension ratings (i.e., how the dimensions are related to each other) for different assessors (Hinrichs & Haanpera, 1976; Sackett & Hakel, 1979), for different types of participants (Bray & Grant, 1966; Huck & Bray, 1976), and for ratings collected at different points in time across the life of the same assessment center in a large organization (King & Boehm, 1982) have typically shown very similar results. This similarity suggests the findings are meaningful and stable.

Factor analysis can also address the question of whether or not the actual structure of across-exercise dimension ratings matches the structure of these dimensions as it was intended by the assessment center designers. Russell (1985) researched this question by comparing the factor structures of assessors' ratings to the proposed four-factor arrangement. Results indicated that even though assessors were told during assessor training to view the dimensional ratings as forming four specified factors (personal qualities, interpersonal skills, problem-solving skills, and communications skills), the actual factor structure did not match this pattern.

By contrast, two studies have shown that the intended clusters of final dimension ratings are reflected to some extent in the ratings of assessors. Shore et al. (1990) found that two intended clusters, namely, performance dimensions and style dimensions, were reflected in the correlations among nine dimensions. Thornton, Clevenger, Tziner, and Dahan (1991) analyzed sixteen dimensions designed to fall into four groups. With the exception of one dimension that was too complex to fit into any factor and one dimension that was "misplaced," the solution matched the intended categories well.

Thus, the factor analysis studies indicate that the dimensions are not representative of completely separate concepts, since only a few factors are needed to explain assessor ratings. On the other hand, more than one general "halo" factor is needed to explain assessors' final dimension ratings. Most of the data indicate that some type of administrative skills factor (e.g., organizing, decision making), some type of interpersonal skills factor (e.g., human relations skill), and some type of activity factor (e.g., energy, forcefulness) are common among assessors' judgments.

The extent to which the factor analysis results actually match the intended clusters of dimensions envisioned by assessment center designers is still an open question: one study showed a poor match, one showed mixed evidence, and a third showed a good match. In addition, it appears that the structure of final dimension ratings is not influenced by type of assessor, type of participant, or time when the data are gathered.

We can also examine studies that have compared final dimension ratings by the assessors with different measures of the same dimensions. The rationale of these studies is that we should find *high* correlations between two methods measuring the same dimensions, and *low* correlations between measures of different dimensions. Two studies have examined this sort of evidence for across-exercise dimension ratings. In the first study, Shore et al. (1990) correlated final dimension ratings with scores on mental ability tests and the 16 PF, a personality test. They found that the dimensions correlated more highly with tests of comparable attributes than with different attributes. For example, the *performance* dimensions, such as originality and work quality, were more highly correlated with mental ability tests, whereas *interpersonal style* dimensions were more highly correlated with appropriate scales on the personality test.

In the second study, ratings from different types of assessors were compared. Thomson (1970) asked psychologist and manager assessors to rate participants on thirteen dimensions. Correlations between the two types of assessors was high. Thomson concluded that assessors were able to differentiate among the various dimensions because the average correlation among the dimension ratings given by both the psychologists and the managers was less than the level of agreement among their judgments. The results suggest the ratings were consistent, the two groups agreed with each other, and each group differentiated among the dimensions they were rating.

In summary, after reviewing the evidence for across-exercise dimension ratings, it appears that the dimensions do not represent completely separate attributes, but it does appear that assessors can make meaningful distinctions among many of them. There seems to be considerably more evidence of the accuracy of final dimension ratings than there is for within-exercise dimension ratings. This is not surprising, since within-exercise ratings are based on the observations of one assessor watching behavior in only one exercise, whereas the final across-exercise dimension ratings are based on the observations of several assessors watching and discussing behavior in several exercises. Finally, the group discussion process results in ratings with a high degree of consistency and accuracy.

Qualities of the Overall Assessment Rating

The trend of more aggregation of assessment information leading to higher accuracy continues: assessors are now combining information about performance on several dimensions into a single judgment of overall competency. As a result, we will see that overall assessment ratings show consistently high levels of accuracy for predicting managerial success.

There is little question that the overall assessment rating is predictive of subsequent progress and performance in management. Numerous reviews of the literature over the past fifteen years have repeatedly shown that the overall assessment rating has an average predictive accuracy of at least .40 for a variety of measures of managerial progress and performance (Cohen, Moses, & Byham, 1974; Gaugler et al., 1988; Howard, 1974; Hunter & Hunter, 1984; Thornton & Byham, 1982). More importantly, the analysis of over one hundred bits of research evidence by Gaugler et al. (1988) showed two things:

1. The assessment center method was accurate in a wide range of situations, that is, showed validity generalization

(Schmidt & Hunter, 1977). In other words, after taking into account variations in the research designs and the characteristics of the subjects used in the many studies, we find that the predictive accuracy of the overall assessment rating is almost always (95 times out of 100) greater than zero. We can be highly confident that if an assessment center is designed and run in the traditional manner described in this book and in the *Guidelines and Ethical Considerations for Assessment Centers*, the overall assessment rating will predict managerial success.

2. There is still a lot of variation in the predictive accuracy of different types of assessment centers that have been conducted in the past, that is, they may still show situation specificity (Schmidt & Hunter, 1977). Further analysis showed that we can identify some of the characteristics that make an assessment center more accurate. Thus, a well-developed assessment center will probably show substantially greater accuracy than the average of .40. It is not unreasonable to expect the accuracy to be .52 or higher. In the past four years, since the Gaugler et al. (1988) analysis, predictive studies continue to show, on average, very substantial relationships between the overall assessment rating and other measures of managerial effectiveness.

The practical application of assessment centers is not totally free of problems. Some differences in predictive accuracy for different criteria continue to appear (McEvoy & Beatty, 1989), and lack of consistency in implementing an assessment center in different locations can diminish validity (Schmitt et al., 1990). On the other hand, at this point, we can say with confidence that the overall assessment rating predicts a wide variety of different kinds of criteria, including career progress (such as promotions and salary increases), success in training programs, performance on the job (evaluated by subsequent supervisors and by trained independent evaluators), and performance on dimensions comparable to those dimensions assessed in the assessment center. Details of some of these studies are described in Chapter 10.

In fact, long ago the issue shifted from "Does the assessment center work?" (even the most severe critics acknowledge that it does) to "Why does the assessment center work?" Now, even that question is greatly clarified, as we will see in Chapter 9. Our review of theory, research, and practice in the areas of human judgment (Chapter 6) and group decision making (in this chapter) provide considerable support for the traditional explanation of why assessment centers work. Assessment centers work because trained assessors, who are knowledgeable about the attributes that lead to job success, watch participants in job simulation exercises, observe and record behavior, classify that behavior into meaningful dimensions, share those observations with other assessors, and pool their judgments to evaluate candidate performance.

Competing hypotheses about why assessment centers work either are largely speculative or have been supported by only limited evidence. This is not to say there is *no* evidence of support for these explanations, as we will see in Chapter 9.

Summary and Conclusions

This chapter has taken us on a long journey through much theoretical and empirical evidence dealing with the integration of assessment information. What have we learned from this information? We can summarize our conclusions by addressing three questions.

- Is the statistical process or the group judgmental process better for making assessment center evaluations? We have seen support for both techniques. Statistical methods may be more appropriate if the organization has done enough assessments over time and can conduct the research analyses to develop a reliable formula for combining information. Group judgmental methods of integration will probably be used by most organizations because they cannot properly develop the statistical methods.

  Furthermore, there is a strong reluctance to turn over decision making about important personnel matters to some "impersonal" statistical formula and remove the human element from the process, regardless of the fact that the mechanical procedure may be somewhat better. Summarizing much research on individual decision making, Peterson and Pitz (1986) noted that

  > "over twenty years of research on...decision aids has produced two clear conclusions. The first is that unaided predictions made by decision makers are not as accurate as predictions derived from a statistical...model. The second is that decision makers will probably not allow

important decisions to be based only on the output of any mechanical method for combining information" (p.163).

One innovation that holds promise is the combination of statistical and judgmental methods. For example, after the assessors agree on final dimension ratings, these ratings can be combined in a statistical formula to give a tentative overall assessment rating. The assessors can then discuss this rating to see if they agree with it or if it should be modified in light of special information regarding that participant. In support of this proposal, a recent study of *individual* judgment by Peterson and Pitz (1986) found that when the predictions from a statistical formula were provided to the judges, their accuracy improved. It remains to be seen whether providing groups with statistical predictions will improve accuracy of the groups' decisions, but some believe it will (Heine, 1991).

- Do group dynamics have a negative impact on the integration discussion? Group dynamics may play a part in assessment center integration discussions, just as they do in any group interaction, but to a lesser extent. In only a minority of integration discussions do we see evidence that the individual assessors are unduly swayed by judgments of the other assessors. The structured process of reporting behaviors and determining dimension ratings minimizes many of the detrimental group effects present in the typical group decision-making situation.

- Does the discussion process make a difference in assessment center judgments? Depending on which research you consider, there is reason to believe that group processes may lead to losses in predictive accuracy, to gains in predictive accuracy, or have no effect at all. In my opinion, predictive accuracy is enhanced if the assessors follow the procedures laid down for the traditional method of observing, classifying, reporting, and integrating the behavioral observations. Accuracy will be high because the evaluations are based on behaviors rather than general impressions, each assessor makes independent judgments before discussing those judgments with others, and the decision process is carefully designed to gather information about multiple dimensions from multiple exercises observed by multiple observers.

The assessment center process leads to accurate final dimension ratings and overall assessment ratings, in contrast to the questionable accuracy of within-exercise dimension ratings. Final dimension ratings are particularly important for diagnostic assessment centers; overall assessment ratings are particularly important for promotion and selection assessment centers.

We turn now to the last major element of a complete assessment center program: feedback of the results to participants and organizational decision-makers. In Chapter 8 we will explore the types of feedback that should be given in selection/promotion, diagnostic, and training assessment centers.

8

Providing Feedback of Assessment Center Results

Key Concepts: Tailoring feedback sessions to support assessment center objectives; disseminating and storing feedback information; examining responses to assessment center feedback.

The assessment center process of making behavioral observations, evaluating performance on dimensions of professional effectiveness, and predicting future success yields a vast amount of information about each individual. We have seen that these observations and evaluations can be made with a high degree of consistency and accuracy. However, whether the information has any practical value for the individual and the organization depends on how it is used. Just because the assessors are able to make accurate observations and judgments does not mean that the information will be helpful to anyone else. The value of the information is dependent on whether or not

- feedback is given in a timely fashion to the appropriate people
- reports are delivered sensitively by a creditable person
- clear examples of both positive and negative results are included in the reports

Organizations have many options when it comes to handling assessment information. The human resource manager (or other manager in charge of assessment center operations) must make many decisions that will have far-ranging implications about the process of supplying feedback. How such decisions are made depends on the purpose of the assessment center, as well as on ethical and professional considerations. The goals in planning a feedback procedure are to devise an effective system for both retaining and disseminating the information and to achieve the original purpose of the assessment center. At the same time, the rights of the individual must be carefully protected.

Matching Feedback to Assessment Purpose

Promotion or selection programs, diagnostic programs, and training programs all require different procedures for providing feedback to management and participants. The purpose of a promotion or selection program is to help the organization identify individuals who have potential for long-range success in the organization; thus, feedback should be given to the individuals who are making selection and promotion decisions. Assessment information should *not* be given to other individuals who are providing independent evaluations of candidates for promotion. Of course, each participant should be told the results of the evaluation. In a diagnostic program the objective is to devise an individualized training program for each participant; thus, feedback should be given to the participant and to the participant's immediate supervisor so that they can set up training activities together. On the other hand, the purpose of a management training or team-building assessment center is to foster skill development during the assessment center itself; therefore, feedback must be given after each exercise so that the participants can learn new skills and practice them in subsequent exercises during the program. Results of these kinds of programs are not typically supplied to the participants' immediate managers.

Rights of the Individual and Responsibilities of the Organization

Each organization must work out a set of policies and procedures that strike a delicate balance. On the one hand, participants have a right to know the results of assessment and to benefit from participation in the program. On the other hand, the organization must protect against unethical use of the information and the threat of a lawsuit.

Employee Rights

The system of gathering, storing, and providing feedback must take into account the rights of the individual employee, as well as the responsibilities of the organization. Employees often have access to their personnel records as a result of (1) the Privacy Act of 1974, which governs federal employees, (2) state laws with similar provisions, or (3) the policies of many large companies that voluntarily provide access to this information (Sovereign, 1984). The individual has the right to know the results of any evaluation that will affect his or her status in the organization. More specifically, if assessment center information is going to be used in making decisions about promotion, in evaluating performance, or in designing training plans, then the individual has the right to know what is in the assessment report (Task Force, 1990).

Even without a law requiring access to the assessment report, it makes good sense to let the individual know how he or she did. The credibility of the system depends on individuals having confidence in its accuracy and fairness. Shuler (in press) has pointed out that any evaluation must have *social validity,* that is, it must be acceptable to the participants. Social validity is based, in part, on the opportunity of the participants to receive information about how the program was conducted and how they fared in the evaluation. Perceptions about selection practices are especially important because applicants and employees generalize from these specific practices about a wide variety of organizational characteristics (Thornton, in press).

Furthermore, giving individuals clear feedback about their evaluations fits with a commitment-type human resources program (Lawrence, 1984). In a commitment relationship, the individual and the organization have an open and equal relationship with each other. The organization treats the individual as a mature and responsible individual, recognizing his or her rights as an equal partner in the employment relationship.

Ethical and professional guidelines for industrial and organizational psychologists also require that assessment center participants receive feedback about their evaluations. Principle 8 of the *Ethical Principles of Psychologists* states that clients have a right to know the results of any assessment procedure they take part in, in language that they can understand. The *Standards for Educational and Psychological Tests*, prepared by a joint committee of the American Educational Research Association, the American Psychological Association, and the National Council on Measurement in Education (1985) states that there should be provision for the individual to learn the results of any testing program. In addition, the *Guidelines and Ethical Considerations for Assessment Center Operations* (Task Force, 1990) states that there should be some provision for feedback of the results of an assessment center. Participants already employed by an organization should be allowed to read any written reports and recommendations; outside applicants for employment should be told the final recommendation if they request that information.

Organizational Interests

The organization also has many interests to protect when it devises a system to gather, retain, and disseminate information about employees. First, the organization must ensure that standardized procedures are being followed (American Educational Research Association et al., 1985) so that the system has *operational validity* (Byham & Temlock, 1972). Operational validity means that a selection procedure is being implemented in a consistent and fair manner across the various divisions and departments where it is being used. Schmitt et al. (1990) have shown that the effectiveness of a well-developed assessment center can vary quite dramatically if the program is not implemented in a consistent manner across different job sites.

Second, organizations must maintain control over the results of an assessment center to protect themselves in the event of a lawsuit or investigation by an equal employment opportunity agency. In light of the litigious nature of our society, especially in the employment arena, organizations must have written policies about personnel decision making and take steps to ensure that these policies are being followed throughout the organization.

Finally, the organization must ensure that the information is used properly. Assessment centers are very expensive operations that involve the valuable time of management assessors. If the program is to benefit the organization and demonstrate its own usefulness for the expense involved, the results must be applied properly.

Other Considerations

The type of feedback given to current participants in an assessment center can influence the effectiveness of future assessments. For example, although it makes sense to give detailed feedback to participants in each specific exercise, a written report of this nature could easily be passed along to someone about to participate in the next assessment program. The advantage to the "informed" participant could alter the subsequent assessment. There is no clear resolution of this conflict. The organization must weigh the benefits and drawbacks of each practice. Most likely, the organization will want to be more protective of the integrity of the exercises in selection and promotion programs; thus, less detailed feedback will be given. In developmental programs, however, more feedback is needed to facilitate learning, and there is less harm done if specific information about exercises is passed along to later participants. Leaks of information about the content of exercises can affect the integrity of the entire assessment program, but experience has shown that general knowledge of the exercises does not destroy the accuracy of assessments.

The human resource manager must also have clear policies about feedback and information retention because practices in these areas determine whether the organization can conduct meaningful research and evaluation studies on the assessment center. It might seem that detailed information from the assessment center should be disseminated widely throughout the organization. The problem with this practice is that managers may base their subsequent performance appraisals on assessment center ratings rather than performance on the job. If the performance appraisals are contaminated with the assessment ratings, it is impossible to evaluate the true accuracy of the assessment center. Therefore, organizations must have clear policies about what information is given to participants, where the reports are kept, who has access to reports, and how long the reports are retained.

Outline of Assessment Feedback

Figure 8.1 provides an outline of topics usually covered in a feedback session. By necessity, this outline is somewhat general because, as we will see later in this chapter, feedback is different for different types of assessment centers.

Figure 8.1
Outline of a Feedback Session

Introduction
    Establish rapport
    Describe your role as the feedback provider
    Encourage questions, comments, and note taking
Describe the process
    Explain the process and its results
    Review assessment center activities
    Describe assessment methodology: exercises, reports,
    team evaluation
Describe the results
    Describe performance dimensions
    Provide overall ratings (if given)
    Review results on individual dimensions
    Explain the meaning of results
Give developmental suggestions
Close on positive note

Source: © New York Telephone Company 1989. Modified with permission
of New York Telephone Company, authored by B. Savage.

Feedback in a Promotion Program

The main purpose of feedback in a promotion program is to give
high-level managers information they can use in making promotion decisions. In addition, the participant should be given information so that he or she thoroughly understands the assessment
process and results.

Feedback to the Individual Participant

In most assessment centers used for promotion decisions, the
participant is given oral feedback by a member of the human
resource staff. In fact, Gaugler et al. (1990) found that in 67
percent of the organizations that responded to their survey, a
human resource administrator conducted the feedback session; in
30 percent of the programs, assessors gave feedback. Feedback in

a promotion program usually consists of a statement of the overall assessment rating, a statement of strengths and weaknesses in the dimensions, and a few supporting examples from the various exercises. This feedback session is usually not very lengthy—lasting thirty minutes to an hour. The person giving feedback should be supportive and sensitive, but must guard against making commitments to the employee. When the overall assessment rating is favorable, the participant must be warned that this does not guarantee promotion. There may not be any immediate openings, and the decision-maker may take into account other information that overrides the assessment center rating. If the assessment center evaluation is negative, the participant needs additional support to understand the reasons for the decision. He or she will probably ask many questions about what can be done next, whether there can be another assessment, if there is an appeal process, and so on. The person providing feedback must have a clear understanding of the organization's policy on all these issues.

Procedural Justice

Providing feedback to an individual who has received a negative evaluation for promotion or selection is particularly difficult. One goal of the feedback session is to help the person see that even though the outcome was not favorable, the process was fair. Theory and research on perceptions of justice (Folger & Greenberg, 1988; Greenberg, 1990) have shown that individuals distinguish between *outcome justice* and *procedural justice*. Outcome justice refers to beliefs about an outcome or decision that affects us; procedural justice refers to beliefs about the process used to arrive at the decision. For example, a sales representative may be disappointed that he was not promoted to district manager but may accept that outcome if he understands that his past performance was considered carefully, that he had ample opportunities to demonstrate his skills and aptitudes, and that his credentials were evaluated equally with those of other candidates. It is natural to be disappointed if a decision is not made in our favor, but we may or may not be satisfied with the procedure that led to that decision. If we believe the process is fair, we are more willing to accept the outcome even though we are not happy with it.

Perceptions of procedural justice are a function of certain features of the decision-making process (Folger & Greenberg, 1985; Greenberg, 1990). We tend to see the process as fair if everyone is treated equitably, if people have equal chances to provide information, and if the decision-maker considers accurate information in an unbiased way. Many such "fair and just" elements are built into the assessment center method. During the feedback session, the assessor or other feedback provider should review these practices so that the participant understands clearly that procedural justice was practiced. For example, it is common practice for feedback providers to give a thorough description of the assessment center process. Information about the process usually includes a description of how the assessors took detailed notes of behaviors in the exercises, classified behaviors into performance dimensions using support materials (such as pre-established behavioral examples of each dimension), shared their observations with other assessors observing other exercises, and integrated their observations in a discussion before arriving at consensus ratings. During this description, the feedback provider usually points out that the various assessors served as checks and balances on each other to avoid any idiosyncratic impressions on the part of a single assessor. Only after describing this process should the feedback provider give feedback on performance.

Feedback to Management

When an assessment center is being used for promotion, the results should be given to the managers who make such decisions. The decision-maker needs to know the results of each individual's assessment and to have some comparative data. The comparative data may be the results for the group as a whole (these candidates might even be ranked) or some larger norm group consisting of people assessed in the program in the past. The comparative information helps to give the decision-maker some perspective on the overall assessment evaluation. For example, he or she might put more weight on the assessment information if it shows that the candidate in question performed at a higher level than most of the other participants.

The decision-maker is most interested in the final overall assessment as to the promotability of the individual. Assessments of strengths and weaknesses on the various dimensions might be useful, too. Of course, the assessment information should be presented in conjunction with other information about the candidate, for example, length of time with the company, types of experience, recent performance records, and recommendations from supervisors. All of these sources provide valuable information about the candidate's suitability for the job.

Figure 8.2 shows an example of a summary sheet for the evaluation of six candidates who were finalists for one position. Note that the overall assessment rating and the various dimension ratings are provided, along with the names of the assessors for that program. (Of course, a complete definition of the dimensions would also be provided.) Knowing the assessors may help the decision-maker interpret the results. Assuming the assessors are credible managers who have been trained well, the decision-maker should be willing to accept the results as meaningful.

Knowing the dimension ratings may allow the decision-maker to overlook a marginal overall assessment rating. For example, Gary Dutton was not recommended for promotion, presumably because he was rated low on interpersonal sensitivity and assertiveness and initiative. On the other hand, he received very high marks on intellectual abilities and decision making. If the decision-maker is looking for someone with those particular strengths, he or she might discount the overall assessment rating and promote Gary.

A brief written report might also be prepared for the decision-maker and for the assessment files. The report might describe each participant's strengths and weaknesses and include examples of behavior in a few of the exercises as supportive evidence. This report might also include ratings on the dimensions and other information not usually given to the participant.

For documentation purposes and for research, a complete file should be prepared with all exercise reports, ratings, and rankings, with demographic information on the participants—age, sex, race, date of hire, and so on. This record should be kept locked in the office of the human resource department. It should not be given to the participant or the decision-maker.

Feedback in a Diagnostic Program

The feedback given to the participant and management in a diagnostic program is quite different from that given in a promotion or selection program. Here the purpose of the assessment is to foster effective developmental planning for the individual; assessment should be only the first step in the planning of a series

Figure 8.2
Assessment Center Summary Sheet

SUMMARY OF APPLICANT RATINGS

("3" is a passing score)

	Gary Dutton	Rick Daves	Ken Lemon	Mary Armor	Steve Blake	Debra Stan
Written Communication	3	4	5	4	3	2
Planning and Organization	3	3	4	4	4	3
Interpersonal Sensitivity	1	4	3	4	4	3
Delegation	3	3	3	3	3	2
Decision Making	5	3	2	4	3	3
Intellectual Abilities	5	3	3	3	3	2
Assertiveness & Initiative	1	3	2	3	3	3
OVERALL ASSESSMENT RATING	2	3	4	4	4	2

Assessors: Martin, Bloom, Lawrence

---

of developmental assignments that will lead to the growth and progress of the individual.

Because of the planning aspects of diagnostic feedback, it is often given to the participant's immediate supervisor by a management assessor who is on the same level or higher than the supervisor. For example, in the Kimberly organization described in Chapter 2, the participants were first-level supervisors and the assessors were third-level managers. These assessors then provided feedback to the participants and to their managers, who were second-level department heads. Because the assessors were at a higher level, they had more influence over the developmental planning efforts of other line managers. Thornton (1976) found that feedback interviews of this type, in conjunction with support materials to help the participants' supervisors, led to better developmental planning for supervisors and technical personnel assessed in a large manufacturing organization. The support materials included a workbook in which the individual and his or her supervisor recorded dimensions in need of improvement, action steps to remediate the weaknesses, and target dates for reviewing progress.

Feedback to the Participant

In a diagnostic program, the participant is usually provided with a written report describing in detail the assessment evaluations. Figure 8.3, at the end of this chapter, shows an example of some portions of such a report. The report gives a clear statement of Bob's relative strengths and weaknesses on the dimensions, and then goes further to provide a thorough diagnosis of each dimension of his performance. For example, rather than just saying Bob is poor on delegation, the report states that he is willing to delegate, but does not give the subordinate any real responsibility and does not use any control mechanisms to determine whether the delegated work is carried out. For planning and organizing, Bob demonstrated a good theoretical approach, but he had difficulties applying the skills. For example, he tends to "live with things" rather than take some action to study an issue or lay out steps to correct a problem. The report includes examples of effective and ineffective behavior in several exercises.

Whereas the report for the promotion program may be only three or four pages long, a diagnostic report tends to be much longer. It may have one page for each of the eight to ten dimensions. A longer report is needed to provide more than just an evaluation on the dimensions; it provides an analysis of that individual's performance on the various facets of each dimension. The assessors may also compare and contrast behaviors relevant to a dimension displayed in different types of situations. For example, the participant's leadership skills might be quite effective in one-on-one situations, yet very poor in groups. The report also contains suggestions for developmental activities that the assessors believe would help the participant improve in the areas of weakness.

Before the assessor prepares the final written report, he or she may meet with the participant to give oral feedback. This meeting, which often takes place soon after the integration discussion, gives the participant a chance to comment on the report and clarify any misunderstandings. During this meeting, the assessor wants to make sure the participant understands the reasons for the various evaluations and gain agreement from him or her regarding developmental needs. In a sense, the assessor is "selling" the participant on the accuracy of the report before it is presented to his or her supervisor. It is important for the participant to accept the report so he or she is willing to make a development plan based on the findings. During the feedback meeting with the participant's supervisor, the assessor will then be able to help the participant get the types of developmental assignments needed for growth. The assessor thus takes on some of the roles of mentor (Hunt & Michael, 1983) in supporting the participant in the advancement of his or her career.

Feedback to Management

Oral feedback and the written report are then given to the participant's supervisor in a meeting between the supervisor, the participant, and the assessor. Here we can see the advantage of having the third-level manager serve as assessor and give the feedback. As a higher-level manager, the assessor may have influence in ensuring that the assessment results will be used to foster the participant's development. Of course, many organizations prefer to have someone from the human resource staff deliver these feedback reports, because assessor/manager time is so valuable. And, in many cases, this is just as effective. On the other hand, it is a not-so-subtle pressure on the boss to know that a higher-level manager is interested in the development of one of his or her people and will be watching as the follow-up efforts unfold.

Feedback in a Training and Organizational Development Program

Whereas feedback in the promotion and diagnostic programs may be provided several days after the assessment center program, the feedback in a training program must be given immediately after each exercise to have any impact. The purpose of a training and organizational development program is to help the participants develop new skills. An important training technique is to provide immediate feedback about performance and then give the learner a chance to practice new modes of behavior. Little learning takes place if the participant goes through all the exercise activities with no guidance and then receives feedback at the end of the program with no opportunity to adjust behaviors in subsequent learning situations (Thornton & Cleveland, 1990). Some large-scale behavioral simulations, similar to assessment centers, are set up so that feedback is not given until the end of the two-day program. Participants may gain some insight into their own ways of handling these situations, but no real skill development can take place unless the person gets a chance to repeat the activity and receive reinforcement for correct behaviors. At IDS Corporation (Braaton, 1989), daily feedback, along with suggestions for improvement, are given to participants so they can practice new skills in subsequent parts of the three-and-a-half-day program.

An example of how immediate feedback and subsequent practice are built into an assessment center was shown in the training program of the Federal Commercial Promotion Agency in Chapter 2. At least two exercises of the same type were included in the program. Feedback after the first exercise allowed the participant to try out new actions in the next exercise and then get another round of feedback. This process ensures that participants develop skills during the program itself; other steps are needed to ensure that these skills transfer to the job situation.

Assessors/Facilitators

The role of the staff members in a training assessment center is somewhat different from the role of assessors in a promotion or diagnostic assessment center. In a training assessment center, the staff member attempts to help the participants learn new skills or helps the group develop better teamwork. Therefore, he or she is often call a facilitator.

Facilitators should have many of the skills needed for other kinds of assessment centers. They must be able to observe and record behavior, to accurately classify behaviors into dimensions, and to articulate these observations to other facilitators and the participants. Some skills needed by assessors in evaluative assessment centers are not as important for facilitators. They are not required to make judgments about the effectiveness of performance on the dimensions or to make predictions about long-range success in the organization. They do not have to have deep insights into organizational requirements.

On the other hand, facilitators must have effective teaching skills, such as excellent oral communication, empathy, and listening ability. They must be able to provide effective feedback about behaviors displayed in the training group in a supportive manner.

Facilitators can be managers or human resource staff members from the organization, or training and development consultants from outside the organization. Consultants can often give valuable insights into group dynamics, since they have no ties to the organization and can observe behaviors objectively.

Peer Feedback

When the assessment center includes group exercises, such as a leaderless group discussion, problem-solving activities, or business games, the participants have a chance to observe the behavior of other participants relevant to job effectiveness. In some programs, the participants are asked to evaluate the performance of other participants, for example, by rating the creativity of others' ideas, rank ordering others in terms of their contribution to group accomplishments, or nominating someone to lead a project team.

Feedback of peer assessment information can be very powerful. Most organizations do not give feedback from peer evaluations in promotion programs, because even though peer descriptions might be valid for predicting success, participants in an assessment program often feel that competitive pressures make the evaluations inaccurate.

In contrast, peer feedback has proven helpful and acceptable in diagnostic and training programs in the United States (Thornton & Byham, 1982) and in Japan (Umeshima, 1989). In these situations, there is little competition and the climate promotes supportiveness and self-insights. Participants usually want to learn all they can about their own developmental needs and how they can improve their skills. Input from peers provides a valuable additional perspective to the feedback from management and staff assessors. In fact, some organizations find peer feedback so valuable and so readily acceptable that they have designed the entire assessment center around peer evaluations. Human resource management staff coordinate the program, and no higher-level management personnel are used as assessors.

Response to Feedback

Numerous surveys have been conducted of participants' reactions to feedback from an assessment center (Dodd, 1977; Thornton & Byham, 1981). The large majority of participants respond favorably, saying that the feedback interview is helpful in understanding their own strengths and weaknesses. They find the feedback provider supportive and willing to give clear examples of the reasons for the assessment results. Of course, feedback is handled very differently in different organizations and may be handled inconsistently by different staff members. Therefore, it is difficult to generalize about all feedback sessions.

There are some common ingredients that make feedback more acceptable to participants. For example, participants like to learn about specific examples of behaviors in more than one exercise that support the evaluations. In addition, they want the feedback to focus on evaluations that represent consensus among the assessors, rather than on the idiosyncratic reactions of one assessor. These characteristics of feedback have been found to be effective in a wide variety of organizational settings (Ilgen, Fisher, & Taylor, 1979; Taylor, Fisher, & Ilgen, 1984).

In an interesting study of the usefulness of an assessment center for developmental purposes, Fleenor (1988) found that both good and poor performers accepted feedback when it was presented by a knowledgeable source, when the feedback included performance-related information, and when the person giving feedback was interested in their development. Furthermore, both good and poor performers subsequently demonstrated improved performance on the job after receiving feedback.

A recent study by Fletcher (1991) provides a rare examination of the longitudinal effects of assessment center participation over a six-month period. Even though immediately following assessment some attitudes increased (e.g., dominance and pursuit of excellence) and other attitudes declined (e.g., need for achievement and work ethic), all these attitudes returned to their initial levels after six months. Unsuccessful candidates appeared to experience the most negative effects over time, with declines in feelings of competitiveness and self-esteem. Fletcher concluded that organizations should give feedback quickly to exploit the learning potential that immediate changes in attitude provide and provide supportive counseling to those whose assessments are low.

Needed Research

There have been no studies of the effects of feedback on assessment center participants beyond the Fleenor study and the polling of participants at the end of various assessment centers. It would be interesting to know what types of feedback lead to greater acceptance of the findings in promotion programs, and whether good feedback leads to more favorable impressions of the organization in selection programs. In diagnostic programs, it would be helpful to understand what types of feedback lead participants to engage in more conscientious developmental planning. Based on research in other fields, we might expect that specific and descriptive (rather than general and evaluative) feedback would be more helpful in training programs, but there has been no research on these issues in the assessment center context.

Summary and Conclusions

We can look on the feedback session as both the beginning and the end. It is the "end" in the sense that feedback is the culmination of all the work that has been done to develop, implement, and execute an assessment center. As we have seen, it is effective only if the dimensions have been chosen correctly, the exercises have been designed properly, and the assessors observe, classify, and judge behavior accurately. "Correctly," "properly," and "accurately" must be interpreted in light of the *purpose* of the assessment center. There is no one best way to carry out each of these steps. In this chapter we have seen how feedback must be tailored to provide the kinds of information needed by decision-makers and participants alike.

Verbal feedback should be given in all types of assessment programs; written feedback should usually be given to employees but need not be given to external applicants. Written feedback is briefer and more general in promotion programs, longer and more detailed in diagnostic programs. The content of feedback in diagnostic and training programs should be much more detailed so that participants can learn from the experience. In contrast, for reasons of security, exercise material should usually not be reviewed in detail in feedback after a selection or promotion program.

Feedback is most commonly given by human resource management staff members, but management assessors can be effective in giving feedback to the participants' immediate supervisors in a diagnostic program, as the first step in developmental planning. Managers, human resource staff, and outside consultants can be helpful facilitators in a developmental program.

Aside from the participant, who should be given the results of an assessment center? There are very good reasons for giving feedback to the participant's immediate supervisor in a diagnostic program, and for *not* giving the immediate supervisor feedback in promotion programs. In a training program, the participant is often the only one who gets feedback.

The feedback session is the "beginning" in the sense that the assessment information must now be put to good use in the organization. In selection and promotion programs, the assessment center results provide input, along with other types of information, to these important personnel decisions. The assessment center ratings should be used in conjunction with other sources of information about the candidate's background, education, work performance, and potential. In developmental programs, the assessment center diagnosis of strengths and weaknesses is only the first step in planning follow-up developmental activities for each individual. The individual and his or her supervisor must sit down and combine the assessment results with information about the individual's performance on the job. Together they should lay out specific action steps. As in the medical field, a diagnosis is not very helpful if no treatment is forthcoming. In training programs, the feedback is an indication of what the person is doing well and what needs to be improved, but for the training to have any effect, there must be opportunities to try out new behaviors and get further feedback.

The assessment center process is particularly good at providing feedback that is helpful for all these purposes. Most organizations find that feedback on assessment center results is well received—compared with feedback on other evaluative information such as performance appraisals—because the assessments are based on specific behavioral observations rather than general impressions. The intense involvement of multiple assessors gives the feedback credibility. Armed with assessment center results, human resource managers find that they are in a good position to help managers make important decisions and launch productive development plans.

Questions remain about what assessment centers really measure and whether they are worth the cost. In the next chapter, we examine in some detail further issues about the accuracy and interpretation of overall assessment center ratings and compare their effectiveness and cost with some alternative assessment methods.

Figure 8.3
Diagnostic Report of Supervisory Skills Workshop

Feedback Report

Participant's Name_____Bob Leonard_____ Date _Feb. 27, 1985____
Reviewed with Department Head_____
Program Staff__ Chuck Stuart ____ Bill Blake _____ Randy Golden

The purpose of this report is to summarize the program staff's observations of the participant, to assist individuals and their supervisors in identifying strengths and development needs, and to help in planning developmental activities.

Overall Summary

Bob appeared to be very sincere and active in this program. He thought the session was slightly more intense than he expected, although he was not noticeably affected by this. He felt that many of the exercises were realistic and job related. We observed distinct strengths and developmental needs in some dimensions, although we observed that degrees of performance in one dimension area were reflected in other dimensions.

Summary of Demonstrated Strengths

Bob demonstrated strengths in *Problem Analysis, Judgement, Oral Communication* and *Sensitivity*. He demonstrated an appreciation of delegation, control, planning and organizing, and leadership. These however were observed to offer room for good improvement.

Summary of Developmental Needs

Developmental needs were observed in *Planning and Organizing, Delegation, Control, Leadership* and *Development of People*. We will illustrate within each dimension how we feel these areas can be enhanced.

Comments

This report is segmented by dimensions. A dimension will include a definition and a narrative description of the participant's behavior in the program.

Each statement is the result of multiple observations by the staff over several exercises. It is our pooled judgement and is supported by specific written observations of behavior. If data is unclear, conflicting, or if we are presenting a gut feeling, it will be noted.

Management Skills

Planning and Organizing

The ability to anticipate as well as to lay out one's work and subordinate's work effectively. To be able to summarize divergent information and effectively coordinate tasks, materials, and manpower.

Observations recorded in this dimension indicate a developmental need exists. Although Bob has a good theoretical approach to Planning and Organizing, some difficulties were encountered in the application of it. We observed examples of Planning and Organizing primarily in the Compensation Committee and the In-Basket. In the Compensation Committee Bob planned the presentation of his candidate very well, and followed through with an effective presentation of the candidate. Bob indicated during his In-Basket interview that his approach was to sort items into: 1. personnel problems, 2. production problems, 3. schedule problems. He stated that on his return, his priorities would be 1. sit down with Bill, 2. get with O'Brian, 3. have introductory meeting with his people.

Examples indicating less planning and organizing occurred in the Background Interview, L.K. Fawcett, and the Interview Simulation.

- Background Interview: When asked what plans and goals he had, he responded, "I don't know." He indicated that he personally doesn't get involved in planning his section's work (unless his help is solicited).

- L.K. Fawcett: Bob didn't schedule the last hour of the day for two plumbers. He put 2 men on a 1 man job because "I didn't know what to do with the other man except have him idle." He interrupted jobs for lunch rather than have plumbers work straight through and take lunch after job.

- Interview Simulation: Although Bob planned his interview to cover past and current job performance, no planning for future goals of improved performance were indicated. As a result, the objective of a commitment to better performance was not obtained. Bob indicated during the feedback interview that he felt this goal and objective was achieved. We discussed this point; I explained that we looked at this rather narrowly. The goal was improved performance and acceptance of the fact that performance had fallen.

Planning and Organizing

We also observed that Bob has a tendency to "live with things" rather than chart out a method of change. When reviewing the work loan problem his section had, he indicated that a "systems study" was made of the operation. Although he recognized the problem; he himself did not initiate this. In the Management Problems exercise, many opportunities were passed up by Bob. For example, Bob got the group's attention by saying "I'm sure there are lots of things you could do . . . ." but then dropped it with no specific plans being made. This feeling will be discussed further in other dimensions.

We encourage Bob to consider *priorities* of his daily assignments, attack the most important issues first and stick with them. We encourage development of the "execution" phase of this planning. Personal assessment of his success in completing these plans will help monitor his growth.

Delegation

Turning over a specific job or responsibility to the appropriate person(s) with some reporting control and accountability: giving adequate, but not overly detailed instructions; ability to use subordinates effectively and to understand where a decision could best be made.

This dimension was observed to be a developmental need. Bob indicated a willingness to delegate, e.g. "try to let them be on their own" (Background and Interview). In the In-Basket, of the 14 items, 9 were sent to Bill, 2 to Suzy, and 2 to Tom O'Brian. Bob's delegation was generally clear and understandable. We did observe two aspects of delegation which offer room for development.

1. He frequently gives instructions to his subordinates, i.e. delegates activities, fact finding, etc. but he was not observed transferring responsibility and/or decision making to subordinates, e.g. "Let's order enough to get some feedback from the trade, but still order from our regular suppliers". "You decide" delegation was not observed.

2. Bob did not use any control mechanisms to check if work was accomplished. He did not give due dates and he did not ask for specific answers to his memos. He did not make a list to follow-up on his requests.

We feel that, as the definition indicates, delegation should include some aspects of responsibility, decision making, and accountability to most effectively utilize subordinates (and to stimulate their own personal development).

9

Evaluating the Accuracy of Assessment Center Results

Key Concepts: Examining the validity of assessment center activities; explaining why assessment centers work; comparing benefits to costs.

The last five chapters have given a detailed view of each of the key elements of the assessment center method. We have seen how dimensions are chosen and how exercises are designed to elicit behavior relevant to those dimensions. We have reviewed the theory and research that explains how individual assessors observe, classify, and evaluate behavior, and how the assessor team forms consistent and accurate dimension ratings and final overall assessment ratings. Finally, we have seen how feedback can be used by upper-level management to aid organizational decision making and by participants and their supervisors to develop managerial and professional skills.

We now step back from our detailed analysis of the elements of the assessment center method to take a broader look at the method itself. Several questions must still be addressed in our consideration of whether assessment centers are a valuable human resource management technique:

- What do assessment centers measure?
- What alternative explanations can be given for why assessment centers work?

- How does the assessment center method compare with other evaluation methods?
- What does it cost to run an assessment center?
- Do assessment centers have utility, that is, do the benefits outweigh the costs?
- How do participants feel about assessment center procedures?

These questions revolve around the general issue of the *validity* of the assessment center method. Validity is a general concept covering evidence that an assessment or development procedure is capable of achieving its stated purposes. Because any given assessment technique can be used for a variety of purposes, many different types of evidence must be considered. For our purposes, we must consider whether the accumulated evidence supports the three main applications of the assessment center method covered in this book: identification of potential for success in higher management positions, diagnosis of job-related skills and competencies, and management training.

We have already laid the groundwork for the answers to these questions in our review of assessment center research. For example, we have seen in Chapter 7 that overall assessment ratings are consistently predictive of managerial success. In addition, dimension ratings provide an accurate diagnosis of strengths and developmental needs, which, in turn, form the basis for developmental planning. We now must address some deeper and tougher questions.

Varieties of Validity of Assessment Centers

The question "What do assessment centers really measure?" must ultimately be answered by empirical research evidence. We must examine this evidence and make inferences based on our best professional judgment. The conclusion—whether or not the assessment center process is of value—cannot be determined by one correlation statistic or one research study. We must examine the many studies that provide evidence of relationships between assessment data and many types of criteria (including performance on the job), relationships between assessment data and other measures, changes in assessment center scores over time, differences in assessments of men and women, of different racial groups, and of different age groups, and patterns of components of assessment ratings. All of this evidence must then be interpreted to provide support for or refutation of the claims we are making about the characteristics measured by the assessment procedure (Landy, 1988). Even though there are many different types of evidence we can examine, validity boils down to an interpretation of all this accumulated evidence (Binning & Barrett, 1989).

To help us make sense of the wide variety of evidence on the assessment center method, we can conveniently classify the evidence into three categories: evidence of content representativeness (i.e., content validity), evidence of relationships with criterion measures (i.e., criteria validity), and evidence of the relationship of the assessment center method and other measures of related constructs (i.e., construct validity, Cronbach & Meehl, 1955).

Content Validity

Information about content validity consists of evidence concerning testing activities. Two requirements must be considered here: (1) do the test materials present a representative sample of situations employees face on the job, and (2) are the required responses to the test materials a representative sample of the performance requirements on the job. Content validity evidence typically consists of judgments by experts that both these requirements have been met. The testing procedure need not cover the *entire* job, but it must cover important and critical job duties (Society for Industrial and Organizational Psychology, 1987).

Judgments about the similarity of exercises to job situations are the most common type of evidence used to demonstrate the validity of assessment centers in individual organizations (Gaugler et al., 1990). Organizations typically defend an assessment center by pointing out that (1) the dimensions are chosen on the basis of job analysis, (2) the exercises include important and frequently encountered job activities, (3) behavior in the exercises can be classified into the critical performance dimensions, and (4) trained assessors can make consistent and accurate observations of participant behavior. Gathering meaningful content validity evidence is not an easy process. Sackett (1987) has pointed out that when using content validity evidence to validate an assessment center, we must look at several features of the assessment situation in addition to the points listed above, such as the instructions given to participants, scoring systems used by the assessors, and methods of interpretation of the assessment results. These features are important because they can affect assessment center ratings.

Evidence of content representativeness is particularly relevant if the test is being used to make inferences about the participants' present level of knowledge and skills. Thus, in the assessment center context, content validity information is most relevant when the program is designed to diagnose current developmental needs (as illustrated in the Kimberly Brothers Manufacturing Company case study in Chapter 2), or when the assessment center is used to measure job-related competencies of applicants.

The procedures set forth in the *Guidelines and Ethical Considerations for Assessment Center Operations* (Task Force, 1989) are designed to ensure that an assessment center has content validity. These guidelines were written by the leading researchers and practitioners of the assessment center method; they reflect state-of-the-art thinking in the field. While it may be true that some early assessment centers, and even some currently in operation, were not designed in this manner, the *Guidelines* represent the way in which most assessment centers are constructed. It is particularly important that the assessment center developer follow each of the prescribed steps—conducting a detailed job analysis, defining behavioral dimensions, designing exercises to elicit relevant behaviors, training assessors adequately, setting up scoring systems, and following systematic procedures for data integration—as all these steps are necessary to demonstrate content validity.

Although there has been some opposition to the process of content validation of assessment centers when they are used to assess management potential (Sackett, 1987), counterarguments have been offered (e.g., Norton, 1981). In my opinion, evidence of content representativeness is quite relevant to understanding the assessment center process. Such evidence is consistent with the pattern of evidence required by researchers into the overall validity of any test (Binning & Barrett, 1989; Landy, 1986). Indeed, it is complementary to the results of statistical studies showing that assessment centers provide accurate predictions of managerial performance.

Predictive Validity

There is little question, even among the most severe critics of the assessment center method, that the overall assessment rating consistently predicts a wide variety of criteria of managerial success.

Table 9.1 summarizes several reviews of the research findings with regard to the predictive validity of overall assessment ratings, starting with Byham's (1970) article in the *Harvard Business Review* and ending with the most recent statistical analysis of prior studies (Gaugler, Rosenthal, Thornton, & Bentson, 1987).

In summary, the best estimate of the relationship between overall assessment center ratings and measures of success in

Table 9.1

Reviews of the Predictive Validity of the Overall Assessment Rating (OAR)

Author	Date	Summary
Byham	1970	OAR identifies managers who make progress in rank; success rate of assessed managers is greater than nonassessed managers; correlation of OAR and performance ranges from .27 to .64.
Cohen et al.	1974	Median correlation with performance is .33, with potential is .63, with promotion is .40.
Thornton & Byham	1982	OAR predicts variety of criteria, e.g., promotions, performance ratings.
Hunter & Hunter	1984	Statistical analysis estimated validity to be .43 in relation to job performance.
Schmitt et al.	1984	Statistical analysis estimated validity to be .41 for a variety of criteria.
Gaugler et al.	1987	Statistical analysis estimated validity to be .37 in relation to progress, performance, ratings, etc.

management is about .40. This means that people who get higher scores on the overall assessment rating will probably be more successful on the job than people who score lower. Data from the Management Progress Study summarized in Table 9.2 clearly illustrate the predictive accuracy of the assessment center. It can be seen that 48 percent of the college graduates who were predicted by the assessment center to reach middle management had actually attained this level in 1965, whereas only 11 percent of those who were not predicted to reach middle management had done so. The figures are even more dramatic for noncollege people: 32 percent of those predicted to reach middle management had done so, whereas only 5 percent of those receiving low ratings had done so. The predictions after eight years and sixteen years show even more accuracy, that is, more and more people assessed highly were actually promoted to middle management. (It can also be seen that many of the low-rated participants with college degrees got promoted by the sixteenth year of the study.)

In this study the assessment center results were never revealed to anyone in the organization and never used for promotion decisions. Therefore, the results are a pure measure of predictive accuracy.

Table 9.2
Evidence of Predictive Accuracy in the Management Progress Study

Predicted to reach middle management	Percentage attaining middle management		
	(8 years or less)	Year 8	Year 16
College sample			
Yes	48	64	89
No or Question	11	32	66
Noncollege sample			
Yes	32	40	63
No or Question	5	9	18

Source: Bray & Grant, (1966); Bray et al. (1974); Howard, (1979).

It should be clear from these results that the assessment center method is valid, that is, the overall assessment rating is related to success in management. It should be noted that the studies included in these reviews were both published and unpublished; that some of the research was carried out for purely academic purposes and some for practical use in the organization; and that some studies involved various criteria ranging from progress in management ranks, ratings of training or on-the-job performance, and observation by independent researchers of job effectiveness. These studies, therefore, represent a broad sampling of unbiased viewpoints.

Variations in Assessment Center Validity

Not all assessment centers have the same level of predictive accuracy. Until recently it was not easy to determine what led some assessment programs to work better than others. The statistical analysis of studies of assessment center validities conducted by Gaugler et al. (1987) provided valuable information about why assessment centers work. As we saw in Chapter 7, the estimated validity of the final overall assessment rating, after taking into account differences in research methods and statistical features such as size of the samples, was .37. More importantly for our present discussion, there was considerable variation in validity results above and below that figure: some correlations with success were .25 or .15, others were as high as .55 or .65. A measure of the variation of these correlations, called the *standard deviation*, was .12. The standard deviation is a useful indicator of how much higher or lower than the average of .37 the correlations might be. Following the statistical procedures in the method we used (called validity generalization; Hunter, Schmidt, & Jackson, 1982), we built a confidence interval around .37. For example, the 90 percent confidence interval goes from .21 to .53. This means that we can have 90 percent confidence that an assessment center will have a correlation with success greater than .21. If we design an effective assessment center, we can expect that its accuracy will be as high as .53, or even greater.

These facts lead to two conclusions. First, the overall assessment rating has predictive accuracy, that is, the validities generalize across a wide variety of samples and organizations. Second, there is considerable variation in the predictive accuracy of the overall assessment ratings derived in the assessment centers studied in the past. This means that the predictive accuracy of an assessment center depends on factors other than differences in the research methods used.

What does the accuracy of the assessment center depend on? The answer to that question was explored in depth in the analysis done by Gaugler et al. (1987) by studying the variables that correlated with the validity of the assessment center. The idea of some variable correlating with validity may be somewhat difficult to grasp. Figure 9.1 illustrates this idea by showing that the validity of assessment centers increases with a particular variable, in this case the number of different types of exercises. This relationship is not perfect; it can be seen that an assessment center with many different types of exercises can still have lower validity. But the trend is clear.

A variable that correlates with the validity coefficients is called a "moderator variable" (Zedeck, 1986). The Gaugler et al. (1987) analysis looked for many different types of moderator variables, including characteristics of participants and assessors, features of the assessment center procedures, and types of assessment devices used.

Figure 9.1
Illustration of a Variable Correlating with the Validity of Assessment Centers

Number of types of exercises	Validity of OAR
6	.55
6	.40
5	.40
4	.25
4	.30
3	.15
2	.08

Several features of the assessment center were found to be correlated with validity across the large group of the studies we reviewed. Assessment centers were more effective when a wide variety of types of assessment techniques was used, when psychologists were added as assessors (along with managers), and when peer evaluations were gathered. These findings give us some clues about the variables that contribute to the higher validities of assessment centers and tell us why assessment centers work.

Further evidence that situational variables affect validities comes from a study of a regionally administered assessment center used to select secondary school principals (Schmitt et al., 1990). It was found that the assessment center was more accurate in predicting a criterion of effectiveness as perceived by teachers when a larger percent of the assessors were principals (as opposed to university professors), when the assessment was conducted in several districts (as opposed to one district), and when the participants had not previously worked closely with the participants. The authors concluded that the quality of implementation of the assessment center is an important determinant of assessment effectiveness.

Construct Validity

Construct validity evidence is broader in scope, consisting of information that supports or refutes the claim that the procedure measures the psychological characteristics of interest (American Educational Research Association et al., 1985). No single study or correlation figure establishes what a test is measuring. Rather, we must examine the accumulated information from many studies in order to interpret the real meaning of the test scores. All of the types of information reviewed so far, that is, evidence of content representativeness and predictive accuracy, and all of the evidence reported in Chapters 6 and 7 must be considered.

The reader will recall that Chapter 6 concluded that assessors could observe behaviors that take place in exercises and classify those behaviors into meaningful dimensions. Ratings on any one dimension of managerial effectiveness by any one assessor based on only one exercise may not be very accurate. A particular problem is that these within-exercise dimension ratings tend to be more highly related to each other than we think they should be. Some general impression that a participant is "doing well" or "doing poorly" may color assessor judgments about all dimensions in a single exercise. This tendency may be caused by asking assessors to determine dimension ratings after a single exercise, a practice that is avoided in the behavioral reporting method.

By contrast, when assessors' ratings on dimensions are based on behaviors across several exercises, their consistency and accuracy is much higher. Taking this one step further, Chapter 7 showed that when several assessors combine their judgments, the consistency and accuracy of final dimension ratings is even higher. Finally, we saw that the assessors can integrate all this information across dimensions and give an overall assessment rating that accurately predicts managerial performance and progress.

To help define the issues we will be discussing in this section, we can consider a fundamental question raised by Klimoski and Brickner (1987) about assessment centers: "Why do assessment centers work?" From their point of view, there is general acknowledgment that assessment centers do work, in the sense that they predict progress in an organization, but there is still widespread opinion about *why* assessment centers work. They summarized these differences by offering five alternative explanations (beyond the traditional one) of why assessment centers work.

The traditional explanation: Assessors make judgments about dimensions or attributes relevant to job success, then derive an overall assessment rating that is predictive of managerial performance.

Actual criterion contamination: Because assessment centers are expensive, people in organizations want to make use of their findings. The overall assessment ratings cannot be kept secret, and they are used for operational decisions. Subsequent decisions, such as promotions, salary increases, and even performance ratings are influenced by the assessment ratings themselves. As a result, the relationship of assessments and criteria will be artificially high.

Subtle criterion contamination: Because the assessors are often managers in the organization, they share the same biases about what constitutes good management with managers who will later provide performance appraisal ratings. Thus, any evidence of predictive accuracy will be "contaminated" and consequently spuriously high; both groups of evaluators may be wrong and may not be evaluating real job performance.

   Self-fulfilling prophecy: As a result of being selected for and participating in an assessment center, employees are given the idea they are competent. Thus, they perform well in the assessment center and get good feedback. Later, they put forth the effort to develop managerial skills and thereby verify the assessors' judgments.

   Performance consistency: Two arguments here are (1) background data about the participants gives assessors information about their past performance, which is then used to predict future performance, and (2) assessors can predict future performance from present performance observed in the work-sample exercises; therefore we can avoid using abstract ideas like dimensions.

   Managerial intelligence: Assessment center ratings reflect the level of intellectual functioning of candidates, but are not evaluations of managerial performance dimensions.

———

Analysis of Alternative Explanations of Why Assessment Centers Work

In the following sections, we will review some of the arguments Klimoski and Brickner (1987) offered to support each of the alternative explanations. In addition, we will review much evidence that refutes the alternatives and leads to the conclusion that the traditional explanation is most tenable.

Actual Criterion Contamination

There is little question that in some assessment centers criterion contamination has been present, that is, the decision to promote individuals was based in part on the assessment ratings. (At the practical level, that is what we hope happens!) However, when evaluating the quality of assessment center research, the issue is whether predictive accuracy is found when actual criterion contamination is *not* present. The answer is very clear: high levels of predictive accuracy are found in many centers where criterion contamination is absent (Thornton & Byham, 1982). More recently, Gaugler et al. (1987) provided evidence, summarized in

Table 9.3, that all types of research designs (e.g., pure research studies, studies with no feedback of the ratings, concurrent validation designs, and studies of operational programs where the assessment data are used for decision making) give about the same estimate of average predictive validity.

The analysis also showed the accuracy of predictions was *not* a function of the type of criterion used to measure managerial success. Assessment ratings predicted not only progress criteria, such as promotions and salary progress (which may be contaminated, but are not necessarily so), but also criteria such as ratings of on-the-job performance, success in training, and ratings by independent evaluators. It is hard to imagine that all of these criteria could be severely contaminated.

In addition, Gaugler et al. (1987) made judgments about the quality of each individual research study with regard to whether criterion contamination was present and whether the study was technically sound in other ways (e.g., was the sample representative of employees, could other reasons explain the results, and so on). They then computed an index of "quality" of the study. The quality of the study was linked to the level of accuracy, so that the *higher* quality studies showed more predictive accuracy than the *lower* quality studies.

Three examples of situations where actual criterion contamination (i.e., knowledge of assessment ratings on the part of people providing criterion ratings) was *not* present will be described. The results of the landmark study of the assessment center method at AT&T (Bray & Grant, 1966; Howard & Bray, 1988) cannot be explained by criterion contamination because no

Table 9.3

Predictive Validity of Assessment Centers Evaluated by Different Research Designs

Research Design	Estimated Validity
Experiment	.36
Predictive study without feedback	.43
Predictive study with feedback	.39
Concurrent validity	.42

Source: Gaugler et al. (1987).

one in the organization, including participants themselves, ever saw the assessment ratings. The results were literally locked up at a remote location outside the company. In another study (Kraut & Scott, 1972), the criterion was promotion to the *second* level of management, which took place long after the assessment center had been conducted and after managers had time to demonstrate performance effectiveness at the first level. In this case it is safe to assume that the decision to promote to the second level was based more on job performance than assessment ratings made several years earlier. In both studies, the overall assessment rating was directly correlated with long-term managerial progress.

A recent example of a long-range study with little chance of criterion contamination was carried out by Tziner, Ronen, & Hacohen (1990). The assessment center predicted two uncontaminated criteria (i.e., ratings by supervisors of performance and potential for further growth) gathered each year for three years after the assessment center was conducted. The results showed that the overall assessment rating and dimension ratings predicted both criteria. Other studies with uncontaminated criteria have also been reported (e.g., Gluski & Sherman, 1989).

In summary, although criterion contamination may exist and, if present, will artificially raise the level of predictive accuracy, there is much evidence that assessment centers can predict a wide variety of criteria that are unlikely to be influenced by assessment center results. Furthermore, many other supportive studies have been conducted where assessment center results were not disseminated in the organization. Actual criterion contamination does not seem to be a plausible explanation of why assessment centers work.

Subtle Criterion Contamination

The argument here is that assessment center research has used poor criteria, that is, ratings of performance and indices of progress are colored by some biased perceptions of work effectiveness. Guion (1987) has used the example that police department administrators have an image of a good police supervisor that includes "being tall." Police department assessment center ratings given by management assessors, as well as ratings of job performance given by managers, were supposedly influenced by this image. According to this argument, the correlations between the assessment center ratings and the criterion ratings were largely due to these shared biases. There are several weaknesses in this argument as it relates to the assessment center research.

First, assessment center research has used a variety of different types of criteria, not just indices of promotion and judgmental ratings by upper-level managers. Table 9.4 shows that predictive accuracy of the assessment ratings is present when different types of criteria are used (Gaugler et al., 1987). Criteria have included judgments by independent third-party observers (Bray & Campbell, 1968), ratings by subordinates (McEvoy & Beatty, 1989; Schmitt et al., 1990), turnover of subordinates in the manager's unit (K.C. Ague, personal communication, March 16, 1971), objective results in a management-by-objectives system for six hundred middle and senior managers (Britz, cited in Spangenberg et al., 1989), and sales performance among telemarketing representatives (Squires et al., 1988).

It is hard to argue that all these criteria are influenced by some irrelevant image of a good employee. Assessment center researchers have faced all of the many criterion problems plaguing industrial and organizational psychologists (Smith, 1976) and have used the best methods available in the field to measure job performance. This counterargument does not mean that we should accept faulty criterion measures (and we do not have to do so because assessment center researchers have used good ones); it does mean that researchers in this area have dealt with the thorny issue of criterion measurement as effectively as other researchers

Table 9.4
Validity of Assessment Centers in Relation to Different Criteria

Type of Criterion	Estimated Validity
Performance	.36
Potential rating	.53
Dimension ratings	.33
Training performance	.35
Career progress	.36

Source: Gaugler et al., (1987).

in other areas of industrial psychology and human resource management.

In summary, subtle contaminations may be present in some criterion ratings, and when present, will probably inflate validity coefficients. At the same time, assessor judgments have predicted a variety of criteria, including ones that are *not* subject to subtle contaminations.

A second weakness of the subtle criterion contamination argument is that a variety of assessors have been used in assessment centers—not just higher-level managers from within the organization. Assessment center staffs have included human resource managers, industrial and organizational psychologists, clinical and counseling psychologists, management consultants, and groups of managers from outside the organization. Even though there is not enough evidence to prove that all of these sources provide equally accurate predictions, some comparisons between types of assessors have been made. Studies have shown that assessment centers using psychologists are just as predictive as centers using managers; when both groups are used, the accuracy is even higher (Gaugler et al., 1987).

A third argument against the subtle criterion contamination hypothesis is that managers who supposedly hold the stereotype of what is a "good manager" cannot seem to make accurate predictions of managerial success without the aid of the assessment center process. There is virtually no evidence that performance appraisal ratings and predictions of success by managers who supervise the candidates can also predict success in higher levels of management (Bernardin & Beatty, 1984; McEvoy & Beatty, 1988; Murphy & Cleveland, 1991). Management's inability to identify personnel with potential for managerial success is what often leads organizations to turn to the assessment center method in the first place (Byham, 1970).

Self-fulfilling Prophecy

There is evidence to support the idea that expectations held by supervisors about employees' performance can have powerful effects on the employees' self-confidence and subsequent job performance (Eden, 1990). The complex process whereby these expectations influence employee performance is less clear. According to one explanation, called the "Pygmalion effect" (Eden, 1984), if the supervisor is led to expect that a subordinate is highly qualified, then the supervisor treats that subordinate in special ways that lead to increased performance. In another process, when the individual himself or herself is told about perceived special talents, that person feels more competent and performs better. Eden (1988, 1990) has provided excellent summaries of studies that have demonstrated these effects in organizational settings and has speculated that similar processes may operate in assessment centers. Turnage and Muchinski (1984) also speculated that the Pygmalion effect may be operating in assessment centers but provided no data. I would say that it is certainly worthy of consideration, and in a practical setting I would try to enhance self-confidence among assessment center participants.

There is clear evidence that the self-fulfilling prophecy phenomenon does not account for much of the effectiveness of assessment centers (Thornton & Byham, 1982). In fact, research evidence shows that predictive accuracy exists when no feedback is given to the participants themselves or to the immediate supervisor (Gaugler et al., 1987). Thus, while participants' expectations about their own competencies may influence performance, studies of assessment center predictions have been conducted when no feedback was provided to alter those expectations, and still the assessment center ratings predicted future success.

Performance Consistency

The first contention here is that the assessors make predictions of future performance based on knowledge of past performance gleaned from the background interview or from the candidates' work record. Such information may enhance predictions, but many assessment centers are conducted in which the assessors do not know the names or backgrounds of the participants; in fact, participants often wear colored arm bands so that their identities are kept secret. This practice perpetuates a long-standing procedure initiated in the studies by the Office of Strategic Service to select espionage agents (Office of Strategic Services, 1948).

The second contention in the performance consistency argument implies that behavior in situational exercises predicts future behavior on the job, and therefore there is no need to make further judgments about attributes or dimensions. Although none of the proponents of this view have described how an alternative practice that did not involve attribute dimensions would actually be carried out, two possibilities seem logical. Assessors could be asked (1) to rate overall performance in each exercise or (2) to sort behaviors into some other logical categories, such as tasks. The first technique has been used; the research evidence on overall exercise ratings was reviewed in Chapter 6. The conclusion was that consistent and accurate ratings can be obtained, but overall exercise ratings are no more consistent and no more predictive of subsequent performance on the job than dimension ratings. This evidence by itself neither refutes or supports the performance consistency argument, because all these assessment centers used human attributes as the guiding principle for job analysis, exercise design, assessor training, and categories for observation and judgment. More importantly, there is no example of an assessment center conducted solely on the basis of exercise ratings, without the use of attribute dimensions as the framework for assessors' observations. Thus, we are left with only speculation that this alternative is an effective procedure.

There *is* evidence that the combination of exercise ratings and dimension ratings correlates more highly with managerial success than either set of ratings alone (Wollowick & McNamara, 1969). Thus, it seems inappropriate to recommend dropping dimension ratings and certainly premature to adopt some other procedure until research evidence is provided.

While there is no evidence in an applied assessment setting that task categories provide a meaningful way to organize behavioral observations, an experimental test of the effectiveness of task ratings was conducted by Adams (1990). She found that there was no difference in the accuracy of ratings using task categories in comparison with attribute categories, although ratings of task categories increased the recall of specific behaviors. More research along these lines is clearly warranted.

Managerial Intelligence

There is no doubt that managerial tasks require intellectual abilities. Aptitude or intelligence tests consistently predict success in managerial positions, and these tests correlate with performance in assessment centers (Klimoski & Brickner, 1987; Thornton & Byham, 1982). The real issue is whether situational exercises measure anything over and above what can be obtained with intelligence tests alone. Again, the Wollowick and McNamara (1969) study showed that they do. They found that the combination of test scores and ratings of dimensions predicted progress more accurately than either the tests or ratings alone. We can conclude that both intelligence test scores and dimension ratings from exercises are predictive of managerial success.

Summary

There is an element of truth in each of the alternative explanations of why assessment centers work, but no *one* of the explanations is totally adequate in explaining assessment center accuracy. At the same time, a review of assessment center research reveals considerable evidence to refute each of the alternative explanations. There is certainly *not* enough evidence to favor one of the alternative explanations over the traditional explanation. In fact, in my opinion, the preponderance of evidence supports the notion that assessment centers work because assessors can and do observe behaviors displayed in situational exercises, classify those behaviors into meaningful categories representing human attributes, make judgments of overall performance, and accurately predict meaningful measures of managerial performance.

The Utility of Assessment Centers: Comparing Benefits and Costs

A human resource management procedure has *utility* if the benefits from the technique exceed the costs by some significant amount. Utility is a way of thinking (Cascio, 1982) about the various costs and benefits that result from the use of a selection or training procedure. Whereas *validity* evidence tells us the extent to which the test correlates with measures of job performance, *utility* tells whether job performance improvements in employees selected using the new assessment procedure are enough to justify the costs of administering the test. Utility analysis requires that we compare the new test with the organization's existing selection procedure to demonstrate that there is some improvement in the benefit/cost ratio.

The most valuable innovation of utility analysis is the ability to express the value of the selection procedure in economic terms. Recent techniques in utility analysis allow us to derive a precise estimate of the benefit of the improved procedure in dollar amounts.

There are many ways that utility analysis can be conducted (Boudreau, 1983; Cascio, 1982, 1987). We will use a formula given by Schmidt, Hunter, McKenzie, & Muldrow (1979) because it shows most clearly the essential ingredients of utility analysis. In addition, this method has been widely used to evaluate personnel selection procedures, including assessment centers. With this method, utility is measured with the following formula:

$$U = t\ Ns\ (r1 - r2)\ SDy\ L\ /\ SR - Ns\ (c1 - c2)\ /SR$$

where t = average tenure of selected people, Ns = the number selected, r1 = validity of the new procedure, r2 = validity of the old procedure, SDy = unrestricted standard deviation in performance in dollar terms, L = ordinate of the normal curve at the selection ratio (a technical term that need not be explained here), SR = selection ratio (i.e., the ratio of the number of people hired to the number of applicants), c1 = cost of new method, and c2 = cost of old method.

The key ingredients of the utility analyses (using slight variations of the utility formula above) from assessment center studies by Cascio and Ramos (1986) and Burke and Frederick (1986) are presented in Table 9.5. In both cases, an assessment center was compared with an interviewing process for selecting managers, because that was the selection method used previously. A high level of utility is demonstrated: the economic gain from the use of the assessment center is at least $2,500 per selectee per year, and can be as high as $21,000 per selectee per year. What

Table 9.5
Results of Two Utility Studies of Assessment Centers

Key Variables	Cascio & Ramos		Burke & Frederick	
	Interview	Assessment Center	Interview	Assessment Center
Validity	.13	.388	.16	.59
Cost per assessee	$300	$688	$383	$2000
Standard deviation of job performance (SDy)	$10,081		$12,789 to 38,333	
Utility (gain per selectee per year)	$2,676		$2,538 to 21,222	

this means is that, even though the assessment center is more expensive than the interview, the benefits of better prediction far outweigh these higher costs. Investments in the more accurate procedure pay off in economic returns. Before we can accept these figures, we must evaluate the credibility of the numbers put into these utility formulae.

Validity Estimates

The validity figures of the assessment centers in these studies are very reasonable and may in fact be too low. In the Cascio and Ramos study, the validity was .388, a value corresponding very closely with the estimate of the average validity found in the analyses reviewed in Chapter 7 and earlier in this chapter. The estimate of .59 in Burke and Frederick is higher, but within the range of validities reported in Thornton and Byham (1982) and Gaugler et al. (1987). In other words, .59 is a high figure, but validities at this level were found in other research studies, and we have some evidence about what factors lead to higher validity.

Another reason to speculate that these validity estimates may be too low is the evidence that the predictive accuracy of assessment centers increases over time. The practical reality of conducting research in organizations dictates that criterion data are collected between a few months and a couple years after the assessments have been made; it is very difficult to wait much longer to gather the success measures. Thus, most of the studies of predictive accuracy cover a relatively short time span. A few organizations have checked the accuracy of predictions over longer periods and found that predictive accuracy improves with time. We saw one example of this pattern in Table 9.2, where the assessments at AT&T were more accurate after eight years and sixteen years than at earlier points in time. IBM has also found that its assessment centers are more accurate over time. Using level of management as the criterion, Wolfson (1988) reported that the predictive accuracy for people assessed in 1984 or earlier was .29, for people assessed in 1982 or earlier was .31, and for those assessed in 1980 or earlier was .37.

Validity of Alternative Procedures

Both the Cascio and Ramos and the Burke and Frederick utility studies involve a comparison of the assessment center with a background interview, the procedure that was used traditionally in these organizations. The assumed validities of the interview were .13 and .16, average validities found in reviews of the literature at the time of the studies. These estimates of the validity of the interview may be lower than the validity of the interview process when it is carried out in a structured, systematic, and standardized manner. Recent reviews (Harris, 1989; Weisner & Cronshaw, 1988) now suggest that the interview can be as accurate as an assessment center, but many organizations start up an assessment center because they find their interviewing process is not effective in identifying effective managers. If the interview process is more accurate than the ones studied in Table 9.5, the utility of the assessment centers will be lower than the estimates reported here.

Another comparison might be made between assessment centers and aptitude tests. Research findings are inconsistent: one review (Schmitt et al., 1984) suggested that assessment centers were more predictive of job performance than aptitude tests, whereas another review (Hunter & Hunter, 1984) concluded that aptitude tests had predictive accuracy greater than our estimate for assessment centers. Looking across these and other studies, it appears that aptitude tests have an average validity that is about the same as assessment centers. Because of this, and because they are less costly, they might appear to be preferable. The problem with this conclusion is that there is very little variability in the validities of aptitude tests (Murphy, 1988). By contrast, we have seen that the accuracy of a well-designed and well-executed assessment center can be much higher.

There are several other arguments that can be given for using the assessment center method. First, paper-and-pencil tests are often not as acceptable as assessment centers to candidates or managers as the basis for making decisions about selection or promotion. Candidates often feel that they do not have a chance to show relevant abilities on aptitude tests. In essence, the tests do not have the "face validity" of situational tests. Furthermore, some applicants believe they do not have control over the outcome of aptitude tests, whereas they believe they can do something to prepare for situational tests and improve the skills required to perform well on them.

Another reason for not using aptitude tests, even though they may be just as valid and less costly, is that many people believe that such tests are unfair to minorities and women. Even though this perception may not be accurate—in fact, aptitude tests do not show differential validity or biased prediction of job success (Hartigan & Widgor, 1989; Schmidt, 1988)—the perception of unfairness is very powerful. Organizations often want to avoid the difficulties of defending an unpopular human resource management procedure, if possible. Because the assessment center method is *perceived* as unbiased, it provides a desirable alternative. Equally important is the evidence that assessment centers have been shown to be fair to minorities and women (Huck & Bray, 1976; Thornton & Byham, 1982).

A final argument for using an assessment center over paper-and-pencil tests is that the results can be much more helpful in understanding the candidates' individual strengths and weaknesses related to placement and later supervision on the job. The rich behavioral information is helpful in understanding how the person will react on the job. By contrast, results of aptitude tests usually give only one or two scores that are not very helpful in this regard.

Costs

An examination of costs in the utility analyses for assessment centers shows, at the low end, just "out-of-pocket" costs for materials, meals, etc. At the high end, the cost includes developing and running the program. The costs of participants' and assessors' time is often omitted because the assessment experience can be considered training for all participants. Thus, the salary expenses are balanced by training benefits and need not be included in the utility formula, which deals only with payoffs from better selection. While there may be some debate about the actual costs to include in the analysis, research by Cascio and Silby (1979) showed that utility results for assessment centers are not very sensitive to the cost figures, in other words, widely different cost figures do not have much influence on final utility figures. These results are not intuitively obvious, but they make sense when the relatively small costs of assessment (e.g., a few hundred dollars) are compared to the very great economic benefits of sound judgment coming from effective managers (e.g., cost savings of thousands of dollars).

Variation in Job Performance: SDy

By contrast, utility analysis is highly sensitive to the value used for SDy, the standard deviation of job performance expressed in dollar terms. SDy is an estimate of the monetary differences in job performance between more effective and less effective managers in the target position. The rationale for this part of the utility analysis can be understood more clearly with an example. If every sales clerk sells about the same amount of merchandise, then the variation in job performance (SDy) is small. By contrast, if some sales clerks sell thousands of dollars' worth of merchandise while others sell only hundreds of dollars' worth, then the variation in job performance (SDy) is large, and a new, more accurate selection procedure will probably have utility for the organization.

Objective measures of the economic effects of variation in job performance are difficult to obtain. Fortunately, the various methods of estimating SDy give approximately the same results (Burke & Frederick, 1986; Reilly & Smither, 1985; Weekly, O'Conner, Frank, & Peters, 1985). Thus, we can have confidence in the overall results of these utility analyses. The Burke and Frederick study (1986) is helpful because a range of SDy figures was included in the study, and we can see the effects on the utility results. Even if we use the lowest estimate of SDy, we can see that the assessment center clearly is a good investment. The payoff is at least $2,500 dollars per year for each manager selected with the assessment center method and may be as great as $21,000 per year per manager.

Other utility studies have been carried out with very similar results. Hogan and Zenke (1986) found that the dollar-value gain for the assessment center for selecting school principals was $58,000. Huck (1987) found that the utility of an assessment center for selecting 29 managers out of 132 candidates was $554,000, translating into a return on investment of 210 percent. Feltham (1988a) found that the utility of an assessment center in England was £550,000 (approximately $1,000,000). Finally, Goldsmith (1989) compared three procedures used to select first-line supervisors in the nuclear division of a public utility: (1) a paper-and-pencil test of judgment combined with autobiographical information (validity = .30); (2) an assessment center (validity = .43); (3) an assessment center combined with two interviews, reference checks, and procedure number one (validity = .55). The utility of the assessment center as opposed to procedure number one was $1,744,445, and the utility of procedure number three as opposed to number one was $9,205,639. We can see the increased benefit from gathering additional valid information. The wide variation in utility figures is a result of studying different types of jobs and different criteria, but the conclusion is clear: assessment centers are sound economic investments.

Other Benefits of Assessment Centers

The utility analyses discussed in the preceding sections show that the economic payoff from selecting better managers far outweighs the additional costs incurred with the assessment center method. However, the utility of an assessment center is even greater because these analyses consider only the primary benefits of selecting better managers. There are many secondary benefits that come from implementing the assessment center method.

Participants learn more from the assessment center experience than from paper-and-pencil tests or one-on-one interviews. In an assessment center, participants gain insights into their own styles of behavior and can observe the ways in which other participants handle the same situations. These benefits come even in a selection or promotion program, where there are no formal training activities. Participants also benefit from the feedback they receive at the end of the program. Even with the often limited feedback that accompanies a selection or promotion program, participants learn how the assessors evaluate their decision-making and interaction styles. And although no formal follow-up activities may be planned to remediate deficiencies, individuals can use the results to launch their own self-improvement plans.

Assessors also benefit from their service on an assessment center staff. Through the assessor training and through their interactions with other assessors, individuals learn many valuable lessons about management, principles of behavioral observation, standards for evaluating subordinates, and successful decision-making techniques. Assessors themselves report that the experience is beneficial (Thornton & Byham, 1982), and, more importantly, research has shown that assessors learn new skills (Lorenzo, 1984). Lorenzo found that, compared to a control group of managers who had no assessor training or experience, the experimental group of managers who were given assessor training and served as assessors for three months showed better skills in interviewing to obtain information, in evaluating that information, and in verbally communicating and defending the information.

Curiously, other research has shown that service as an assessor in a lower-level assessment center program did not make managers more effective as participants in a higher-level assessment center program (Struth, Frank, & Amato, 1980). The authors offer several possible explanations for the lack of advantage in the higher-level program: different skills were being assessed in the higher-level program; the managers did not assess highly because they were being compared with truly outstanding participants in the higher-level program; or the managers learned valuable skills from their participation as assessors, but not the skills needed in the higher-level assessment program.

Setting up an assessment center can have additional benefits to the organization far beyond those mentioned. Alon (1977) has pointed out that there were many positive effects on his organization following the assessment center. Working together on the definitions of dimensions and the assessment of candidates led to a better "alignment of perspectives among all levels of management regarding a model of supermarket store manager" (p. 229). Managers learned from each other about the behavior that contributes to the effective operation of the entire organization, thereby furthering the development of the company itself.

Summary and Conclusions

The assessment center method has shown high levels of predictive accuracy in relation to a variety of indicators of managerial performance and success. There is little question that a well-designed assessment center will help an organization identify individuals with a high level of potential for managerial success. In addition, the assessment of strengths and weaknesses in managerial competencies can form the basis of human resource management programs to diagnose training needs, plan developmental actions, train managers, and build effective management teams.

The assessment center method is complex, and we are still learning about what attributes it actually measures. As with any test or measurement procedure, our understanding of its strengths and weaknesses is constantly changing as evidence accumulates. There has been much speculation about what assessment centers actually measure, but no substantial, direct evidence to support any of the alternatives has been put forth. Thus, the traditional explanation of why assessment centers work seems most defensible. Assessors observe behavior, classify behavior into meaningful categories representing human attributes, and derive overall assessment ratings. Even though critics can marshal some evidence that one of the alternative explanations is partially tenable, that evidence is not adequate to overturn the traditional explanation. Dimensions, in the form of human attributes, provide a useful basis for many aspects of the assessment center method, such as describing job requirements, guiding the design of exercises, helping to train assessors, providing mental frameworks for the observation and rating of behavior, and giving feedback to participants and their supervisors. My recommendation is to continue using human attributes as the basis for assessment center operations.

Assessment centers are expensive, but worth it. The costs of developing, implementing, and maintaining an assessment center can be large, especially if the time of participants and assessors is included. But the benefits far outweigh the costs. Economic analyses have clearly demonstrated the payoff of a well-run assessment center in terms of better selection of managers. In addition, there are many other benefits from an assessment center that do not come with testing or interviewing programs. Participants gain insights into managerial competencies, and assessors learn skills relevant to management. Both groups see the assessment process as relevant and fair in comparison with other human resource management practices for management evaluation.

10

The Future of Assessment Centers

Assessment centers have made many valuable contributions to the selection and development of personnel over the past forty years. In Chapter 1 we saw examples of how assessment centers have been used for several different human resource management purposes, including managerial selection, promotion, diagnosis of development needs, and management training. In later chapters we looked at the wide variety of ways that assessment centers can be designed and implemented. Our review to this point suggests that these assessment center applications are based on sound theories of decision making and social judgment. In addition, the empirical research evidence provides substantial support for the predictive accuracy of assessments of managerial competence and long-range potential for management success.

While there is much evidence to support the assessment center method, there have also been serious questions raised about what the method really measures and whether it is worth the expense. Critics often cite evidence that brings into question three key points: the ability of assessors to make judgments about separate dimensions of managerial effectiveness, the need for the integration discussion among assessors, and the effectiveness of the assessment center method in comparison with other assessment methods, such as tests and interviews.

In summary, there is currently strong debate about several issues with regard to the assessment center method. In this chapter, we will review some of the current trends and make some predictions about the future of assessment centers. But first we will take a brief look at where the assessment center method stands in the present.

Response to Assessment Centers

One way of understanding the status of assessment centers is to examine how various groups presently evaluate the method. The next sections examine reactions of participants, assessors, unions, and the courts.

Response by Participants

Numerous surveys (e.g., Dodd, 1977; Fleenor, 1988; Teel & Dubois, 1983; Thornton & Byham, 1981) of participants who have gone through an assessment center show that they respond quite favorably to the procedure. Typical findings show that: participants believe the exercises measure relevant managerial qualities and provide a fair chance to exhibit job-related skills; participants perceive the exercises as difficult and challenging, but even though they feel stress throughout the program, they see the pressures as realistic and reasonable; the majority report they understand the feedback and believe it will be useful for development; and overall endorsement of the assessment process is high and most participants would recommend it to a colleague.

Response by Assessors

Similar survey research with managers who have served as assessors has shown that they have equally positive reactions: they find the assessor training helpful as a means of learning about managerial performance dimensions as well as sharpening their observation and evaluation skills; serving as an assessor is time-consuming and stressful (and assessors seldom get complete relief from their regular job duties), but they believe the experience is worth the effort; and the skills they learn as assessors transfer to their job duties.

One potential problem with long-standing assessment center programs is that assessors can get "stale" after serving on several programs over a period of many months (Jeanneret, 1989). In such situations, human resource staff members must guard against any unwarranted modifications of standard assessment center procedures, for example, not taking adequate notes or failing to thoroughly discuss differences in ratings to reach consensus. The accuracy of an assessment center can be undermined if the program is implemented in an unstandardized way.

Response from Unions

Selection and promotion decisions have traditionally been a prerogative of management and have fallen outside the realm of negotiations with labor unions. More recently, organizations have seen the value of involving unions in a wider variety of decision making about management functions. The Team Columbus Project (1990) provides an exciting example of a joint union-management effort to design and implement an assessment center to select team players and team leaders in a new manufacturing organization. In this project, McDonnell Douglas and the International United Automobile Workers worked together to select the staff members for a new aerospace facility. Joint efforts on the assessment center were just one part of a broader, cooperative plan to revitalize the operation. Union members, trained as assessors, worked with members of management to design two different assessment centers—one for manufacturing employees and one for first-level supervisors. This group operated as a self-managing team in the design, implementation, and evaluation of the new selection efforts. The union representatives reported that the collaborative efforts in the assessment center led to better understanding between the parties, feelings of trust rather than antagonism, development of skills, and pride of ownership in the new organization. In addition, the team experienced a reduction in turnover rates, less absenteeism, and no grievances after the assessment center program was implemented. Of course, these improvements cannot all be attributed to the assessment center; other concurrent changes in the organization also contributed to these outcomes.

Response from the Courts

The assessment center method has been a part of personnel selection procedures that have been challenged in court cases alleging unfair discrimination. Most of these cases have been in the public sector and have involved promotional examinations in police and fire departments. While the issues have varied somewhat from one situation to another, the common complaints by plaintiffs have been that the assessment centers were not job-relevant, were administered in an inconsistent manner, and were biased against racial minorities.

The first ten cases appeared in the 1970s; the results were summarized in Thornton and Byham (1981). At that time, Thornton and Byham reported that the assessment center had successfully weathered these challenges; there was no instance where the court ruled against the assessment center method. The successful defense was due in large part to the extensive research evidence behind the assessment center method, including job analyses, empirical evidence that the method provided consistent and accurate evaluations, evidence that the method is fair to minorities and women, and tight controls to ensure administrative consistency.

New court cases involving assessment centers have arisen in recent years. In 1985, the assessment center used by the City of Omaha (Mendenhall, 1989) to select police sergeants was challenged in much the same way as it had been in 1975. Once again, the use of the assessment center was upheld by the court. The city won the case because it demonstrated that all assessors had been trained thoroughly, that all exercises were administered in a standardized fashion, that behavioral observations had been made and recorded on standard forms, and that, even though multiple assessors did not observe every exercise, role players in two of the exercises provided input to the evaluations. Equally important, the city provided data to demonstrate agreement among individual assessors, and among different assessor teams, in the evaluation of exercise performance.

Burroughs and Cook (1990) reported the ruling of the U.S. District Court in Florida, which supported the procedures and techniques comprising the traditional assessment center method. Metropolitan Dade County entered a consent decree with the Progressive Officers Club, Inc., to use an assessment center, along with tests and other procedures, to select police officers for promotion to the rank of lieutenant. Several minority sergeants and the police association later charged that the assessment center itself was invalid and discriminatory. The court ruled that (1) there was no disproportionate rejection of blacks from the assessment center, (2) the assessment center was justified by business necessity, (3) only observable work behaviors were being tested, (4) the managerial skills being assessed could not be learned in a brief on-the-job training (thus were appropriate for assessment), (5) evidence that the exercises were representative of major activities supported the job-relatedness of the assessment center, and (6) on-the-job performance evaluations of work as a sergeant did not provide a viable alternative for selecting the best candidates.

These cases show that the courts have been supportive of the assessment center method when it is carried out carefully, as prescribed by the *Guidelines and Ethical Considerations for Assessment Center Operations* (Task Force, 1989). In addition, the cases provide support for the belief that the assessment center method can survive the scrutiny of the courts, where plaintiffs' expert witnesses challenge many aspects of the selection procedure. In no case has a court ruled against an organization using an assessment center.

Why Assessment Centers Fail

Over the past twenty years I have been involved with numerous assessment centers. During that period I have planned, initiated, implemented, conducted, observed, consulted on, evaluated, and listened to stories about many assessment centers. I have seen a number of assessment centers fail, and I have learned a great deal from those experiences. I believe there are several possible reasons why assessment centers fail.

Some assessment centers fail before they ever get started— mostly because of poor planning. In some cases, the appropriate people are not involved in the preliminary discussions. In others, not enough care is taken to enlist the support of upper-level management. Occasionally, shifts in personnel leave no one to champion the idea of an assessment center, and plans for it are never acted upon. In still other cases, the assessment center is not the appropriate solution to the human resource problem, and it is simply not adopted.

Some assessment centers are never implemented because the preliminary work was more burdensome than the organization had anticipated. During the job analysis or exercise development work, the organization sometimes decides these efforts are too time-consuming. In one case, a union strike required that managers spend time on operational matters, and the developmental work for an assessment center was suspended and never started again.

In other organizations, the assessor training is the breaking point. In one instance, the assessors realized how much work would be involved and decided it was too much. In another assessor training program at a large hospital, the "participant" (an administrative intern from a local university) argued aggressively about the practice feedback and the assessors got frightened off.

Other assessment centers fail because the results are misused or not used at all. A common problem is that the findings from a diagnostic or developmental program are used to make promotion decisions. The credibility of subsequent efforts is therefore destroyed. In one program, nothing was done with the results. The organization ran the assessment center, identified talented people and developmental needs, but then did not follow up on the results. Participation in the assessment center created expectations among the employees; however, since the organization did nothing to respond to those expectations, there was widespread dissatisfaction. Of course, this was a criticism of the support system surrounding the assessment center, not the assessment center itself. Human resource managers can learn from this criticism that the assessment center techniques themselves must be embedded in a system of coordinated activities, a topic we will explore in the next section.

Some assessment centers fail because evaluations show they do not predict success, in other words, there is no demonstrated relationship between the evaluations and later performance on the job. The reason for this might be that the assessment center evaluations were faulty or that job performance was not measured accurately. In one case, the assessment center lost company support because one person who received a low assessment was hired anyway and proved quite successful on the job.

Assessment centers sometimes fail due to lack of support from senior managers in the form of time, money, facilities, and verbal endorsement. Lack of top-level support can destroy even the most well-run program. Support from key executives is important for all types of assessment centers, but especially for developmental assessment centers, which rely heavily on managerial follow-up activities. In many organizations, top executives are not very good at developing people because they have concentrated on the technical or financial success of the business. They may not see the need for special diagnostic and training efforts, and they may not know how to use the results of the assessment program. On occasion, some top managers fear that the identification of "developmental needs" will be interpreted by others as serious weaknesses or deficiencies, and fail to use the results. As a consequence, middle-level managers serving as assessors may become discouraged about the usefulness of the assessment center. If top executives do not recognize and reward good performance by the assessors, sanctioning, by default, poor performance, the assessment staff will begin to believe that the program is not valued and become lax in their duties. One result of this problem is that assessors take shortcuts and produce poor quality reports and feedback.

Jeanneret (1989) provided an excellent case study summarizing many thoughts on how *not* to run an assessment center. In the case study, the same assessors were used repeatedly over a long period of time and became "stale." The same exercises were used for several years, and their content leaked out. Subsequent participants were coached by their peers on how to behave *before* they participated in the exercises. Assessors worked with participants on the job, and this may have led to some upward or downward biases in evaluations. The job requirements for the target job changed but these changes were not reflected in dimensions or exercises. Finally, feedback was either poorly given or nonexistent. It is no wonder that this assessment center did not compare favorably with an individual assessment procedure that was later set up in the company.

Conducting Successful Assessment Centers

In order to avoid many of the problems enumerated above, two general strategic principles should guide the human resource manager in the development and implementation of an assessment center: (1) the assessment center must be technically sound, and (2) the assessment center must be used with complementary programs so as to fit with the larger human resource system in the organization. It is surprising that applications of the assessment center method do not always follow these principles, as they are well articulated in the *Guidelines and Ethical Considerations for Assessment Center Operations* (Task Force, 1989) and in many professional articles and books on the subject.

Building a Sound Assessment Center

The practical details of designing and running an assessment center are far beyond the scope and purpose of this book. For the purposes of this book, I can only summarize by stating that developing a good assessment center involves philosophical work, technological work, and administrative work. The philosophical work involves writing a clear statement of the purposes of the program and the policies that will govern its operation. According to the *Guidelines*, the policy statement should address the following points: the objectives of the assessment center, who will be assessed and how they will be selected, who will be the assessors and how they will be trained and certified, how assessment reports will be used and who will have access to them, and how the program will be evaluated. In addition, writing a brochure to distribute to prospective participants will sharpen the organization's thinking about the assessment center. The *Guidelines* state that the organization is obligated to inform participants about what the program entails prior to the assessment center. The following information should be provided: the objectives of the center, procedures for selecting participants, alternatives to participation and consequences of not participating, the composition of the assessor team and how assessors will be trained, materials to be used, how results will be used, feedback procedures, opportunities for reassessment, who has access to reports, and who is responsible for administering the program.

The technological work includes conducting careful job analyses, selecting the right dimensions, designing exercises, preparing supporting materials, and training assessors. This book discusses many critical issues affecting these efforts. The interested reader can obtain details from "how-to" books cited in earlier chapters.

The administrative work of running an assessment center is critical to its success. Many details of operations must be carefully planned, including location of the center, materials used, and schedules. A human resource manager in charge of an assessment center can gain valuable tips on its operation by obtaining training from a consultant specializing in assessment center programs, by attending the International Congress on the Assessment Center Method (which always has a mixture of presentations on practice, research, and theory of assessment), or by visiting an organization that currently operates an assessment center.

Embedding the Assessment Center in the Human Resource System

The second strategic principle guiding the success of an assessment center is to ensure that is part of a well-coordinated system of human resource practices. No assessment center can stand alone in an organization, and each one must be an integrated part of the larger human resource management system. This principle applies to all types of assessment centers, especially when they are used for promotion, diagnosis, or training.

Promotion Programs. A promotional assessment center should be just one part of a set of procedures that assess the qualifications needed for success in higher-level positions. Other assessment procedures might include a review of credentials and previous experience by the human resource department, appraisal of performance on the current job by the immediate supervisor, a set of tests to measure basic skills and knowledge, an interview by a human resource specialist, an interview by a manager in the hiring unit, and a medical examination. Thornton and Byham (1982) have described how an entire system of personnel activities can be built around a list of well-defined dimensions of job effectiveness. Any one dimension should be assessed by more than one procedure, for example, oral communication skills might be assessed in several interviews, the performance appraisal, and the assessment center, whereas delegation abilities might be assessed only in the assessment center and in the interview with the hiring department. This sort of approach works if there is a written plan for gathering coordinated pieces of assessment information.

Diagnostic and Development Programs. A diagnostic assessment center should be just the first step in a well-planned system to identify training needs, carry out developmental planning, and conduct actual training. For many years, Kodak's Colorado Division used such a system for three levels of managers: nonsupervisory managers in technical and administrative positions (e.g., engineers and accountants), first-level supervisors, and second-level department heads. The system included an assessment center, a career-planning activity, multiple feedback sessions, a developmental planning activity, training in coaching skills for managers, and a revised performance appraisal in which managers were evaluated on their accomplishments in developing their staff members.

The assessment center followed the traditional pattern described in this book. Specific dimensions and exercises were somewhat different for the three levels of personnel. The career-planning activity was a two-hour session at the end of the assessment exercise. It involved short presentations by a consultant, discussion among groups of managers, and worksheets to help the participants understand their own strengths and weaknesses, identify alternative career paths, and lay out steps to achieve career goals. The program was designed to show participants that they could take charge of their own careers and take steps to improve their skills. One goal was to get them ready to receive the assessment center feedback. Feedback then followed the pattern described in Chapter 8, first with the participant alone, and then with the participant and his or her manager.

Participants and their immediate supervisors used feedback from the assessment center and information about job performance to fill out a development planning booklet. They chose three or four dimensions for follow-up work. For each dimension needing improvement, a developmental plan was set forth, as illustrated in Figure 10.1. To improve on the dimension "Initiative," for example, the participant and her supervisor listed the specific area to be developed: "actively seek new business—rather than wait for client departments to call." They also listed actions to be taken, such as "make regular contacts" and "set priorities," along with the specifics of what would be done and with whom. The plan included statements of how and when the participant and her manager would determine progress. The purpose of the booklet was to help the participant and the supervisor translate the assessment center evaluations into concrete plans for development.

Like many other organizations, Kodak found that participants' supervisors needed help in laying out plans for follow-up development activities. Some suggestions, such as attending a training program, come readily to mind, but there are many others. Kodak developed a list of readings, special job assignments, coaching activities, and off-the-job activities (e.g., participating in Toastmasters to develop presentation skills) for each of the dimensions. A valuable resource guide for developmental planners is the *Successful Manager's Handbook* written by Davis, Hellervik, and Sheard (1986).

Because much of an individual's development takes place on the job, the immediate supervisor must be a good coach. Kodak found that supervisors needed to improve their coaching skills. Therefore, the company developed a training program in coaching to support this on-the-job development of subordinates. Finally, Kodak modified its performance appraisal forms to

Figure 10.1
Supervisory Development Plan

EXAMPLE	SUPERVISORY DEVELOPMENT PLAN			

Name	*Jean Deaux*			
Supervisor's Name	*Peter Smith*			

	Supervisory Training Dates	Transition	Workshops	Performance
		3/82	*8/82*	

Development Category   *Initiative*

Specific Area for Development   *Actively seek "new business" — rather than wait for client departments to call*

Development Actions What actions will I take?	Approaches How — and with whom — do I do it?	Progress How will we determine if I'm making progress?	Review Dates	Target Date
Current Accounts *Make regular contacts*	*Plan periodic meetings* *Make more "initiating" phone calls* *Get on client department's mailing list for status reports*	*Reports on increased number of contacts* *On mailing list*	*11/82* *1/83* *3/83* *11/82*	 *3/83* *1/83*
Set priorities	*Supervisor review priorities of contacts and projects*	*- - -*	*11/82* *12/82*	
New Accounts *Find out more about client department's long-range plans*	*Meet with department management (supervisor might accompany at first)* *Get invited to planning staff meetings (supervisor may have to help arrange with client department)*	*Proposal on "how we can help you with your project" very soon (say, within 10 days) after client department announces the project*	*12/82*	*1/83*

make "development of people" a part of the evaluation of all managers. This change clarified for everyone that managers were responsible for using the assessment center results to lay out and implement a developmental plan for their subordinates.

Kodak's example shows clearly how the assessment center itself can be just one part of a more complex system of human resource programs needed to foster managerial development. Other parts of the system are targeted at the individual's motivation to take advantage of the assessment center results (the career-planning activity), the follow-up training activities (the list of resources), and the skill and motivation of the boss (coaching training and the change in the performance appraisal criteria).

Training and Organization Development Programs. An assessment center designed to train managerial skills and develop teamwork among managers needs a different system of supports. For this application, the climate of the broader organization must be compatible with the values and goals of the assessment center program. Consider an assessment center designed to teach open communications, supervisory practices that involve subordinates in decision making, and innovation and risk taking among managers. The success of even the most well-run assessment program will be short-lived if the participants return to a setting that runs on formal rules, autocratic decisions, and punishment for minor failures. The principles of the training program must be supported in other ways in the organization, for example, in statements by the chief executive officer, actions by top-level managers, dealings with unions and outside organizations, and decisions and practices in the personnel office. Changing the way an organization operates is not easy; all the burden cannot fall on an assessment center (or any other technique) used for management training.

Future Challenges

One of the predictions we can make with great confidence is that there will *not* be a decrease in the use of assessment centers in organizations throughout the United States and the world in the foreseeable future. One might think that all the challenges and questions asked about assessment centers in technical and scientific journals, practitioner journals, and the legal arena would indicate that the practice of assessment center operations will diminish. This is not the case. In fact, there are many signs that the assessment center enterprise is growing consistently:

- Numerous research articles continue to appear in professional journals;
- Programs on assessment centers continue to be presented at scientific and practitioner conventions, such as those of the Society for Industrial and Organizational Psychology, the Academy of Management, and the International Congress on the Assessment Center Method;
- The assessment center method is being used with increased frequency in public sector organizations, including city municipalities, state agencies, public school districts, and federal agencies;
- The use of assessment centers is increasing in many countries around the world, including the United States (Byham, 1986, 1989), Great Britain (Robertson & Makin, 1986), and China (Lu, 1988, 1990);
- Participation at the International Congress on the Assessment Center Method continues to grow and reached a record-high attendance level of over 250 in Toronto, Ontario, Canada, in 1991;
- A survey of over two hundred organizations (Gaugler et al., 1990) revealed that assessment centers are being used for a wide variety of purposes;
- Numerous consulting organizations throughout the United States, Europe, South Africa, Israel, and Japan specialize in designing and implementing assessment centers;
- The largest consulting organizations providing assessment center service, among them Development Dimensions International, Personnel Development Incorporated, Assessment Designs, and Electronic Selection Systems Corporation, report that their assessment business has been increasing in recent years.

All this activity, however, does not mean that the assessment center of the future will necessarily be the same as the assessment center of the past. In fact, there are many indications that some applications of the assessment center method are changing in important regards. Specifically, it appears that practitioners are taking two paths in using the method. The first path represents a continuation of the traditional approach to assessment centers. This approach is the one described in the *Guidelines* and featured in this book. We might call these "Assessment Centers" with capital letters. The second path, which we might call generically the "assessment center method," represents a set of innovations that involve one or more of the principles of the traditional Assessment Center.

What directions does the path of the innovations in the assessment center method seem to be taking? Byham (1989) pointed out that the method is being "deformalized." That is, the standard elements of an Assessment Center, required by the *Guidelines,* are being relaxed or changed to make the procedure more streamlined and flexible. Changes can be seen in the way exercises are administered, how performance is evaluated, and how observations are integrated. Administrative changes might mean that participants and assessors do not actually come together as a group. Instead, participants might engage in exercises (e.g., an in-basket or case study) at remote locations; videotapes of an oral presentation might be made; the background interview might be conducted over the telephone; and the in-basket might be administered via a computer hookup to a central location. It should be noted that this "disassembled" procedure does not permit the use of group exercises, such as the leaderless group discussions or complex business games.

Observing and scoring procedures can also be varied. For example, an assessor can watch a videotape of an oral presentation when his or her schedule permits. Alternatively, the videotapes might be sent to a central location where specially trained assessors evaluate and integrate the results. Computers are also being used to aggregate dimension ratings after the assessor uses a behavior checklist to record the behaviors he or she observed (Heine, 1989).

Further changes can be made in the process of the integration discussion. Assessors may not meet face-to-face in a formal integration discussion. Instead, they may submit reports and evaluations of performance that are compiled by a computer. The computer program can be set up to project the final dimension ratings using a formula that weights each score according to the importance of the corresponding dimension or according to the experience of the assessors in the organization. The results are then sent back to assessors, who in turn determine ratings of overall performance; these overall ratings are then compiled centrally. All of these innovations have been tried out in one or more organizations, but very little evaluation research has been conducted to prove their consistency and accuracy.

Hollenbeck (1990) reported the results of a telephone survey conducted with nine leaders in the field of assessment center methodology, in which he asked: "Where are we? How is assessment different from what it used to be?" and "Where are we going?" He found agreement on several points. These experts noted that many organizations are flattening their structure, using more participative management styles, altering the role and style of managers, and recognizing that people may move between organizations more frequently. In response, assessment centers have adapted in many ways. Hollenbeck noted eight trends:

1. Business is booming, not only in assessment centers, but in assessment in general. As a result of recent down-sizing and labor shortages, organizations face an increased need to identify effective managers.

2. In contrast to the earlier emphasis on selection in assessment practices, there has been a shift toward development. Due to labor shortages and the need to make existing staff more competent in a wider range of management skills, organizations are using assessment centers for developmental purposes.

3. "The disappearing center" was noted. Although not eliminated by any means, the traditional program, in which participants and assessors meet for three to five days, has been replaced by arrangements in which subsets of simulations are administered at separate times.

4. Assessment has become computerized and video-aided. These devices are used to present stimuli and record responses. The responses can then be viewed, evaluated, and scored later.

5. Different types of employees are being assessed. The assessment of entry-level personnel and individual (non-management) contributors has been added to the traditional assessment of managers.

6. Dimensions are being defined differently. Detailed behavioral descriptions of dimensions are replacing labels based on general traits.

7. Computerized checklists are being used as the recording format for assessors. Checklists, in turn, are compiled by a computer into dimension ratings or predictions of performance. Statistical prediction models are being used more frequently to combine assessment ratings.

8. The use of assessment centers is increasing in the public sector. (Reprinted with permission.)

Based on these trends, Hollenbeck and the experts involved in his survey made the following predictions for the future of assessment centers: more computerization, more job-specific assessment, fewer paper-and-pencil tests, more dimension-specific simulations, more technical advances in simulations, fewer actual "centers" where participants and assessors meet over a period of days, and the institution of a national "skills index" card for each participant. This last idea sounds like a farfetched, "brave new world" approach, but the governor of Michigan has proposed just such a system for state workers, in which each worker would carry a card with a list of his or her capabilities. Many ethical, professional, and technical questions come to mind and would have to be answered before we could expect wide endorsement of this proposal.

Barriers to Advancement in Assessment

In this closing section, I will identify a few of the challenges faced by the assessment center enterprise. If assessment centers are to move in the directions noted above, and if they are to help organizations deal with business challenges in the future, they must be developed and studied just as intensely as they have been in the past. This suggests a magnificent opportunity for practitioners and researchers in the human resource management field. There is concern, however, that because we have done so much evaluation research in the past, and because organizations may resist further research due to budget constraints, innovations will proliferate without solid research to determine their effectiveness.

Developmental Assessment

The clear trend seems to be toward more developmental applications of the assessment center method. Three obvious concerns arise. First, the various dimensions must be distinct enough from one another to generate results that are useful in prescribing different types of training programs. As I have emphasized throughout this book, the assessment center must be designed and implemented so as to provide final dimension ratings that measure distinct competencies. If the assessment center is supposed to measure more than five or six separate dimensions, then it must contain several exercises, the assessors must be painstakingly trained to observe and classify behaviors into conceptually distinct dimensions, and the integration discussion must allow a thorough diagnosis of performance on each dimension. With pressures to streamline the process and make it more efficient, the quality of the dimension ratings may not allow for the adequate identification of separate strengths and weaknesses.

Second, the assessment results must give clear prescriptions for development. For the results to be most effective in a development program, they must provide specifics about the kinds of follow-up training programs that will benefit the participant. In other words, the assessment team must lay out a developmental program for the individual that matches his or her specific needs and provides training in a way that suits the individual's learning styles. For example, one employee might benefit most from attending a formal seminar on a particular skill, whereas another employee might benefit from on-the-job experiences. This implies some type of relationship between the type of training and the characteristics of the individual learner (Cronbach & Snow, 1977), in which one treatment is more effective for individuals with certain characteristics and another treatment is more effective for individuals with different characteristics. Unfortunately, psychologists are not very advanced in identifying the specific combinations of training methods and individuals that work best together (Dance & Neufeld, 1988; Speece, 1990). What appears to be particularly difficult is assessing the characteristics that influence learning effectiveness. The topic of "learning styles" (Keefe, 1987) has attracted much attention but has not produced clear directions for how to measure styles and apply them in practical settings. The state of the art is even less well developed in the management training arena. In the first place, there is very little evidence available to substantiate the effectiveness of management training techniques per se (Latham, 1988). Secondly, there is even less evidence to show that a technique is more effective with certain types of managers. Much more research is needed to understand how assessment centers can diagnose participants' needs, not only in terms of their strengths and weaknesses on various dimensions, but also in terms of how follow-up training should be delivered to yield maximum benefit for the individual.

The third concern about the increased use of assessment centers for developmental purposes is that there has been little research into the effectiveness of these applications. Most of the research has dealt with the predictive accuracy of assessment centers designed for selection and promotion purposes. We cannot assume that the research showing this type of predictive accuracy means that assessment centers are useful for developmental purposes as well.

Assessing Dimensions for the "Manager of the Future"

There has been much discussion about the changes in managerial responsibilities needed to meet the demands of the 1990s and beyond (Offerman & Gowing, 1990). With changes in organizational structure and culture (Schein, 1990), global competitiveness and the changing composition of the work force (Morrison & Von Glinow, 1990), and new teamwork requirements (Sundstrom, DeMeuse, & Futrell, 1990), it follows that dimensions of managerial effectiveness will change. Dimensions such as "strategic planning," "entrepreneurialship," "ability to manage work," and "transformational leadership" have been identified as important for managerial effectiveness in the future. Now these abstract notions must be made more concrete, in the form of behaviors we can assess objectively. There is every reason to believe that simulation technology can provide the means to assess these dimensions just as effectively as they have the more traditional dimensions, such as delegation, planning and organizing, and communication skills. In fact, some assessment programs have already been developed to assess some of the more abstract dimensions. For example, the Japanese concepts of "wa" (harmony) and "kaizan" (improvement) have been the target of assessment for the selection of associates (automobile assembly-line workers) and team leaders (first-level supervisors) in joint venture organizations with Japanese companies in the United States (Henry, 1988).

This same type of innovation in assessment is needed at the executive and general management level. DeVries and White (1989) and White and DeVries (1990) have observed that the dimensions we should be assessing at the executive level are different from the attributes important at middle and lower levels. For example, strategic thinking, dealing with ambiguity and uncertainty, and developing effective teams are all necessary skills for executives. In addition, there is a set of basic beliefs, including values and attitudes, that interact with knowledge and skills to determine executive effectiveness. Assessment centers have not traditionally provided assessments of these executive-level attributes.

Studies by the Center for Creative Leadership have shown that successful executives thrive on challenge and learn from chaotic situations. Assessment centers have not evaluated the abilities to learn from experience; they are almost always "one shot" evaluations. What is needed, according to DeVries and White (1989), is some way to assess the executive periodically and to understand his or her resilience and adaptability over time. In addition, assessment centers need to assess the specific employee-to-job fit, not just the more general executive management attributes. In short, the assessment system must include a better means of placing the individuals in situations that will test, stretch, and develop them. To do this, we need better means of assessing job characteristics in relation to their developmental potential.

Continued Research Efforts

The innovations in assessment center technology are exciting and encouraging. In virtually every aspect of the assessment center method, we see extensive experimentation:

- New dimensions and revised definitions of traditional dimensions
- New exercises
- Computerized presentation of exercises
- New procedures for recording observations
- Automated methods of reporting results
- New methods for integrating results

What should concern all of us—practitioners, critics, academics, theoreticians, and observers—is the need to accumulate evidence to support these innovations. We need to know whether a seemingly small change alters the consistency and accuracy of assessment center results. The assessment center method has enjoyed its widespread success because of the extensive basic and applied research conducted by numerous large and small organizations. Will a comparable level of research be carried out to investigate the innovations?

There is reason to question this. Research units in human resource management departments have been trimmed substantially in recent years as a part of the general move to reorganize and eliminate staff positions. We have seen reductions in the number of industrial and organizational psychologists in large organizations, such as AT&T, the Bell companies, SOHIO, and General Motors—many of which have been active in assessment center research and practice. Maybe the slack will be picked up by governmental agencies, where assessment centers are thriving (Hollenbeck, 1990). There is certainly more to learn about the many innovations we are seeing in assessment center methodology.

Appendix

Guidelines and Ethical Considerations For Assessment Center Operations

Task Force on Assessment Center Guidelines
Endorsed by the Seventeenth International Congress
on the Assessment Center Method
May 17 1989—Pittsburgh, Pennsylvania

These guidelin⁀s replace the 1979 Standards and Ethical Considerations for Assessment Center Operations. The primary purpose of this document is to provide professional guidelines for users of the assessment center method. As such, these guidelines include explanations of the most important concepts common to all assessment centers and suggestions which if followed should maximize the benefits obtained from use of this method. These guidelines have been developed and endorsed by practitioners who specialize in the use of the assessment center method.

Table of Contents

Source: Published by the International Personnel Management Association, Alexandria, Virginia. Reprinted with permission.

A. Task Force Members & Organizations Who Have Contributed to These Guidelines

Task Force for 1979 Edition

Albert Alon—Miracle Food Mart (Canada)
Dale Baker—U.S. Civil Service Commission
Douglas W. Bray, Ph.D.—AT&T
William C. Byham, Ph.D.—Development Dimensions International
Steven L. Cohen, Ph.D.—Assessment Designs, Inc.
Lois A. Crooks—Educational Testing Service
Donald L. Grant, Ph.D.—University of Georgia
Milton D. Hakel, Ph.D.—Ohio State University
Lowell W. Hellervik, Ph.D.—University of Minnesota
James R. Huck, Ph.D.—Western Airlines
Cabot L. Jaffee, Ph.D.—Assessment Designs, Inc.
Frank M. McIntyre, Ph.D.—Consulting Associates
Joseph L. Moses, Ph.D. (Chairman)—AT&T
Nicky B. Schnarr—I.B.M.
Leonard W. Slivinski, Ph.D.—Public Service Commission (Canada)
Thomas E. Standing, Ph.D.—Standard Oil of Ohio
Edwin Yager—Consulting Associates

Task Force for 1989 Edition

Virginia Boehm—Assessment & Development Associates
Doug Bray (co-chair)—Development Dimensions International
William Byham—Development Dimensions International
Ann Marie Carlisi—Bell South
Jack Clancy—Clancy and Associates
Joep Esser—Mars B.V.
Reginald Ellis—Canadian National Railway
Fred Frank—Electronic Selection Systems Corp.
Ann Gowdey—Connecticut Mutual
Dennis Joiner—Joiner and Associates
Rhonda Miller—New York Power Authority
Marilyn Quaintance—Laventhol & Horwath,
    Office of Personnel Management
Robert Silzer—Personnel Decisions Inc.
George Thornton (co-chair)—Colorado State University

B. Background

The rapid growth in the use of the Assessment Center method in recent years has resulted in a proliferation of applications in a variety of organizations. Assessment Centers currently are being used in industrial, educational, military, government, and other organizational settings. Practitioners have raised serious concerns that reflect a need for standards or guidelines for users of the method. The Third International Congress on the Assessment Method Meeting (May 1975) in Quebec endorsed the first set of guidelines. These were based on the observation and experience of a representative group of professionals representing many of the largest users of the method.

Developments in the following five years concerning Federal guidelines related to testing, as well as professional experience with the original guidelines, suggested that the guidelines should be evaluated and revised. Therefore, the 1979 guidelines included the essential items from the original guidelines and changes in the direction of: 1. Further definitions, 2. Clarification of impact on organizations and participants, 3. Expanded guidelines on training, 4. Additional information on validation.

Since 1979 the use of assessment centers has spread dramatically to many different organizations assessing individuals representing widely diverse types of jobs. During this period pressures to modify the assessment center method have come from three different sources. First, there have been attempts to streamline the procedures to make them less time consuming and expensive. Second, there have been put forth theoretical arguments and empirical research evidence which some people have interpreted to mean that the assessment center method does not work as its proponents originally believed and that the method should be modified. Third, many procedures purporting to be assessment centers have not complied with previous guidelines because they were too ambiguous. Revisions in this third edition are designed to incorporate needed changes and to respond to some of the concerns raised in the last 10 years.

The current revision of these guideline was begun at the Fifteenth International Congress on the Assessment Center method (April 1987) in Boston when Dr. Douglas Bray conducted a discussion with many attendees. Subsequently, Bray and Dr. George Thornton solicited additional comments from a group of assessment center practitioners. The (1989) Task Force named above provided comments on drafts of a revision prepared by Bray and Thornton. A subsequent draft was circulated and discussed at the Sixteenth Congress in May, 1988 in Tampa.

The present guidelines were written in response to comments at the 1988 Congress and from members of the Task Force. These guidelines were endorsed by a majority of the Task Force and by participants at the Seventeenth Congress in May 1989 in Pittsburgh.

Changes from prior editions include: 1. Specification of the role of job analysis. 2. Clarification of the types of attributes to be assessed an J whether or not attributes must be used. 3. Delineation of the processes Jf observing, evaluating, and aggregating information. 4. Further specification of assessor training.

C. Purpose

This document is intended to establish professional guidelines and ethical considerations for users of the Assessment Center method. These guidelines are designed to cover both existing and future applications. The title "assessment center" is restricted to those methods which follow these guidelines.

These guidelines will provide (a) guidance to human relations specialists, Industrial/Organizational Psychologists, and others designing assessment centers, (b) information to managers deciding whether or not to institute an assessment center, and (c) instruction to assessors serving on the staff of an assessment center.

D. References

The guidelines have been developed to be compatible with the following documents:

American Educational Research Association, American Psychological Association and National Council on Measurements in Education. (1985). *Standards for educational and psychological testing*. Washington, DC: American Psychological Association, 1985.

Society for Industrial and Organizational Psychology Inc., American Psychological Association. (1987). *Principles for the validation and use of personnel selection procedures*. (Third Edition) College Park, MD: author.

E. Assessment Center Defined

An Assessment Center consists of a standardized evaluation of behavior based on multiple inputs. Multiple trained observers and techniques are used. Judgments about behavior are made, in major part, from specifically developed assessment simulations. These judgments are pooled in a meeting among the assessors or by a statistical integration process. In an integration discussion, comprehensive accounts of behavior, and often ratings of it, are pooled. The discussion results in evaluations of the performance of the assessees on the dimensions or other variables which the assessment center is designed to measure. Statistical combination methods should be validated in accord with professionally accepted guidelines.

There is a difference between an Assessment Center and assessment center methodology. Various features of the assessment center methodology are used in procedures which do not meet all of the guidelines set forth here. Such personnel assessment procedures are not covered by these standards; each should be judged on its own merits. Procedures which do not conform to all the guidelines here should not be represented as Assessment Centers or imply that they are assessment centers by using the term "assessment center" as a part of the title.

The following are the essential elements necessary for a process to be considered an Assessment Center.

1. A job analysis of relevant behaviors must be conducted to determine the dimensions, attributes, characteristics, qualities, skills, abilities, motivation, knowledge, or tasks that are necessary for effective job performance and to identify what should be evaluated by the assessment center.

The type and extent of the job analysis depends on the purpose of assessment, complexity of the job, the adequacy and appropriateness of prior information about the job, and the similarity of the new job to jobs which have been studied previously.

If past job analyses and research are used to select dimensions and exercises for a new job, evidence of the comparability of the jobs must be provided.

When the job does not currently exist, analyses can be done of actual projected tasks which will compose the new job.

2. Behavioral observations by assessors must be classified into some meaningful and relevant categories, such as dimensions, attributes, characteristics, aptitudes, qualities, skills, abilities, knowledge, or tasks.

3. The techniques used in the assessment center must be designed to provide information for evaluating the dimensions, etc. previously determined by job analysis.

4. Multiple assessment techniques must be used. These can include tests, interviews, questionnaires, sociometric devices, and simulations. The assessment techniques are developed or selected to tap a variety of behavior and information relevant to the predetermined dimensions, etc. The assessment techniques will be pretested prior to use to ensure that the techniques provide reliable, objective, and relevant behavioral information for the organization in question. Pretesting might entail trial administration with participants similar to Assessment Center candidates, thorough review by subject matter experts as to accuracy and representativeness of behavior sampling, evidence from the use of these techniques for similar jobs in similar organizations, etc.

5. The assessment techniques must include sufficient job-related simulations to allow multiple opportunities to observe the candidate's behavior related to each dimension, etc. being assessed.

A simulation is an exercise or technique designed to elicit behaviors related to dimensions, etc. of performance on the job requiring the participants to respond behaviorally to situational stimuli. Examples of simulations include group exercises, in-basket exercises, interview simulations, fact-finding exercises, etc.

If a single comprehensive assessment technique is used, then it must include distinct job related segments. For simple jobs, one or two job related simulations may be used if the job analysis clearly indicates that only one or two simulations sufficiently simulate a substantial portion of the job being evaluated.

The stimuli contained in a simulation parallel or resemble stimuli in the work situation, although they may be in different settings. The desirable degree of fidelity is a function of the purpose of the assessment center: fidelity may be relatively low for early identification and selection programs for non-managerial personnel, and may be relatively high for programs designed to diagnose training needs for experienced managers. Assessment center designers should be careful that content of the exercises does not favor certain assessees (e.g. assessees in certain ethnic, age, or sex groups) for irrelevant reasons.

6. Multiple assessors must be used for each assessee.

When selecting a group of assessors the following characteristics should be considered: diversity of ethnicity, age, gender and functional work area.

Peer-and self-assessment may be gathered as assessment information.

The maximum ratio of assessees to assessors is a function of several variables, including the type of exercises used, the dimensions sought, the roles of the assessors, the type of integration carried out, the amount of assessor training, the experience of the assessors, and the purpose of the assessment center. A typical ratio of assessees to assessors is 2 to 1. A participant's supervisor should not assess him or her in an assessment center.

7. Assessors must receive thorough training and demonstrate performance guidelines as outlined in Section G prior to participating in an assessment center.

8. Some systematic procedure must be used by assessors to record accurately specific behavioral observations at the time of their occurrence; this might involve handwritten notes, behavioral observations scales, behavioral checklists, etc.

9. Assessors must prepare some report or record of the observations made in each exercise in preparation for the integration discussion.

10. The integration of behaviors must be based on a pooling of information from assessors and from techniques at a meeting among the assessors or through a statistical integration process validated in accord with professionally accepted standards.

During the integration discussion, assessors should report information from the assessment techniques, but not information irrelevant to the purpose of the assessment process.

The integration of information may be accomplished by consensus or some other method of arriving at a joint decision. Methods of combining assessors' evaluations of information heard in the assessor discussion must be supported by research evidence showing reliable and valid aggregations of the observations.

The following kinds of activities *do not* constitute an Assessment Center.

1. Panel interviews or a series of sequential interviews as the sole technique.

2. Reliance on a single technique (regardless of whether a simulation or not) as the sole basis for evaluation. A single comprehensive assessment technique which includes distinct job related segments, i.e. large complex simulations with several definable components and with multiple opportunities for observations in different situations, are not precluded by this restriction.

3. Using only a test battery composed of a number of pencil and paper measures, regardless of whether the judgments are made by a statistical or judgmental pooling of scores.

4. Single assessor assessment, i.e. measurement by one individual using a variety of techniques such as pencil and paper tests, interviews, personality measures or simulations.

5. The use of several simulations with more than one assessor where there is no pooling of data; i.e., each assessor prepares a report on performance in an exercise, and the individual reports (unintegrated) are used as the final product of the center.

6. A physical location labeled as an "Assessment Center" which does not conform to the requirements noted above.

F. Organizational Policy Statement

Assessment Centers need to operate as a part of a human resource system. Prior to the introduction of a center into an organization, a policy statement should be prepared and approved by the organization. This policy statement should address the following areas:

1. Objective — This may be selection, diagnosis for development, early identification, affirmative action, evaluation of potential, evaluation of competency, succession planning, or any combination of these.

2. Assessees — The population to be assessed, the method for selecting assessees from this population, procedures for notification, and policy related to assessing should be specified.

3. Assessors — The assessor population (including sex and ethnic mix), limitations on use of assessors, number of times assigned, evaluation

of assessor performance and certification requirements, where applicable, should be specified.

4. **Use of Data** — The flow of assessment records, who receives reports, restrictions on access to information, procedures and controls for research and program evaluation purposes, feedback procedures to management and employee, and the length of time data will be maintained in files should be specified.

5. **Qualifications of Consultant(s) or Assessment Center Developer(s)** — The internal or external consultants responsible for the development of the center should be identified and their professional qualifications and related training listed.

6. **Validation** — There should be a statement specifying the validation model being used. If a content oriented validation strategy is used, documentation of the relationship of the job content to the dimensions and exercises should be presented along with evidence of reliability to in observation and rating of behavior. If evidence is being taken from prior validation research, which may have been summarized in meta-analyses, the organization must document that the current job and assessment center are comparable to the jobs and assessment centers studied elsewhere. If local validation has been carried out, full documentation of the study should be provided. If validation studies are underway, there should be a time schedule indicating a validation report will be available.

G. Assessor Training

Assessor training is an integral part of the Assessment Center program. Assessor training should have clearly stated training objectives and performance guidelines.

The following are some issues related to training:

1. Training Content

Whatever the approach to assessor training, the objective is obtaining reliable and accurate assessor judgments. A variety of approaches may be used, as long as it can be demonstrated that reliable and accurate assessor judgments are obtained. The following minimum training goals are required.

a. Thorough knowledge of the organization and job being assessed.

b. Thorough knowledge and understanding of the assessment techniques, relevant dimensions etc., to be observed, expected or typical behaviors, examples or samples of actual behaviors, etc.
c. Thorough knowledge and understanding of the assessment dimensions etc., definitions of dimension, relationship to job performance, examples of effective and ineffective performance.
d. Demonstrated ability to record and classify behavior in dimensions, including knowledge of forms used by the center.
e. Thorough knowledge and understanding of evaluation and rating procedures, including how data are integrated.
f. Thorough knowledge and understanding of assessment policies and practices of the organization, including restrictions on how assessment data are to be used.
g. Thorough knowledge and understanding of feedback procedures, where appropriate.
h. Demonstrated ability to give accurate oral and written feedback, when feedback is given by the assessors.
i. Demonstrated knowledge and ability to play objectively and consistently the role called for in interactive exercises, e.g. one-on-one simulations or fact-finding exercises, when this is required of assessors.

2. The length of assessor training may vary due to a variety of considerations that can be categorized into three major areas:

    a. Trainer and Instructional Design Considerations

- The instructional mode(s) utilized
- The qualifications and expertise of the trainer
- The training and instructional sequence

    b. Assessor Considerations

- Previous knowledge and experience with similar assessment techniques
- The use of professional psychologists
- Experience and familiarity with the organization and the target position(s) or target level
- The frequency of assessor participation

    c. Assessment Program Considerations

- The difficulty level of the target position
- The number of dimensions, etc. to be rated

- [ ] The anticipated use of the assessment information (immediate selection, broad placement considerations, development, etc.)
- [ ] The number and complexity of the exercises
- [ ] The division of roles and responsibilities between assessors and others on the assessment staff
- [ ] The degree of support provided assessors in the form of observation guides.

It should be noted that *length* and *quality* of training are not synonymous. Precise guidelines for the exact minimum number of hours or days required for assessor training are difficult to specify. However, extensive experience has shown that for the initial training of assessors who have no experience in an assessment center which conforms to the guidelines in this document, it is desirable to have at least two days of assessor training for each day of the administration of assessment center exercises. Assessors who have experience with similar assessment techniques in other programs may require less training so long as they meet the performance guidelines below. More complex assessment centers with varied formats of simulation exercises may require additional training.

In any event, assessor training is an important aspect of an assessment program. The true test of training quality should be provided by the performance guidelines and certification outlined below.

3. Performance Guidelines and Certification — Each Assessment Center should have clearly stated minimal-performance guidelines for assessors.

These performance guidelines should, as a minimum, include the following areas:

a. The ability to administer an exercise, if the assessor serves as exercise administrator.
b. The ability to recognize, observe, and report the behaviors measured in the center.
c. The ability to classify behaviors into the appropriate dimensions, etc.
d. The ability to rate behavior in a standardized fashion.

Some measurement is needed to indicate that the individual being trained is capable of functioning as an assessor. The measurement of assessor performance may vary and could include data in terms of (1) rating performance, (2) critiques of assessor reports, (3) observation as an evaluator, etc. It is important that, prior to their actual duties, assessor performance is evaluated to ensure that individuals are sufficiently trained to function as assessors and that such performance is periodically monitored to ensure that skills learned in training are applied.

Each organization must be able to demonstrate its assessors can meet minimal performance guidelines. This may require the development of additional training or other action for assessors not meeting these performance guidelines.

The trainer of assessors should be competent to develop the assessor skills stated above and to evaluate the acquisition of these skills.

4. Currency of Training and Experience

The time between assessor training and initial service as an assessor must not exceed 6 months. If a longer period has elapsed, a refresher course should be attended.

Assessors who do not have recent experience as an assessor (i.e. fewer than 2 assessment centers over two consecutive years), should attend a refresher course before they serve again.

H. Informed Participation

The organization is obligated to make an announcement *prior* to assessment so that participants will be fully informed about the program. While the information provided will vary across organizations, the following basic information should be given to all prospective participants.

Ideally, this information should be made available in writing prior to the center. A second option is to use the material in the opening statement of the center.

1. Objective — The objectives of the program and the purpose of the Assessment Center.

2. Selection — How individuals are selected to participate in the center.

3. Choice — Any options the individual has regarding the choice of participating in the Assessment Center as a condition of employment, advancement, development, etc.

4. Staff — General information on the assessor staff to include composition and assessor training.

5. Materials — What Assessment Center materials are collected and maintained by the organization.

6. Results — How the Assessment Center results will be used. The length of time the assessment results will be maintained on file.

7. Feedback — When and what kind of feedback will be given the participants.

8. Reassessment — The procedure for reassessment (if given).

9. Access — Who will have access to the Assessment Center reports and under what conditions.

10. Contact — Who will be the contact person responsible for the records. Where will the results be stored.

I. Validation Issues

A major factor in the widespread acceptance and use of Assessment Centers is directly related to an emphasis on sound validation research. Numerous studies demonstrating the predictive validity of individual assessment center programs have been conducted and reported in the professional literature in a variety of organizational settings.

The historical record of the validity of this process cannot be taken as a guarantee that a given assessment program will or will not be valid in a new setting.

Ascertaining the validity of an Assessment Center program is a complicated technical process, and it is important that validation research meet both professional and legal guidelines. Research should be conducted by individuals knowledgeable in the technical and legal issues pertinent to validation procedures.

In evaluating the validity of Assessment Center programs, it is particularly important to document the selection of the dimensions, etc. assessed in the center. In addition, the relationship of assessment exercises to the dimensions, attributes or qualities assessed should be documented as well.

Validity generalization studies of assessment center research suggest that overall assessment ratings derived in a manner conforming to these guidelines show considerable predictive validity. Such findings support the use of a new assessment center in a different setting if the job, exercises, assessors, and assessees in the new situation are similar to those in the validation research and similar procedures are used to observe, report, and integrate the information. The validity generalization studies of the predictive validity of the overall assessment rating do not necessarily establish the validity of the procedure for other purposes, e.g. diagnosis of training needs, accurate assessment of level of skill in separate dimensions, the developmental influence of participation in an assessment center, etc.

The technical standards and principles for validation appear in *Principles for the Validation and Use of Personnel Selection Procedures* (Society for Industrial and Organizational Psychology, Inc. 1987) and *Guidelines for Educational and Psychological Testing* (APA, 1985).

J. Rights of the Participant

In the United States the Federal Government enacted the Freedom of Information Act and Privacy Act of 1974 to ensure that certain safeguards are provided for an individual against an invasion of personal privacy. Some broad interpretations of these acts are applicable to the general use of Assessment Center data.

Assessment Center activities typically generate a volume of data on an individual who has gone through an Assessment Center. These assessment data come in many different forms, ranging from observer notes, reports on performance in the exercises, assessor ratings, peer ratings, paper and pencil tests, and final Assessment Center reports. This list, while not exhaustive, does indicate the extent of collection of information about an individual.

The following guidelines for use of these data are suggested:

1. Assessees should receive feedback on their performance at the Center and be informed of any recommendations made. Assessees who are members of the organization have a right to read any

formal summary written reports concerning their own performance and recommendations which are prepared and made available to management. Applicants to an organization should be provided at a minimum what the final recommendation is, and if possible, the reasons for the recommendation, if requested by the applicant.

2. For reasons of test security, Assessment Center exercises are exempted from disclosure, but the rationale and validity data concerning ratings of dimensions, etc., and recommendations should be made available upon request of the individual.

3. If the organization decides to use assessment results for purposes that can impact the assessees other than those originally announced, the assessees involved must be informed.

4. The organization should inform the assessee what records and data are being collected, maintained, used, and disseminated.

References

Abelson, R.P. (1981). Psychological status of the script concept. *American Psychologist, 36,* 715–729.

Adams, S.R. (1990). Impact of assessment center method and categorization scheme on schema choice and observational, classification, and memory accuracy. Unpublished doctoral dissertation, Colorado State University, Ft. Collins, CO.

Adams, S.R., & Thornton, G.C. III. (1987). *Organizational impressions: The role the selection process plays.* Unpublished manuscript.

Alba, J.W., & Hasher, L. (1983). Is memory schematic? *Psychological Bulletin, 93,* 203–231.

Alon, A. (1977). Assessment and organizational development. In J.L. Moses & W.C. Byham (Eds.), *Applying the assessment center method.* New York: Pergamon Press.

American Airlines (1976). *A preliminary report on the validity of the key manager human resources center.* Unpublished manuscript.

American Board of Professional Psychology (1988). *The assessment center procedure for the diplomate examination in clinical psychology.* Columbia, MO.

American Educational Research Association, American Psychological Association, and National Council on Measurement in Education. (1985). *Standards for educational and psychological tests.* Washington, DC: American Psychological Association.

American Psychological Association. (1981). Ethical principles of psychologists. *American Psychologist, 36,* 633–638.

Anastasi, A. (1988). *Psychological testing* (6th ed.). New York: Macmillan.

Anderson, N.H. (1974). Cognitive algebra: Integration theory applied to social attribution. In L. Berkowitz (Ed.), *Advances in experimental social psychology* (Vol. 7, pp. 1–101). New York: Academic Press.

Anderson, N.H. (1981). *Foundations of information integration theory.* New York: Academic Press.

Archambeau, D.J. (1979). Relationships among skill ratings assigned in an assessment center. *Journal of Assessment Center Technology, 2,* 7–10.

Argyris, C.F., & Schon, D. (1974). *Theory in practice.* San Francisco, CA: Jossey-Bass.

Arvey, R.D., & Faley, R.H. (1988). *Fairness in selecting employees* (2nd ed.). Reading, MA: Addison-Wesley.

Asher, J.J., & Sciarrino, J.A. (1974). Realistic work sample tests: A review. *Personnel Psychology, 27,* 519–533.

Baker, T.A. (1986). *Multitrait-multimethod analysis of performance ratings using behaviorally anchored and behavioral checklist formats.* Unpublished master's thesis, Old Dominion University, Norfolk, VA.

Bandura, A. (1977). *Social learning theory.* Englewood Cliffs, NJ: Prentice Hall.

Bandura, A. (1982). Self-efficacy mechanism in human agency. *American Psychologist, 37,* 122–147.

Bandura, A. (1986). *Social foundations of thought and action.* Englewood Cliffs, NJ: Prentice Hall.

Barker, L.I., Wahlers, K.J., Cegala, D.J., & Kibler, R.J. (1983). *Groups in process.* Englewood Cliffs, NJ: Prentice Hall.

Bass, B.M. (1950). The leaderless group discussion. *Personnel Psychology, 3,* 17–32.

Bass, B.M. (1954). The leaderless group discussion. *Psychological Bulletin, 51,* 465–492.

Beitz, C. (1985). *Executive skills assessment center for development.* U.S. Army War College.

Bender, J.M. (1973). What is "typical" of assessment centers? *Personnel, 50*(4), 50–57.

Bentz, V.J. (1967). The Sears experience in the investigation, description, and prediction of executive behavior. In F.R. Wickert & D.E. McFarland (Eds.), *Measuring executive effectiveness,* (pp. 147–205). New York: Appleton-Century-Crofts.

Bentz, V.J. (1980). *Overview of Sears research with multiple assessment techniques.* Chicago, IL: Sears

Bernardin, H.J., & Beatty, R.W. (1984). *Assessing human behavior at work.* Boston, MA: Kent.

Bernardin, H.J., & Walter, C.W. (1977). Effects of rater training and diary keeping on psychometric error in ratings. *Journal of Applied Psychology, 62,* 64–69.

Binning, J.F., & Barrett, G.V. (1989). Validity of personnel decisions: An examination of the inferential and evidential bases. *Journal of Applied Psychology, 74,* 478–494.

Boehm, V.R., & Hoyle, D.F. (1977). Assessment and management development. In J.L. Moses & W.C. Byham (Eds.), *Applying the assessment center method* (pp. 203–224). New York: Pergamon Press.

Boice, R. (1983). Observation skills. *Psychological Bulletin, 93,* 3–29.

Borman, W.C. (1977). Consistency of rating accuracy and rating errors in the judgment of human performance. *Organizational Behavior and Human Performance, 20,* 238–252.

Borman, W.C. (1978). Exploring the upper limits of reliability and validity in job performance ratings. *Journal of Applied Psychology, 63,* 135–144.

Borman, W.C. (1982). Validity of behavioral assessment for predicting recruiter performance. *Journal of Applied Psychology, 67,* 3–9.

Borman, W.C., Eaton, N.K., Bryan, J.D., & Rosse, R.L. (1983). Validity of army recruiter behavior assessment: Does the assessor make a difference? *Journal of Applied Psychology, 68,* 415–419.

Boudreau, J.W. (1983). Economic considerations in estimating the utility of human resource productivity improvement programs. *Personnel Psychology, 36,* 551–576.

Braaten, L. (1990). Can assessment add value to the selection and development of sales managers? In C.W. Stucker (Ed.), *Proceedings of the 1989 National Assessment Conference* (pp. 18–21). Minneapolis, MN: Personnel Decisions, Inc.

Brannick, M.T., Michaels, C.E., & Baker, D.P. (1989). Construct validity of in-basket scores. *Journal of Applied Psychology, 74,* 957–963.

Bray, D.W. (1964). The management progress study. *American Psychologist, 19,* 419–429.

Bray, D.W., & Campbell, R.J. (1968). Selection of salesmen by means of an assessment center. *Journal of Applied Psychology, 52,* 36–41.

Bray, D.W., Campbell, R.J., & Grant, D.L. (1974). *Formative years in business: A long-term AT&T study of managerial lives.* New York: Wiley.

Bray, D.W., & Grant, D.L. (1966). The assessment center in the measurement of potential for business management. *Psychological Monographs, 80* (17, Whole No. 625), 1–27.

Burke, M.J., & Frederick, J.T. (1986). A comparison of economic utility estimates for alternative SDy estimation procedures. *Journal of Applied Psychology, 71,* 334–339.

Burroughs, W.A., & Cook, D., Jr. (1990). Court rules on assessment center case. *The Industrial/Organizational Psychologist, 27*(3), 57–61.

Bycio, P., Alvares, K.M., & Hahn, J. (1987). Situational specificity in assessment center ratings: A confirmatory factor analysis. *Journal of Applied Psychology, 72,* 463–474.

Byham, W.C. (1970). Assessment center for spotting future managers. *Harvard Business Review, 48*(4), 150–160, plus appendix.

Byham, W.C. (1971). The assessment center as an aid in management development. *Training and Development Journal, 25* (12), 10–22.

Byham, W.C. (1977). Assessor selection and training. In J.L. Moses & W.C. Byham (Eds.), *Applying the assessment center method.* New York: Pergamon Press.

Byham, W.C. (1986). *The assessment center method and methodology: New applications and technologies* (Monograph 7). Pittsburgh, PA: Development Dimensions International.

Byham, W.C. (1989). What's new with assessment centers. In C.W. Stucker (Ed.), *Proceedings of the 1989 National Assessment Conference,* (pp. 22–25). Minneapolis, MN: Personnel Decisions, Inc.

Byham, W.C. (1990). *Dimensions of effective performance for the 1990s.* Pittsburgh, PA: Development Dimensions International.

Byham, W.C., & Temlock, S. (1972). Operational validity—a new concept in personnel testing. *Personnel Journal, 51,* 639–647, 654.

Campbell, D.T., & Fiske, D.W. (1959). Convergent and discriminant validation by the multitrait-multimethod matrix. *Psychological Bulletin, 56,* 81–105.

Campbell, J.P., Dunnette, M.D., Lawler, E.E. III, & Weick, K.E. (1970). *Managerial behavior, performance and effectiveness.* New York: McGraw-Hill.

Campbell, W.J. (1986). *Construct validation of role-playing exercises in an assessment center using BARS and behavioral checklist formats.* Unpublished master's thesis, Old Dominion University, Norfolk, VA.

Cascio, W.F. (1982). *Costing human resources: The financial impact of behavior in organizations.* Boston, MA: Kent.

Cascio, W.F. (1987). *Applied psychology in personnel management* (3rd ed.). Englewood Cliffs, NJ: Prentice Hall.

Cascio, W.F. (1989). *Assessment data and personnel decisions.* Paper presented at the 1989 National Assessment Conference, Minneapolis, MN.

Cascio, W.F., & Ramos, R.A. (1986). Development and application of a new method for assessing job performance in behavioral/economic terms. *Journal of Applied Psychology, 71,* 20–28.

Cascio, W.F., & Silbey, V. (1979). Utility of the assessment center as a selection device. *Journal of Applied Psychology, 64,* 107–118.

Caspy, T., Ben-Ari, R., & Margalit, O. (1990). Predictive validation of assessment center using various performance appraisal criteria. Unpublished manuscript.

Chaiken, S., & Stangor, C. (1987). Attitudes and attitude change. In M.R. Rosenzweig & L.W. Porter (Eds.), *Annual Review of Psychology,* (Vol. 38, pp. 575–630). Palo Alto, CA: Annual Reviews.

Cherrington, D.J. (1983). *Personnel management: The management of human resources.* Dubuque, IA: Brown.

Cochran, D.S., Hinckle, T.W., & Dusenberry, D. (1987). Designing a developmental assessment center in a government agency: A case study. *Public Personnel Management, 16*(2), 145–152.

Cohen, B.M., Moses, J.L., & Byham, W.C. (1974). *The validity of assessment centers: A literature review.* Monograph II. Pittsburgh, PA: Development Dimensions Press.

Cooper, W.W. (1981). Ubiquitous halo. *Psychological Bulletin, 90,* 218–244.

Cronbach, L.J. (1970). *Essentials of psychological testing.* New York: Harper & Row.

Cronbach, L.J., & Meehl, P.E. (1955). Construct validity in psychological tests. *Psychological Bulletin, 52,* 281–302.

Cronbach, L.J., & Snow, R.E. (1977). *Aptitudes and instructional methods.* New York: Irvington.

Dance, K.A., & Neufeld, R.W.J. (1988). Aptitude-treatment interaction research in the clinical setting: A review of attempts to dispel the "patient uniformity" myth. *Psychological Bulletin, 104,* 192–213.

Davis, B.L., Hellervik, L.W., & Sheard, J.L. (1986). *Successful manager's handbook.* Minneapolis, MN: Personnel Decisions, Inc.

Dawes, R.M. (1979). The robust beauty of improper linear models in decision making. *American Psychologist, 34,* 571–582.

Denning, D.L., & Grant, D.L. (1979). Knowledge of the assessment process: Does it influence candidate ratings? *Journal of Assessment Center Technology, 2*(2), 7–12.

DeVries, D.L., & White, R.P. (1989). Forgotten factors in executive assessment. In C.W. Stucker (Ed.), *Proceedings of the 1989 National Assessment Conference* (pp. 33–39). Minneapolis, MN: Personnel Decisions, Inc.

Dodd, W.E. (1977). Attitudes toward assessment center programs. In J.L. Moses & W.C. Byham (Eds.), *Applying the assessment center method* (pp. 161–183). New York: Pergamon Press.

Dugan, B. (1988). Effects of assessor training on information use. *Journal of Applied Psychology, 73,* 743–748.

Ebbesen, E.B. (1981). Cognitive processes in inferences about a person's personality. In E. Higgins, C. Herman, & M. Zanna (Eds.), *Social cognition: The Ontario symposium* (Vol. 1, pp. 247–276). Hillsdale, NJ: Erlbaum.

Eden, D. (1984). Self-fulfilling prophecy as a management tool: Harnessing Pygmalion. *Academy of Management Review, 9,* 64–73.

Eden, D. (1988). Creating expectation effects in OD: Applying self-fulfilling prophecy. In *Research in organizational change and development* (Vol. 2, pp. 235–267). Greenwich, CT: JAI Press.

Eden, D. (1990). *Pygmalion in management: Productivity as a self-fulfilling prophecy.* Lexington, MA: Lexington Books.

Einhorn, H.J., Hogarth, R.M., & Klempner, E. (1977). Quality of group judgment. *Psychological Bulletin, 84,* 158–172.

Equal Employment Opportunity Commission, Civil Service Commission, Department of Labor, & Department of Justice. (August 25, 1978). *Uniform Guidelines on Employee Selection Procedures,* Federal Register, *43*(166), 38290–38309.

Feldman, J. (1981). Beyond attribution theory: Cognitive processes in performance appraisal. *Journal of Applied Psychology, 66,* 127–148.

Feltham, R. (1988a). Validity of a police assessment centre: A 1-19-year follow-up. *Journal of Occupational Psychology, 61,* 129–144.

Feltham, R. (1988b). Assessment centre decision making: Judgmental vs. mechanical. *Journal of Occupational Psychology, 61,* 237–241.

Finkle, R.B. (1976). Managerial assessment centers. In M.D. Dunnette (Ed.), *Handbook of industrial and organizational psychology* (pp. 861–888). Chicago, IL: Rand McNally.

Finkle, R.B., & Jones, W.S. (1970). *Assessing corporate talent: A key to managerial manpower planning.* New York: Wiley Interscience.

Fishbein, M., & Aijen, I. (1975). *Belief, attitude, intention, and behavior. An introduction to theory and research.* Reading, MA: Addison-Wesley.

Fiske, S.T., & Taylor, S.E. (1984). *Social cognition.* Reading, MA: Addison-Wesley.

Flanagan, J.C. (1954). The critical incident technique. *Psychological Bulletin, 51,* 327–349.

Fleenor, J.W. (1988). *The utility of assessment centers for career development.* Unpublished doctoral dissertation, North Carolina State University.

Fleishman, E.A., & Quaintance, M.K. (1984). *Taxonomies of human performance: The description of human tasks.* Orlando, FL: Academic Press.

Fletcher, C. (1991). Candidates' reactions to assessment centres and their outcomes: A longitudinal study. *Journal of Occupational Psychology, 64,* 117–127.

Fletcher, C.A., & Dulewicz, V. (1984). An empirical study of a UK-based assessment centre. *Journal of Management Studies, 21,* 83–97.

Fogli, L. (1985). *Coremart.* Pheasant Hill, CA: Author.

Folger, R., & Greenberg, J. (1985). Procedural justice: An integrative analysis of personnel systems. In K.M. Rowland and G.R. Ferris (Eds.), *Research in personnel and human resources management* (Vol. 3, pp. 141–183). Greenwich, CT: JAI Press.

Foster, S.L., & Cone, J.D. (1986). Design and use of direct observation. In A.R. Cimincro, K.S. Calhoun, & H.E. Adams (Eds.), *Handbook of behavioral assessment* (2nd ed.) (pp. 253–322). New York: Wiley.

Frank, F.D. (1990). *Video testing: An alternative to assessment centers.* Paper presented at the 18th International Congress on the Assessment Center Method.

Frederiksen, N., Saunders, D.R., & Wand, B. (1957). The in-basket test. *Psychological Monographs, 71*(9, Whole No. 438).

French, W.L. (1982). *The personnel management process* (5th ed.). Boston, MA: Houghton Mifflin.

Gael, S. (1983). *Job analysis: A guide to assessing work activities.* San Francisco, CA: Jossey-Bass.

Gatewood, R.D., & Feild, H.S. (1987). *Human resource selection.* Chicago, IL: Dreyden Press.

Gatewood, R., Thornton, G.C. III, Henessey, H.W., Jr. (1990). Reliability of exercise ratings in the leaderless group discussion. *Journal of Occupational Psychology, 63,* 331–342.

Gaugler, B.B., Bentson, C., & Pohley, K. (1990). *A survey of assessment center practices in organizations.* Unpublished manuscript.

Gaugler, B.B., Rosenthal, D.B., Thornton, G.C. III, & Bentson, C. (1987). Meta-analysis of assessment center validity. *Journal of Applied Psychology, 72,* 493–511.

Gaugler, B.B., & Thornton, G.C. III. (1989). Number of assessment center dimensions as a determinant of assessor accuracy. *Journal of Applied Psychology, 74,* 611–618.

Gavin, J.F., & Hamilton, J.W. (1975). Selecting police using assessment center methodology. *Journal of Police Science and Administration, 3*(2), 166–176.

Ghiselli, E.E., Campbell, J.P., & Zedeck, S. (1981). *Measurement theory for the behavioral sciences.* San Francisco, CA: Freeman.

Gluski, B.J., & Sherman, A.M. (1989, May). *Results of concurrent and content validation studies for supervisory assessment center transported from manufacturing to insurance services.* Paper presented at the International Congress on the Assessment Center Method, Pittsburgh, PA.

Goldsmith, R.F. (1990). Utility analysis and its application to the study of the cost effectiveness of the assessment center method. In K.R. Murphy & F.E. Saal (Eds.), *Psychology in organizations: Integrating science and practice* (pp. 95–110). Hillsdale, NJ: Erlbaum.

Goldstein, A.P., & Sorcher, M. (1974). *Changing managerial behavior.* New York: Pergamon Press.

Goldstein, I.L. (1986). *Training in organizations: Needs assessment, development, and evaluation* (2nd ed.). Monterey, CA: Brooks/Cole.

Gorsuch, R.L. (1983). *Factor analysis* (2nd ed.). Hillsdale, NJ: Lawrence Erlbaum.

Greenberg, J. (1990). Organizational justice: Yesterday, today and tomorrow. *Journal of Management, 16,* 399–432.

Greenwood, J.M., & McNamara, W.J. (1967). Interrater reliability in situational tests. *Journal of Applied Psychology, 51,* 101–106.

Guilford, J.P. (1954). *Psychometric methods.* New York: McGraw-Hill.

Guion, R.M. (1965). *Personnel Testing.* New York: McGraw-Hill.

Guion, R.M. (1987). Changing views for personnel selection research. *Personnel Psychology, 40,* 199–213.

Hackman, J.R., & Morris, C.G. (1978a). Group process and group effectiveness: A reappraisal. In L. Berkowitz (Ed.), *Group processes* (pp. 57–66). New York: Academic Press.

Hackman, J.R., & Morris, C.G. (1978b). Group tasks, group interaction process, and group performance effectiveness: A review and proposed integration. In L. Berkowitz (Ed.), *Group processes* (pp. 1–55). New York: Academic Press.

Hammond, K.R., McClelland, G.H., & Mumpower, J. (1980). *Human judgment and decision making: Theories, methods, and procedures.* New York: Praeger.

Hampson, S.E., John, O.P., & Goldberg, L.R. (1986). Category breadth and hierarchical structure in personality: Studies of asymmetries in judgments of trait implications. *Journal of Personality and Social Psychology, 51,* 37–54.

Harris, H. (1949). *The group approach to leadership testing.* London: Routledge and Paul.

Harris, M.M. (1989). Reconsidering the employment interview: A review of recent literature and suggestions for future research. *Personnel Psychology, 42,* 691–726.

Hartigan, J.A., & Wigdor, A.K. (1989). *Employment testing.* Washington, DC: National Academy Press.

Hastie, R. (1986). Experimental evidence of group accuracy. In B. Grofman & G. Owen (Eds.), *Decision research.* Greenwich, CT: JAI Press.

Hastie, R., & Carlston, D. (1980). Theoretical issues in person memory. In R. Hastie, T.M. Ostrom, E.B. Ebbeson, R.S. Wyer, D.L. Hamilton, & D.E. Carlston (Eds.), *Person memory: The cognitive basis of social perception* (pp. 1–54). Hillsdale, NJ: Erlbaum.

Hastie, R., & Kumar, P. (1979). Person memory: Personality traits as organizing principles in memory for behavior. *Journal of Personality and Social Psychology, 37,* 25–38.

Heine, D. (1989). *Is computerized scoring the answer?* Paper presented at the International Congress on the Assessment Center Method, Pittsburgh, PA.

Heine, D. (1991). *Alternative methods of data integration in assessment centers.* Debate at the Nineteenth International Conference on the Assessment Center Method, Toronto, Ontario, Canada.

Heine, D.M., & Struth, M.R. (May, 1989). *Computerized assessment centers.* Paper presented at the 17th International Congress on the Assessment Center Method, Pittsburgh, PA.

Hemphill, J.K. (1959). Job descriptions for executives. *Harvard Business Review, 37*(5), 55–67.

Henry, S.E. (1988). *Nontraditional applications of assessment centers: Assessment in staffing plant start-ups.* Paper presented at the meeting of the American Psychological Association, Atlanta, GA.

Herriot, P., Chalmers, C., & Wingrove, J. (1985). Group decision making in an assessment centre. *Journal of Occupational Psychology, 58,* 309–312.

Higgins, E.T., & Bargh, J.A. (1987). Social cognition and social perception. In M.R. Rosenzweig & L.W. Porter (Eds.), *Annual review of psychology* (Vol. 38). Palo Alto, CA: Annual Reviews.

Hill, G.W. (1982). Groups vs. individual performance: Are N + 1 heads better than one? *Psychological Bulletin, 91,* 517–539.

Hinrichs, J.R. (1976). Comparison of "real life" assessments of management potential with situation exercises, paper-and-pencil ability tests, and personality inventories. *Journal of Applied Psychology, 53,* 425–432.

Hinrichs, J.R. (1978). An eight-year follow-up of a management assessment center. *Journal of Applied Psychology, 63,* 596–601.

Hinrichs, J.R., & Haanpera, S. (1976). Reliability of measurement in situational exercises: An assessment of the assessment center method. *Personnel Psychology, 29,* 31–40.

Hintzman, D.L. (1986). "Schema abstraction" in a multiple-trace memory model. *Psychological Review, 93,* 411–428.

Hintzman, D.L. (1988). Judgment of frequency and recognition memory in a multiple-trace memory model. *Psychological Review, 95,* 528–551.

Hoffman, L.R. (1978a). The group problem-solving process. In L. Berkowitz (Ed.), *Group processes* (pp. 57–66). New York: Academic Press.

Hoffman, L.R. (1978b). Group problem solving. In L. Berkowitz (Ed.), *Group processes* (pp. 67–113). New York: Academic Press.

Hogan, J., & Zenke, L.L. (1986). Dollar-value utility of alternative procedures for selecting school principals. *Educational and Psychological Measurement, 46,* 935–945.

Hollenbeck, G.P. (1990). The past, present, and future of assessment centers. *The Industrial/Organizational Psychologist, 28*(2), 13–17.

Howard, A. (1974). An assessment of assessment centers. *Academy of Management Journal, 17,* 115–134.

Howard, A. (1979). Assessment center predictions sixteen years later. Paper presented at the 7th International Congress on the Assessment Center Method, New Orleans, LA.

Howard, A. (1989). When does assessment *not* predict? In C.W. Stucker (Ed.), *Proceedings of the 1989 National Assessment Conference* (pp. 59–63). Minneapolis, MN: Personnel Decisions, Inc.

Howard, A., & Bray, D.W. (1988). *Managerial lives in transition: Advancing age and changing times.* New York: Guilford Press.

Howard, A., & Bray, D.W. (1989, May). *When assessment doesn't predict.* Paper presented at the International Congress on the Assessment Center Method, Pittsburgh, PA.

Huck, J.R. (1974). *Determinants of assessment center ratings for white and black females and the relationship of these dimensions to subsequent performance effectiveness.* Unpublished doctoral dissertation, Wayne State University, Detroit, Michigan.

Huck, J.R. (1987, April). *Costing the value of human resources: A look at the economic utility of an assessment center selection process.* Paper presented at the Institute for Personnel Management, Stellenbosch, South Africa.

Huck, J.R., & Bray, D.W. (1976). Management assessment center evaluations and subsequent job performance of black and white females. *Personnel Psychology, 29,* 13–30.

Hunt, D.M., & Michael, C. (1983). Mentorship: A career training and development tool. *Academy of Management Review, 8,* 475–485.

Hunter, J.E., & Hunter, R.F. (1984). Validity and utility of alternative predictors of job performance. *Psychological Bulletin, 96,* 72–98.

Hunter, J.E., Schmidt, F.L., & Jackson, G.B. (1982). *Meta-analysis: Cumulating research findings across studies.* Beverly Hills, CA: Sage.

Ilgen, D.R., Fisher, C.D., & Taylor, M.S. (1979). Consequences of individual feedback on behavior in organizations. *Journal of Applied Psychology, 64,* 340–371.

Jackson, S.E., Schuler, R.S., & Rivero, J.C. (1989). Organizational characteristics as predictors of personnel practices. *Personnel Psychology, 42,* 727–786.

Jacobsen, L., & Sinclair, N. (1990, March). *Assessing the writing of teacher candidates: Connecticut's method of holistic assessments.* Paper presented at the 18th International Congress on the Assessment Center Method, Anaheim, CA.

Janis, I.L. (1982). *Groupthink* (2nd ed.). Boston, MA: Houghton Mifflin.

Jeanneret, P.R. (1989). Can an assessment center and individual assessments co-exist in the same organization? In C.W. Stucker (Ed.), *Proceedings of the 1989 National Assessment Conference* (pp. 64–67). Minneapolis, MN: Personnel Decisions, Inc.

Jeffrey, K.M., & Mischel, W. (1979). Effects of purpose on the organization and recall of information in person perception. *Journal of Personality, 47,* 397–419.

Johnson, M.K., & Raye, C.L. (1981). Reality monitoring. *Psychological Review, 88,* 67–85.

Jones, E.E., & Davis, K.E. (1965). A theory of correspondent inferences: From acts to dispositions. In L. Berkowitz (Ed.), *Advances in experimental and social psychology* (Vol. 2, pp. 220–266). New York: Academic Press.

Jones, G.T. (1972). *Simulations and business decisions.* Middlesex, England: Penguin.

Kane, J.S., & Lawler, E.E. (1978). Methods of peer assessment. *Psychological Bulletin, 85,* 555–586.

Kazdin, A.E. (1984). *Behavior modification in applied settings* (3rd ed.). Homewood, IL: Dorsey.

Keefe, J.W. (1987). *Learning style: Theory and practice.* Reston, VA: National Association of Secondary School Principals.

Kehoe, J.F., Weinberg, K., & Lawrence, I.M. (1985, August). *Dimension and exercise effects on work simulation ratings.* Paper presented at the meeting of the American Psychological Association, Los Angeles, CA.

King, L.M., & Boehm, V.R. (1990, September). *Assessment center judgment stability across time periods and assessors.* Paper presented at the 88th Annual Convention of the American Psychological Association, Montreal.

Kintsch, W., & van Dijk, T.A. (1978). Toward a model of text comprehension and production. *Psychological Review, 85,* 363–394.

Klimoski, R., & Brickner, M. (1987). Why do assessment centers work? The puzzle of assessment center validity. *Personnel Psychology, 40,* 243–260.

Knowles, M.S. (1970). *The modern practice of adult education: Andragogy versus pedagogy.* New York: Association Press.

Knowles, M.S. (1973). *The adult learner: A neglected species.* Houston, TX: Gulf Publishing Co.

Kogan, N., & Wallach, M.A. (1967). Risk-taking as a function of the situation, the person, and the group. In T.M. Newcomb (Ed.), *New directions in psychology* (Vol. 3, pp. 111–266). New York: Holt.

Konz, A.M. (1988). *A comparison of dimension ratings and exercise ratings in assessment centers.* Unpublished doctoral dissertation, University of Maryland.

Kraut, A.I., & Scott, G.J. (1972). Validity of an operational management assessment program. *Journal of Applied Psychology, 56,* 124–129.

Lamm, H., & Myers, D.G. (1978). Group-induced polarization of attitudes and behavior. In *Advances in Experimental Psychology* (Vol. 11). New York: Academic Press.

Landy, F.J. (1986). Stamp collecting versus science: Validation as hypothesis testing. *American Psychologist, 41,* 1183–1192.

Latané, B., & Darley, J.M. (1970). *The unresponsive bystander: Why doesn't he help?* New York: Appleton-Century-Crofts.

Latham, G.P. (1988). Human resource training and development. *Annual Review of Psychology, 39,* 545–582.

Laughlin, P.R. (1980). Social combination processes of cooperative problem-solving groups on verbal intellective tasks. In M. Fishbein (Ed.), *Progress in social psychology.* Hillsdale, NJ: Erlbaum.

Laughlin, P.R., & Ellis, A.L. (1986). Demonstrability and social combination processes on mathematical intellective tasks. *Journal of Experimental Social Psychology, 22,* 177–189.

Laughlin, P. R., & McGlynn, R.P. (1986). Collective induction: Mutual group and individual influence by exchange of hypotheses & evidence. *Journal of Experimental Social Psychology, 22,* 567–589.

Lawrence, P. R. (1984). Trends in human resource management. In R.E. Walton & P.R. Lawrence (Eds.), *Human resource management trends and challenges.* Boston, MA: Harvard Business School Press.

Leitenberg, H. (1976). *Handbook of behavior modification and behavior therapy.* Englewood Cliffs, NJ: Prentice Hall.

Levine, J.M., & Moreland, R.L. (1990). Progress in small group research. *Annual Review of Psychology, 41,* 585–634.

Libby, R., Trotman, K.T., & Zimmer, I. (1987). Member variation, recognition of expertise and group performance. *Journal of Applied Psychology, 72,* 81–87.

Linville, P.W., Fischer, G.W., & Salovey, P. (1989). Perceived distributions of the characteristics of in-group and out-group members: Empirical evidence and a computer simulation. *Journal of Personality and Social Psychology, 57,* 165–188.

Locksley, A., Borgida, E., Brekke, N., & Hepburn, C. (1980). Sex stereotype and social judgment. *Journal of Personality and Social Psychology, 39,* 821–831.

Locksley, A., Stangor, C., & Hepburn, M. (1984). The ambiguity of recognition memory tests of schema theories. *Cognitive Psychology, 16,* 421–428.

Lopez, F.M., Jr. (1966). *Evaluating executive decision making: The in-basket technique* (AMA Research Study No. 75). New York: American Management Association.

Lorenzo, R.V. (1984). Effects of assessorship on managers' proficiency in acquiring, evaluating, and communicating information about people. *Personnel Psychology, 37,* 617–634.

Louiselle, K.G. (1986). *Confirmatory factor analysis of two assessment center rating procedures.* Paper presented at the Seventh Annual IO/OB Graduate Student Conference, Minneapolis, MN.

Lozada-Larsen, S.R. (1990, March). *EXCEL: A tool for the analysis of managerial work.* Paper presented at the 18th International Congress on the Assessment Center Method, Anaheim, CA.

Lu, H. (1988). *Human resource development and assessment: Theory and practice in China.* Toronto, Canada: Toronto-Global Publishing.

Lu, H. (1990). *Cross-cultural issues in the teaching of assessment centers.* Shanghai, China: Jiaotong University.

Major, B. (1980). Information acquisition and attribution processes. *Journal of Personality and Social Psychology, 39,* 1010–1023.

Margersion, C., & Kakabadse, C. (1984). *How American chief executives succeed.* New York: American Management Association.

McClelland, D.C. (1987). *Competency assessment: Future prospects and developments.* Paper presented at the International Congress on the Assessment Center, Boston, MA.

McConnell, J.J., & Parker, T. (1972). An assessment center program for multiorganizational use. *Training and Development Journal, 26*(3), 6–14.

McCormick, E.J. (1979). *Job analysis: Methods and applications.* New York: AMACOM.

McEvoy, G.M., & Beatty, R.W. (1989). Assessment centers and subordinate appraisals of managers: A seven-year examination of predictive validity. *Personnel Psychology, 42,* 37–52.

McEvoy, G.M., Beatty, R.W., & Bernardin, H.J. (1987). Unanswered questions in assessment center research. *Journal of Business and Psychology, 2*(2), 97–111.

McGrath, J.E., & Kravitz, D.A. (1982). Group research. *Annual Review of Psychology, 33,* 195–230.

McIntyre, R.M. (1989, May). *Accreditation of trained assessors: Reasons and methods.* Paper presented at the International Congress on the Assessment Center Method, Pittsburgh, PA.

McIntyre, R.M., & Vanetti, E. (1988, August). *The effects of priming in a simulated assessment center environment.* Paper presented at the meeting of the American Psychological Association, Atlanta, GA.

Meehl, P.E. (1954). *Clinical versus statistical prediction: A theoretical analysis and a review of the evidence.* Minneapolis, MN: University of Minnesota.

Mendenhall, M.D. (1989, May). *Successful legal defense of the assessment center method: A first-hand account.* Paper presented at the International Congress on the Assessment Center Method, Pittsburgh, PA.

Menzmer, D. (1990, March). *California Highway Patrol management development center.* Paper presented at the International Congress on the Assessment Center Method, Anaheim, CA.

Miner, F.C. (1984). Group versus individual decision making: An investigation of performance measures, decision strategies, and process losses/gains. *Organizational Behavior & Human Performance, 33,* 112–114.

Mintzberg, H. (1975). The manager's job: Folklore and fact. *Harvard Business Review, 53,* 49–61.

Mischel, W., Jeffry, K.M., & Patterson, C.J. (1974). The layman's use of trait and behavioral information to predict behavior. *Journal of Research in Personality, 8,* 231–242.

Mitchel, J.O. (1975). Assessment center validity: A longitudinal study. *Journal of Applied Psychology, 60,* 573–579.

Morrison, A.M., & von Glinow, M.A. (1990). Women and minorities in management. *American Psychologist, 45,* 200–208.

Moscovici, S. (1985). Social influence and conformity. In G. Lindzey & E. Aronson (Eds.), *Handbook of social psychology* (pp. 347–412). New York: Random House.

Moses, J.L. (1973). The development of an assessment center for the early identification of supervisory potential. *Personnel Psychology, 26,* 569–580.

Moses, J.L., & Boehm, V.R. (1975). Relationship of assessment center performance to management progress of women. *Journal of Applied Psychology, 60,* 527–529.

Murphy, K.R. (1988). Psychological measurement: Abilities and Skills. In C.L. Cooper & I. Robertson (Eds.), *International Review of Industrial and Organizational Psychology.* New York: Wiley.

Murphy, K.R., & Cleveland, J.N. (1991). *Performance appraisal: An organizational perspective.* Boston, MA: Allyn and Bacon.

Murphy, K.R., & Constans, J.I. (1987). Behavioral anchors as a source of bias in ratings. *Journal of Applied Psychology, 72,* 573–579.

Murphy, K.R., & Constans, J.I. (1988). Psychological issues in scale format research: Behavioral anchors as a source of bias in rating. In R.L. Cardy, S.M. Puffer, J.M. Newman (Eds.), *Advances in information processing in organizations* (Vol. 3, pp. 135–153). Greenwich, CT: JAI Press.

Murphy, K.R., Jako, R.A., & Anhalt, R.L. (1991). *The nature and consequences of halo error: A critical analysis.* Unpublished manuscript.

Murphy, K.R., & Kroeker, L.P. (1988). *Dimensions of job performance.* San Diego, CA: Navy Personnel Research and Development Center, NPRDC-TN88-39.

Myers, D.G., & Lamm, H. (1976). The group polarization phenomenon. *Psychological Bulletin, 83,* 602–627.

Nathan, B.R., & Lord, R.G. (1983). Cognitive categorization and dimensional schemata: A process approach to the study of halo in performance ratings. *Journal of Applied Psychology, 68,* 102–114.

Neidig, R.D., & Martin, J.C. (1979). *The FBI's Management Aptitude Progam Assessment Center (report no. 2): An analysis of assessors' ratings.* (TM79-2). Washington, DC: Applied Psychology Section. Personnel Research and Development Center, U.S. Civil Service Commission.

Neidig, R.D., Martin, J.C., & Yates, R.E. (1978). *The FBI's Management Aptitude Program Assessment Center: Research report no. 1* (TM78-3). Washington, DC: Applied Psychology Section. Personnel Research and Development Center, U.S. Civil Service Commission.

Nevo, B. (1989, May). *The practical and theoretical value of examinee feedback questionnaires (EFeQ).* Paper presented at the conference, "The individual and organizational side of selection and performance evaluation and appraisal." Universität Hohenheim, Stuttgart, Germany.

Nevo, B., & Jager, R. (1986). *Psychological testing: The examinee perspective.* Gottingen, Germany: Hogrefe.

Nisbett, R., & Ross, L. (1980). *Human inference strategies and shortcomings of social judgment.* Englewood Cliffs, NJ: Prentice Hall.

Noe, R.A., & Steffy, B.D. (1987). The influence of individual characteristics and assessment center evaluation on career-exploration behavior and job involvement. *Journal of Vocational Behavior, 30,* 187–202.

Norton, S.D. (1981). The assessment center process and content validity: A reply to Dreher and Sackett. *Academy of Management Review, 6,* 561–566.

Nunnally, J. (1978). *Psychometric theory*. New York: McGraw-Hill.

Offerman, L.R., & Gowing, M.K. (1990). Organizations of the future: Changes and challenges. *American Psychologist, 45,* 95–108.

Office of Strategic Services Assessment Staff (1948). *Assessment of men: Selection of personnel for the Office of Strategic Services*. New York: Rinehart.

O'Hare, K., & Love, K.G. (1987). Accurate selection of police officials within small municipalities: "*Et tu* assessment center?" *Public Personnel Management, 16* (1), 9–14.

Outcalt, D. (1988, May). *A research program on General Motor's foreman selection assessment center: Assessor / assessee characteristics and moderator analysis*. Paper presented at the 16th International Congress on the Assessment Center Method, Tampa, FL.

Peterson, D.K., & Pitz, G.F. (1986). Effect of input from a mechanical model on clinical judgment. *Journal of Applied Psychology, 71,* 163–167.

Petty, R.E., & Caccioppo, J.T. (1986). The elaboration likelihood model of persuasion. *Advances in Experimental Social Psychology, 19,* 123–205.

Pigors, P., & Pigors, F. (1961). *Case method in human relations: The incident process*. New York: McGraw-Hill.

Pigors, P. (1976). Case method. In R.L. Craig (Ed.), *Training and development handbook* (2nd ed.). New York: McGraw-Hill.

Pynes, J.E., & Bernardin, H.J. (1989). Predictive validity of an entry-level police officer assessment center. *Journal of Applied Psychology, 74,* 831–833.

Reilly, R.R., Henry, S., & Smither, J.W. (1990). An examination of the effects of using behavior checklists on the construct validity of assessment center dimensions. *Personnel Psychology, 43,* 71–84.

Reilly, R.R., & Smither, J.W. (1985). An examination of two alternative techniques to estimate the standard deviation of job performance in dollars. *Journal of Applied Psychology, 70,* 651–661.

Rhodes, D.W., & Walker, J.W. (1984). Management succession and development planning. *Human Resources Planning, 7,* 157–173.

Ritchie, R.R., & Moses, J.L. (1983). Assessment center correlates of women's advancement into middle management: A 7-year longitudinal analysis. *Journal of Applied Psychology, 68,* 227–231.

Robertson, I.T., Gratton, L., & Sharpley, D. (1987). The psychometric properties and design of managerial assessment centres: Dimensions into exercises won't go. *Journal of Occupational Psychology, 60,* 187–195.

Robertson, I.T., & Makin, P.J. (1986). Management selection in Britain: A survey and critique. *Journal of Occupational Psychology, 59,* 45–57.

Rohrbaugh, J. (1979). Improving the quality of group judgment: Social judgment analysis and the Delphi technique. *Organizational Behavior and Human Performance, 24,* 73–92.

Rokeach, M. (1973). *The nature of human values.* New York: Free Press.

Rosch, E. (1978). Principles of categorization. In E. Rosch & B. Lloyd (Eds.), *Cognition and categorization* (pp. 28–49). Hillsdale, NJ: Erlbaum.

Rosch, E., Mervis, C.G., Gray, W.D., Johnson, D.M., & Boyes-Braem, P. (1976). Basic objects in natural categories. *Cognitive Psychology, 8,* 382–439.

Russell, C.J. (1987). Person characteristic versus role congruency explanations for assessment center ratings. *Academy of Management Journal, 30,* 817–826.

Ryan, A.M., & Sackett, P.R. (1987). A survey of individual assessment practices by I/O psychologists. *Personnel Psychology, 40,* 455–488.

Ryan, A.M., & Sackett, P.R. (1989). Exploratory study of individual assessment practices: Interrater reliability and judgments of assessor effectiveness. *Journal of Applied Psychology, 74,* 568–579.

Rynes, S.L., Heneman, H.G. III, & Schwab, D.P. (1980). Individual reactions to organizational recruiting: A review. *Personnel Psychology, 33,* 529–542.

Sackett, P.R. (1982). A critical look at some common beliefs about assessment centers. *Public Personnel Management Journal, 2,* 140–147.

Sackett, P.R. (1987). Assessment centers and content validity: Some neglected issues. *Personnel Psychology, 40,* 13–25.

Sackett, P.R., & Dreher, G.F. (1982). Constructs and assessment center dimensions: Some troubling empirical findings. *Journal of Applied Psychology, 67,* 401–410.

Sackett, P.R., & Dreher, G.F. (1984). Situation specificity of behavior and assessment center validation strategies: A rejoinder to Neidig and Neidig. *Journal of Applied Psychology, 69,* 187–190.

Sackett, P.R., & Hakel, M.D. (1979). Temporal stability and individual differences in using assessment information to form overall ratings. *Organizational Behavior and Human Performance, 23,* 120–137.

Sackett, P.R., & Wilson, M.A. (1982). Factors affecting the consensus judgment process in management assessment centers. *Journal of Applied Psychology, 67,* 10–17.

Savage, B.L. (1989, May). *Feedbacks.* Paper presented at the International Congress on the Assessment Center Method, Pittsburgh, PA.

Sawyer, J. (1966). Measurement and prediction, clinical and statistical. *Psychological Bulletin, 66,* 178–200.

Schein, E.H. (1970). *Organizational psychology.* Englewood Cliffs, NJ: Prentice Hall.

Schein, E.H. (1990). Organizational culture. *American Psychologist, 45,* 109–119.

Schippmann, J.S., Prien, E.P., & Katz, J.A. (1990). Reliability and validity of in-basket performance measure. *Personnel Psychology, 43,* 837–859.

Schmidt, F.L. (1988). The problem of group differences in ability test scores in employment selection. *Journal of Vocational Behavior, 33,* 279–292.

Schmidt, F.L., & Hunter, J.E (1977). Development of a general solution to the problem of validity generalization. *Journal of Applied Psychology, 62,* 529–540.

Schmidt, F.L., Hunter, J.E., McKenzie, R., & Muldrow, T. (1979). The impact of valid selection procedures on workforce productivity. *Journal of Applied Psychology, 64,* 609–626.

Schmitt, N. (1977). Interrater agreement in dimensionality and combination of assessment center judgments. *Journal of Applied Psychology, 62,* 171–176.

Schmitt, N., Gooding, R.Z., Noe, R.A., & Kirsch, M. (1984). Meta-analyses of validity studies published between 1964 and 1982 and the investigation of study characteristics. *Personnel Psychology, 37,* 407–422.

Schmitt, N., Schneider, J.R., & Cohen, S.A. (1990). Factors affecting validity of a regionally administered assessment center. *Personnel Psychology, 43,* 1–12.

Schneider, B., & Konz, A.M. (1989). Strategic job analysis. *Human Resource Management, 28*(1), 51–63.

Schoenfeld, C.P., & Heine, D.M. (1990, March). *Selection of entry-level jobs for non-traditional manufacturing.* Paper presented at the International Congress on the Assessment Center Method, Anaheim, CA.

Schweiger, D.M., Sandberg, W.R., & Rediner, P.L. (1989). Experiential effects of dialectical inquiry, devil's advocacy, and consensus approaches to strategic decision making. *Academy of Management Journal, 32,* 745–772.

Sherman, S.J., Judd, C.M., & Park, B. (1989). Social cognition. *Annual Review of Psychology, 3,* 281–326.

Shore, T.H., Thornton, G.C. III, & Shore, L.M. (1990). Construct validity of two categories of assessment center dimension ratings. *Personnel Psychology, 43,* 101–115.

Shuler, H. (in press). Social validity of selection situations: A concept and some empirical results. In H. Schuler, J.L. Farr, & M. Smith (Eds.), *Personnel selection and assessment: Individual and organization perspectives.* Hillsdale, NJ: Lawrence Erlbaum.

Silverman, W.H., Dalessio, A., Woods, S.B., & Johnson, R.L. (1986). Influence of assessment center methods on assessors' ratings. *Personnel Psychology, 39,* 565–578.

Silzer, R.F., & Louiselle, K. (1990, March). *Statistical versus assessor data: Application and recent research.* Paper presented at the 18th International Congress on the Assessment Center Method, Anaheim, CA.

Slivinski, L.W., Grant, K.W., Bourgeois, R.P., & Pederson, L.D. (1977). *Development and validation of a first-level management assessment centre.* Ottawa, Canada: Public Service Commission of Canada.

Smith, A.B. (1989). *A comparison of two assessment center integration methods.* Unpublished doctoral dissertation, Colorado State University.

Smith, E.E., & Medin, D.L. (1981). *Categories and concepts.* Cambridge, MA: Harvard University Press.

Smith, P.C. (1976). Behaviors, results, and organizational effectiveness: The problem of criteria. In M.D. Dunnette (Ed.), *Handbook of industrial and organizational psychology* (pp. 745–775). Chicago, IL: Rand McNally.

Smith, P.C., & Kendall, L.M. (1963). Retranslation of expectations: An approach to the construction of unambiguous anchors for rating scales. *Journal of Applied Psychology, 47,* 149–155.

Sniezek, J.A., & Henry, R.A. (1989). Accuracy and confidence in group judgment. *Organizational Behavior and Human Decision Processes, 43,* 1–28.

Sniezek, J.A., & Henry, R.A. (1990). Revision, weighting, and commitment in consensus group judgment. *Organizational Behavior and Human Decision Processes, 45,* 66–84.

Society for Industrial and Organizational Psychology. (1987). *Principles for the validation and use of personnel selection procedures* (3rd ed.). College Park, MD: Author.

Sovereign, K.L. (1984). *Personnel law.* Reston, VA: Reston.

Spangenberg, H.H., Esterhuyse, J.J., Visser, J.H., Briedenhann, J.E., & Calitz, C.J. (1989). Validation of an assessment centre against BARS: An experience with performance-related criteria. *Journal of Industrial Psychology, 15*(2), 1–10.

Speece, D.L. (1990). Aptitude-treatment interactions: Bad rap or bad idea? *The Journal of Special Education, 24*(2), 139.

Squires, P., Torkel, S.J., Smither, J.W., & Ingate, M.R. (1988, August). *Validity and generalizability of a role-play test to select telemarketing representatives.* Paper presented at the meeting of the American Psychological Association, Atlanta, GA.

Steiner, I. (1972). *Group process and productivity.* New York: Academic Press.

Struth, M.R., Frank, F.D., & Amato, A. (1980). Effects of assessor training on subsequent performance as an assessor. *Journal of Assessment Center Technology, 3*(2), 17–22.

Stumpf, S.A. (1988). Business simulations for skill diagnosis and development. In M. London & E.M. Mone (Eds.), *Career growth and human resources strategies* (pp. 195–206). New York: Quorum Books.

Sundstrom, E., DeMeuse, K.P., & Futrell, D. (1990). Work teams: Applications and effectiveness. *American Psychologist, 45,* 120–133.

Swann, W.B. (1984). Quest for accuracy in person perceptive: A matter of pragmatics. *Psychological Review, 91,* 457–477.

Task Force on Assessment Center Guidelines. (1989). Guidelines and ethical considerations for assessment center operations. *Public Personnel Management, 18*(4), 457–470.

Taylor, C.R. (1990, March). *Strategic job analysis.* Paper presented at the International Congress on the Assessment Center Method, Anaheim, CA.

Taylor, M.S., Fisher, C.D., & Ilgen, D.R. (1984). Individual reactions to performance feedback in organizations: A control theory perspective. In R. Rowland & G. Ferris (Eds.), *Research in personnel and human resources management* (Vol. 2, pp. 81–124). Greenwich, CT: JAI Press.

Team Columbus (1990, March). *A joint UAW/DAC venture in the assessment process.* Paper presented at the 18th International Congress on the Assessment Center Method, Anaheim, CA.

Teel, K., & DuBois, H. (1983). Participants' reactions to assessment centers. *Personnel Administrator, 28,* 85–91.

Tetlock, P.E. (1983). Accountability and the complexity of thought. *Journal of Personality and Social Psychology, 45,* 74–83.

Tetlock, P.E. (1985). Accountability: The neglected social context of judgment and choice. In L.L. Cummings & B.M. Staw (Eds.), *Research in organizational behavior* (Vol. 7, pp. 297–332). Greenwich, CT: JAI Press.

Thomas, J.N. (1990, March). *The validity of video-based assessment processes: Do they predict job performance?* Paper presented at the International Congress on the Assessment Center Method, Anaheim, CA.

Thomson, H.A. (1970). Comparison of predictor and criterion judgments of managerial performance using the multitrait-multimethod approach. *Journal of Applied Psychology, 54,* 496–502.

Thornton, G.C. III (1976). *The effects of feedback in developmental planning.* Paper presented at the Fourth International Congress on the Assessment Center Method, Portsmouth, NH.

Thornton, G.C. III (in press). The effect of selection practices on applicants' perceptions of organizational characteristics. In H. Schuler, J.L. Farr, & M. Smith (Eds.), *Personnel selection and assessment: Individual and organization perspectives.* Hillsdale, NJ: Lawrence Erlbaum.

Thornton, G.C. III, & Byham, W.C. (1982). *Assessment centers and managerial performance.* New York: Academic Press.

Thornton, G.C. III, & Cleveland, J.N. (1990). Developing managerial talent through simulation. *American Psychologist, 45,* 190–199.

Thornton, G.C. III, Clevenger, J., Tziner, A., & Dahan, M. (1991). *Structure of final dimension ratings in an assessment center.* Unpublished paper.

Turnage, J.J., & Muchinsky, P.M. (1984). A comparison of the predictive validity of assessment center evaluations versus traditional measures of forecasting supervisory job performance: Interpretive implications of criterion distortion for the assessment paradigm. *Journal of Applied Psychology, 69,* 595–602.

Tziner, A., & Dolan, S. (1982). Validity of an assessment center for identifying future female officers in the military. *Journal of Applied Psychology, 67,* 728–736.

Tziner, A., Ronen, S., & Hacohen, D. (1990). *The assessment center once more under the surgeon's knife: A long-term validation study in a non–North American organization setting.* Unpublished manuscript.

Umeshima, M. (1989). *Combining outside assessors with peer assessors.* Paper presented at the 17th International Congress on the Assessment Center Method, Pittsburgh, PA.

Walsh, J.P., Weinberg, R.M., Fairfield, M.L. (1987). The effects of gender on assessment center evaluations. *Journal of Occupational Psychology, 60,* 305–309.

Wanous, J.P. (1977). Organizational entry: The individual's viewpoint. In J.R. Hackman, E.E. Lawler, & L.W. Porter (Eds.), *Perspectives on behavior in organizations* (pp. 126–135). New York: McGraw-Hill.

Wanous, J.P. (1992). *Organizational entry: Recruitment, selection, and socialization of newcomers* (2nd ed.). Reading, MA: Addison-Wesley.

Wanous, J.P., & Youtz, M.A. (1986). Solution diversity and the quality of group decisions. *Academy of Management Journal, 29,* 149–159.

Weekly, J.A., Frank, B., O'Conner, E.J., & Peters, L.H. (1985). A comparison of three methods of estimating the standard deviation of performance in dollars. *Journal of Applied Psychology, 70,* 122–126.

Weisner, W.H., & Cronshaw, S.F. (1988). A meta-analystical investigation of the impact of interview format and degree of structure on the validity of the employment interview. *Journal of Occupational Psychology, 61,* 275-290.

Weldon, E., & Gargano, G.M. (1985). Cognitive effort in additive groups: The effects of shared responsibility on the quality of multiattribute judgments. *Organizational Behaviors and Human Decision Processes, 36,* 348–361.

Weldon, E., & Mustari, E.L. (1988). Felt dispensability in groups of coactors: The effects of shared responsibility and explicit anonymity on cognitive effort. *Organizational Behavior and Human Decision Processes, 36,* 348–361.

Wernimont, P.F., & Campbell, J.P. (1968). Signs, samples, and criteria. *Journal of Applied Psychology, 52,* 372–376.

White, R.P., & DeVries, D.L. (1990). Making the wrong choice: Failure in the selection of senior-level managers. *Issues and Observations, 10*(1), 1–6.

Wiggins, J.S. (1973). *Personality and prediction: Principles of personality assessment.* Reading, MA: Addison-Wesley.

Wingrove, J., Jones, A., & Herriot, P. (1985). The predictive validity of pre- and post-discussion assessment centre ratings. *Journal of Occupational Psychology, 58,* 189–192.

Wolfson, A.D. (1988, August). *Assessing general management skills in technical functions.* Paper presented at the annual meeting of the American Psychological Association, Atlanta, GA.

Wolfson, A.D., & Mischkind, L.A. (1989, May). *Illuminating the errors of assessment.* Paper presented at the International Congress on the Assessment Center Method, Pittsburgh, PA.

Wollowick, H.B., & McNamara, W. J. (1969). Relationship of the components of an assessment center to management success. *Journal of Applied Psychology, 53,* 348–352.

Wyer, R.S., Jr., & Srull, T.K. (1986). Human cognition in its social context. *Psychological Review, 93,* 322–359.

Zedeck, S. (1971). Problems with the use of "moderator" variables. *Psychological Bulletin, 76,* 295–310.

Zedeck, S. (1986). A process analysis of the assessment center method. In B.M. Staw & L.L. Cummings (Eds.), *Research in Organizational Behavior* (Vol. 8, 259–296). Greenwich, CT: JAI Press.

Index